The Origin of
HUMAN
NATURE
A ZEN BUDDHIST LOOKS AT EVOLUTION

"In *The Origin of Human Nature,* Dr. Albert Low breathes new life into old terms – the transcendent, consciousness, awareness, evolution, creativity, intention – not by going around science, but by going through it. In the current frenzy to purge science of purpose, meaning, direction, and values, Low's insights are a welcome resource. One might say that our survival depends on the wisdom in this book." *Larry Dossey, MD, author of* The Extraordinary Healing Power of Everyday Things

"The old religious models don't seem to work for us these days. And so we have turned to secularity, to the cooler gaze of science, especially the neo-Darwinism of Richard Dawkins and others. Albert Low shows that the bloom of their answer – the random-mutation mechanistic evolutionary system – that once seemed so promising, cannot account for our capacity for love, appreciation of beauty, altruism, creativity or intelligence. And it cannot offer us meaning or direction. So we find ourselves in an uncomfortable place of ambiguity... *The Origin of Human Nature* offers a model that lives creatively in just that ambiguity." *Professor Robert Forman, Professor Emeritus of Comparative Religion, CUNY, founding Co-Editor of* The Journal of Consciousness Studies *and author of* Grassroots Spirituality

"In this intelligently written book Albert Low gives us a modern *Guide for the Perplexed*; a richly thoughtful reflection on the roots of human nature that glows with a deep respect for both science and the spirit." *Allan Combs, author of* The Radiance of Being

"The battles over evolution are fought by two sides that are far too rigid in their thinking, the Biblical literalists on the one hand and the mechanistically committed materialists on the other. But our human and spiritual nature is much bigger than fanatic literalism or scientistic dogmatism, and Low's refreshing book offers a more open direction to explore the potentials of evolution for real human beings." *Charles T. Tart is Core Faculty at the Institute of Transpersonal*

Dedicated to

Tony Stern

The Origin of
HUMAN NATURE

A ZEN BUDDHIST LOOKS AT EVOLUTION

ALBERT LOW

sussex
ACADEMIC
PRESS
Brighton • Portland • Toronto

2 4 6 8 10 9 7 5 3

First published 2008 in Great Britain by
SUSSEX ACADEMIC PRESS
PO Box 139
Eastbourne BN24 9BP

Distributed in North America by
SUSSEX ACADEMIC PRESS
ISBS Publisher Services
920 NE 58th Ave #300, Portland, OR 97213, USA

British Library Cataloguing in Publication Data
A CIP catalogue record for this book is available from the British Library.

Library of Congress Cataloging-in-Publication Data
Low, Albert.
   The origin of human nature : a Zen Buddhist looks at
   evolution / Albert Low.
   p. cm.
   Includes bibliographical references and index.
   ISBN 978-1-84519-260-0 (pb : alk. paper)
   1. Consciousness. 2. Consciousness—Religious aspects.
   I. Title.

B105.C477L696 2008
294.3′422—dc22

                 2007028505

Typeset and designed by SAP, Brighton & Eastbourne
Printed and bound by CPI Group (UK) Ltd, Croydon, CR0 4YY
This book is printed on acid-free paper.

Contents

Preface

"Modern Biology is characterized by a number of ideological prejudices that shape the form of its explanations and the way its researches are carried out."

R .C. LEWONTIN[1]

Can the prevailing materialistic/mechanistic philosophy provide an adequate foundation for an acceptable theory of the origin of human nature? This question has been the motive for writing this book. I began asking the question a number of years ago during a stay in Kingston, Ontario. A couple of friends were kind enough to invite my wife and me to 'house sit' for a month while they were away on vacation. It was a beautiful house in the university town of Kingston, one of the most serene towns in Ontario, bordering on Lake Ontario. The house had a lovely lawn that stretched down to the lake and, as the weather was so beautiful that long summer, we were able to sit in the shade of a tree and spend long, lazy hours reading in peace.

I had taken along a number of books with me to read, and among them was one about evolution — *The Blind Watchmaker* by Richard Dawkins. Throughout my life I have been a student of human nature and have had a life-long interest in psychology, philosophy, Eastern religion, Western Science in general and evolution theory in particular. Many years ago I had read Darwin's two principle books — *The Origin of Species* and *The Descent of Man* — and was enchanted by them. I had felt a great deal of sympathy with his theories and much admiration for his courage in publishing them. But as I read Richard Dawkins' book, I felt a mounting dis-ease, a sense of something being awfully wrong.

When I was a fair way through Dawkins' book my wife and I decided to take a break from reading and go downtown to see the Buskers Festival, the festival of street entertainers. Kingston plays host each year to the Buskers of Canada and buskers from all over Canada attend.

Naturally the buskers attract crowds of people who go to watch them at work.

It was a lovely summer's evening, and strolling among the good natured crowds all of them out for a pleasant and entertaining evening, with a clear evening sky above and the sun glinting off the lake forming a back drop to it all, I felt a deep sense of satisfaction: this was humanity at its best. I marveled at the entertainers, most of who gave amazing displays of inventiveness and dexterity. I remember one, a young fellow riding a monocycle on a tightrope playing a mouth organ, and another who, skipping around on the same tightrope, juggled flaming torches. There were musicians, dancers, and conjurers, all enjoying the opportunity to display their artistry, while the crowds applauded and laughed along with them. I wondered at the dedication of these entertainers: the hours of practice and their willingness to fail and fail again until they had reached such perfection that when they performed it all seemed so simple.

When we got home we sat for a while in the darkening night watching the sun sink into the lake and I could not help wondering more about what we had witnessed. I wondered not only about the entertainers, but also about the inventiveness and creativity of human beings generally. In North America and Europe almost any city or even town of any size has art galleries overflowing with paintings and sculpting; each town has libraries full of books on every imaginable subject. Human beings have built cathedrals and pyramids, skyscrapers and bridges. Whole civilizations have come and gone. We have walked on the moon and have explored Mars by proxy. Symphonies have thrilled millions, and the theatre and films have given us spectacles to enthrall. Great religions — Christian, Judaic, Buddhist, Hindu, Muslim — have inspired humankind and opened up to us a way to the transcendent. With the Internet, cell phone, and high definition TV we now are one world, thanks to the genius and creativity of human beings.

I could not help thinking of Dawkins' book as a background against all of this. He begins the book by saying, "This book is written in the conviction that our own existence once presented the greatest of all mysteries, but that it is a mystery no longer because it has been solved." All the time that I had walked around that evening this phrase had kept drumming in my head like a mantra, and as I sat there in the growing dusk it came back to me in full force.

Richard Dawkins is a *neo-Darwinian*, the name given to what is the mainstream theory of evolution. As I will show later, this theory is, in a way, a betrayal of Darwin's original idea, but nevertheless it is the theory taught by universities and schools. Dawkins is one of the chief exponents of the theory and his book *The Blind Watchmaker*, according to the blurb on the back cover, is brilliant and controversial: it "demonstrates that evolution by natural selection, the unconscious, automatic, blind yet essentially non-random process discovered by Darwin — is the only answer to the biggest question of all: why do we exist." *The Times* of London stated, on the same back cover, "His subject is nothing less than the meaning of life, and he attacks it with the evangelical fervor of a clergy man and the mind of a scientist." His solution to the mystery of life was the neo-Darwinian solution. The mysteries of life, and therefore of the mind, of human genius, of love and altruism were mysteries no more, he says, because we are machines.

The neo-Darwinian theory is a materialistic-mechanistic theory that tells us that matter is the element from which all is derived, and the evolution of life is no different to the evolution of matter. This evolution is powered by random mutations in genes, which modify the organism they produce, and an unconscious, uncaring, natural selection eliminates the unfit. The end products are increasingly complex machines. I realized as I sat there that this theory does not solve the mystery of life; it ignores it. Thinking over all the immensity of human nature, and the marvel of the human mind, I could not help wonder how such a simplistic theory could have received such wide and authorative acceptance.

How can anyone, let alone very intelligent and well-meaning scientists, willingly accept that a series of accidents accounts for the emergence of human genius: the genius exemplified by great artists such as Leonardo da Vinci, Michelangelo, Picasso, the literary genius of Dostoyevsky, Tolstoy, and Shakespeare, the scientific genius of Einstein, Darwin, and Neils Bohr, the musical genius of Bach, Beethoven and Mozart? The majority of people, of course, apart from scientists, do not accept it. According to the 2004 Gallup poll[2] almost 90 percent of Americans polled rejected the neo-Darwinian solution to the mystery of life. Only 12 percent agreed with it. Fifty percent believed that God created the earth and all that lives on earth according to the way described by Genesis. This too is marvelous in its way: that so many people are prepared to put aside so much evidence painstakingly accumulated by the various sciences that points unequivocally to a steady evolution of life forms, and are willing to rely simply upon dogma for their understanding. It may very well be that many of these people are willing to do this, indeed feel compelled to do this, because they believe that the only alternative is to accept that life is a meaningless charade. If we are indeed but complicated machines, what else can life be other than meaningless?

The other 40 percent of the Americans that were polled accept the fact of evolution, but feel that some creative agency must have had a hand in the evolutionary process. Recently Michael Behe, a professor at LeHigh University, has given voice to some of this 40 percent. He revived Intelligent Design as a further alternative. Some systems, he believes, are irreducibly complex and could not have evolved in the gradual way demanded by Darwin's theory. He concluded that God must have been involved in creating them. The flurry of intense debate that Behe stirred up shows how deeply concerned so many of us are about our origins.

The question is, how did you and I come to be? What were the forces that through the long eons of evolution finally made it possible for me to write this book and you to read it? None of the three — random mutation, Genesis, or Intelligent Design — gives a satisfactory answer. Accidents are the very opposite of creativity, although from an objective point of view we may sometimes have great difficulty distinguishing between them. An accident is by its very nature unintentional; yet creativity is, as I will discuss later, dependent upon intention. Accident is without direction, while creativity goes in the direction of greater simplicity[3] and unity. An accident, being fortuitous, has no history, whereas creativity is the continuation of a process and is dependent upon what has preceded it.

The word 'God' is loaded and its meaning changes according to whoever uses it as well as how it is used. The God of the Christian and the God of the Muslim are quite different gods, as the followers of both religions affirm. Furthermore the god of a televangelist and the god of someone like Mother Theresa are different gods, just as the God of the Israelites and the God of the present-day Catholic are different. The word God is so vague it means little to say, "Human nature is possible because God created everything," or "God designed irreducibly complex systems."

But let us return to the question, "Why has the mechanistic theory been so widely accepted among scientists as the solution to the mystery of life." Dawkins tells us, "Each of us is a machine like an airliner only more complicated."[4] When Dawkins and other like-minded scientists are with their families and friends, when they conduct their researches and argue with their colleagues, they do not look upon these people as machines. They see them as human beings with minds and intentions, with hopes and fears. But then, when they turn their minds to consider human beings in the abstract — as elements in a theory — they transform those same members of their family, their friends, their colleagues and *themselves* into machines. They do not say, "Let us suppose that we look at human beings as mindless machines and see how far we get with our understanding." That would be a perfectly legitimate way for a scientist to behave. Eliminating the wild variable of consciousness to see how far we can get without using the concept would be a fruitful way of conducting research. In fact for some scientists it has been a very fruitful way. But the neo-Darwinians do not do this. Dawkins says quite flatly, " Each of us is a machine", and he means what he says.

Thinking about this over the years has convinced me that we are all victims of our assumptions, and the neo-Darwinians are no exception. We make, or more often accept, assumptions about the way the world is and about the way others and we are. These become so familiar to us that later we forget they are assumptions and they become what Harvard professor Richard Lewontin called ideologies. Then we say this *is* the way the world is.

For example, it was once taken for granted that the world was a flat plate, that it was stationary and was at the center of the universe that revolved around it. To question this was to be regarded either as mad or as a servant of the devil. We now know that these were assumptions turned into dogmas that were taken for granted and, for centuries, remained unexamined. Another assumption was that human beings were at the pinnacle of creation and were specially created by God. Darwin questioned that assumption and said that human beings are the last in line of a long evolution extending back millions of years. Many of us are now prepared to see the idea that human beings were created by God is indeed simply an assumption, a way of thinking about the world, and so have either abandoned it altogether or have kept it simply as the best explanation about the way things are. But we now have the assumption that evolution was made possible by random mutation whose results have been refined by natural selection. Is it not time that we examined that assumption as well?

As we know many people had great difficulty accepting that the earth was not the center of the universe. The problem was not that they had to change their mind about what they thought. That the world was flat was not, for them, a thought; it was the way things were. When told that the earth was not the center of the universe they were not being asked to change one idea for another; they had to allow their world to be destroyed in order that another, different, world could take its place. As we see, 50 percent of Americans are also unable to make the change from humans being the unique creation of God to humans being the last in the evolutionary chain. They are unable to abandon a world in which a God creates them individually and cares for each one, and replace it with a materialist/mechanical world without sense or meaning; for them to do so would be spiritual suicide.

Scientists pride themselves on their objective way of viewing the world, a way undistorted by unexamined assumptions and wishful thinking. Yet, pondering on why so many scientists are prepared to put up with a simplistic solution to the mystery of life, it became obvious to me that one reason is because they assume that they are free from assumptions and bias. And so I made a list of the more influential of their unexamined assumptions. I do not say that all scientists have all of them, but most have some. For many, they are not assumptions at all, but the way things are, the way the world is; just as for Dawkins, that we are machines is not an assumption but the way we are.

Assumptions of neo-Darwinians

1   The world is a material world out of which, as it becomes increasingly complex, life and consciousness arise.
2   Organisms, including human beings, being complicated matter, can be studied using the same scientific approach that has been used in studying physical matter.
3   Everything can, in principle, be known.
4   Evolution occurs through accidental mutations refined by natural selection.
5   To understand the evolution of the species and human nature

one must start at the time of the earliest forms of life and trace evolution forward from that time.

6   The struggle to survive is essentially passive. Natural selection can be compared to a winnowing process that occurs when, for example, one sieves gravel to select only pieces of a given size.

7   Classical logic is adequate for gaining an understanding of life processes.

8   Evolution has no direction.

9   The need to survive is the sole life motivator. For the neo-Darwinian, the need to pass on one's genes is the sole motivator.

10 Evolution is a continuous process. No new elements may be introduced later into the evolutionary process to explain the appearance of new forms or qualities.

The real difficulty lies in the first two assumptions. If neo-Darwinian theory were presented as an explanation of the evolution of the *form* of organisms, it would not, perhaps, present quite the same difficulties as it creates with its claim that it has solved the mystery of life. It is because it makes this claim that I shall be questioning all of these assumptions except the last one. Without a doubt what I will say will either *be severely contested or ignored altogether*. For scientists to accept it will mean that they too would have to give up, not a set of beliefs or assumptions, but the way the world is for them. It is only fair therefore that I should state as clearly and as unequivocally as I can my own assumptions.

My assumptions

1   The world is a living world and consciousness is inherent to it.

2   Evolution occurs through a series of discrete creative moments, evolution is not a mechanical process and cannot be studied using the same assumptions as are used in the physical sciences.

3   The knowable is an island within the unknowable.

4   Evolution occurs through creativity, the results of which are then refined by natural selection.

5   One must start with what is best and greatest in human beings and account for its evolution.

6   The struggle for survival is both active and metaphorical. Two

dogs fighting for limited food resources is an example of active struggle to survive. As intelligence, creativity, courage and endurance determine the survivor, the same qualities winnow out the weaker and less fit to survive. These qualities would then gradually become part of the evolutionary sieve.

7 Classical logic is not adequate for gaining an understanding of life processes. We need a logic of creativity that includes classical logic, but goes beyond it.

8 Evolution goes in the direction of increasing intelligence.

9 The need to survive, the need to procreate, and the need to create are the motivators of life.

10 Evolution is a continuous, creative process. No additional elements may be introduced later into the evolutionary process to explain the appearance of new forms or qualities.

As I thought that summer in Kingston about the existing theories of evolution –creationism, neo-Darwinian, and Intelligent Design — I felt that some alternative had to be found. We do not just want a theory of the evolution of the human *form* but a theory of the evolution of human *nature*, which would of course include a theory of the evolution of mind. To have produced human beings, with their consciousness, intelligence, creativity, evolution must in some way be an intelligent, creative process. If this is so, if evolution is creative, no additional Creator is necessary. Certainly, accidents must have had something to do with it, but, if evolution and creativity are more or less synonymous, and it seems to me that somehow they are, then accidents cannot be the sole agent of change.

One of the problems with the way evolution has normally been studied is that theorists have worked from the bottom up so to speak. The theory starts at a very uncertain past and with the simplest of things — inanimate matter. This matter, the theory says, becomes increasingly complex and finally human beings appear on the scene. As nothing has been added to the process than what was initially there — inanimate matter — then human beings are very complex forms of inanimate matter. A preferable theory of the evolution of human nature and the human mind would start *with* human nature, *with* the fact of creativity and intelligence, and work back while asking ourselves how we have got to where we are.

Human beings like Christ, Buddha, Plato, Einstein, Michelangelo,

Bach, the great Zen and Sufi masters, the Christian Saints and Mystics such as Mother Theresa, St. Therese d'Avila, St Julian of Norwich, all have lived on earth. This is a fact as solid as any scientific fact. How are we to account for this? Many people have a strong religious urge, an urge that comes from the sense of something perfect, unattainable through the senses, yet nevertheless more real than the urge for sex or food. How can we account for this urge? How can we show how the evolution of the best and greatest in human beings — capacity for love, appreciation of beauty, altruism, creativity and intelligence — has been possible? No new properties, by some divine designer, nor even by an emergent sleight of hand, may be later added to the process of evolution. Only what is there at the beginning can participate throughout the whole process. No miraculous interventions, no special cases, no fudging the books of life may be allowed. But, instead of starting in the remote and uncertain past and moving to the present, we should start at the certain and immediate present and go back to the remote past.

Does all of this matter?

In the Introduction, I will show that the way we think about others and ourselves, about our origins and destiny, about the way we relate to each other and the rest of Nature, does matter, not simply to academics and scientists, but to each one of us educated and uneducated alike. If we truly believe that we are complicated machines living among other complicated machines, objects living among other objects, we will act accordingly. Racism, anti-Semitism, and racial profiling generally, which deny others their humanity, are scourges that need never be except that we look at others through the lens of prejudice and misinformation.

It matters in another way. John Horgan,[5] in his book *The Undiscovered Mind* leaves his readers in no doubt that the psychological sciences are in a state of disarray. This may well be because the life sciences generally have no firm foundation on which to build. Andrew Brown in *The Darwin Wars*[6] points out that the present trend of biological research tells us that beauty and elegance mean nothing to the universe and that this research "presents us with a terrible dilemma. *We can have truth or ethics but not both*" [*my emphasis*]. I would like to offer a possible way by which a new foundation for the life sciences may be constructed, a foundation that has Darwin's theory of evolution as its stimulus. This foundation will offer us the possibility of rediscovering that beauty and elegance does matter to the universe, as well as offering us a way to side step the terrible dilemma because, when we build upon it, we can have both truth and ethics.

What are my qualifications?

I appreciate that I am like Daniel walking into the lions' den. I will challenge some of the conclusions of well-qualified scientists who are highly respected, and who have written many widely read and well-received books. So, what are my qualifications? In one way I have none. None, that is to say, from the academic point of view. Yet, in this is my greatest asset. Let us remember that it was a young boy who saw the emperor had no clothes, not the wise counselors or the high-powered courtiers. Academic qualifications give status, prestige, authority, which, in turn, confers creditability. Even so, up to a point, the more qualifications one has, the less likely one is to risk challenging current orthodoxy. It is from that orthodoxy that so much that passes for qualifications and authority draws its power.

I say that in one way I have none, because in another way I am highly qualified to undertake the task that I have set myself: to open up a new way to answer the question, "How is it possible that human nature has evolved?" I have spent my life with the question, "What is a human being?" enquiring into it from the perspective of Zen Buddhism, as well as from the perspective of Western philosophy, psychology and evolutionary science. Zen Buddhism is a way, a practice. It has no dogmas or beliefs; it prescribes no rituals or ceremonies.[7] Buddha likened his teaching to a raft that one uses to 'cross over' or awaken beyond experience. He asked his disciples, "After you have crossed a river on a raft, do you then carry the raft on your heads?" To help them get beyond dogmas and beliefs and so 'cross over', a Zen master told his disciples to "Think the unthinkable!" When someone asked him how to do this he replied, "Without assumptions, theories, concepts or dogmas."

Long practice of 'thinking the unthinkable', of thinking beyond experience in this way, is to think differently. One awakens to an entirely new way of looking at the world and at our place in it. In what follows I try to show what this means by looking at the origin and evolution of human nature. At one time I thought of using a sub-title for this book "Meditations on what it means to be human." The questions, "What am I?" and by extension, "What is a human being?" are central issues of Zen practice. So I am not going to tell of 'what Zen thinks about evolution', or give the Zen philosophy of life, because ultimately there is no Zen to think or to philosophize.

I have added copious notes, both from the sayings of Zen masters and from Western teaching, because I want to show that although what I say comes out of meditation it nevertheless has universal value. I have not looked at any of these as sources for what I am saying; I quote them simply to show that what I say is not without precedent.

I have worked throughout the last forty years within the Zen Rinzai tradition whose roots are the same as the roots of human creativity,[8] and whose province is the transcendent aspects of the mind. For the first twenty of these forty years I worked under the guidance of a qualified Zen Master, spent two to three hours a day in meditation and, in addition, attended frequent weeklong retreats, all with this single question in focus: "What is a human being?" (What am I?). For the last twenty-seven years I have taught students, among whom have been university professors, doctors, psychiatrists, psychologists, lawyers, Jesuit priests and nuns. In 2003 I was awarded an Honorary Doctorate of Laws from Queen's University, a prestigious Canadian University, for academic attainment and community service.

I draw on some of what I have labored over during these last forty years in order to write what follows. I do not pretend to be able to say the last word. On the contrary, what I wish to do by writing this book is open up a new way to think about life, evolution and above all what has made possible the evolution of human nature. My earlier book, *Creating Consciousness* takes off where this book ends, and deals with many of the aspects that just cannot be dealt with in this introductory book. But even together the two books only form a prolegomena to what might one day be a much more productive understanding of the evolution of life and of human beings than we have at the moment. Psychologists, sociologists, philosophers and students of spirituality all could contribute to such an understanding. Possibly, as I shall emphasize, we have no greater intellectual need at the moment than a reality based understanding of the origins and development of the human being, an understanding that could revitalize the humanities and the life sciences.

An unavoidable problem, which creates difficulties for the reader, will accompany what I will be saying. I will often refer to a *transcendent* reality that lies beyond the range of our language and logical thought processes. By this I do not mean some mystical reality accessible only to spiritual adepts, but a reality, which, though immediate and ever-present to us all, just cannot be grasped in words and thoughts. I will have to rely on the good faith of the reader to be willing to follow me through a few dark and difficult (although, I hope) fascinating passages.

Chapter 3 may present some initial difficulties. It is an important chapter as it shows how we can talk about consciousness in very primitive organisms, but it is not 'easy' reading. Please do not worry if at first you do not completely follow the argument about 'knowing' and 'being' that I am making. The essential message of the chapter is presented in its opening paragraphs, and concluding summary paragraph. Throughout the book I refer back to these paragraphs repeatedly as they give one of the main themes of the book. Once you have read to the end of the book, the argument presented in this chapter will become easier to understand in the light of all that has been said.

Chapter 13 may also present some difficulties but it is an essential chapter and opens the way to understanding the origin of anxiety, anger and depression as well as love, creativity and the religious. In short it is the entrance to an understanding of human nature and gives an entirely original view of it. Because of this novelty I have had to create new words or use one or two words in new ways. Anyone who is blazing a trail has the same difficulty. The flurry of new words and expressions in computer science is an example of what I mean.

I will demonstrate the truth of several of the basic concepts that I shall be using by some very simple experiments, which anyone can repeat.

Darwin's theory is incomplete, as it does not show how the evolution of human nature has been possible. I will not question the facts that genetics, paleontology, and evolutionary research generally have discovered. But I will question the *context* within which these discoveries are evaluated, and within which conclusions have been drawn. This context is restricting, too confining to contain all that we need to understand about life and its processes. Working from the top down enables us to develop a wider context and to draw different conclusions. There will be no QED, no final punch line in conclusion. The theory of evolution does not lend itself to any final proof, such as one finds in the theories in physics and chemistry. Instead I will offer a step-by-step, cumulative argument, each chapter taking from and building on previous chapters. I will moreover present some of the key points in such a way that the reader may verify the validity of these points for himself or herself.

An apology and an explanation

I must add a word of apology and explanation to women who will read this book. I refer throughout to 'he' and 'him'. When talking about a scientist in general I will say, "*he* says this or *he* thinks that". I understand that this may well grate on some women's nerves. No doubt they will ask themselves, "Does he not think that women scientists can say and think things too?" I must assure whoever asks this that I certainly agree that women scientists are as scientifically astute as men: my wife, daughter and granddaughters would dare me to think otherwise. However, I feel that the question of style is as important as being politically correct. To say on each occasion 'he or she', or 'him or her' can become tedious; to alternate between he and she seems pedantic. I have therefore decided throughout this book to use 'he' as it has been used for centuries without any inference that women are to be excluded from what is being said.

Acknowledgments

I would like to acknowledge the help that the following people have given.

My thanks go to my wife Jean for her courageous and exacting editing, and for her unfailing support, to Monique Dumont and Jacqueline Vischer for their careful editing and their invaluable encouragement, to Tony Stern whose belief in my work has been an inspiration, to Paul Cash for his wisdom and excellent advice, to Alfonso Montuori and Bill Byers for the many discussions that we have had that have helped immeasurably in the development of these ideas, to Sandra Olney for her encouragement, and to my son John Low who read and commented on the developing Ms. Finally I would like to add a word of thanks to my editor and publisher Tony Grahame for his confidence in my work and for his courage in publishing it.

"I suggest that the universe, or its evolution, is creative, and that the evolution of sentient animals with conscious experiences has brought about something new. These experiences were first of a more rudimentary and later of a higher kind; and in the end that kind of consciousness of self and that kind of creativity emerged which, I suggest, we find in man."

KARL POPPER[1]

"It is clear that genes per se were not 'drivers' of evolution."

SEAN CARROLL[2]

"Let us therefore do something quite radical, something quite forbidden by our current views of science. Let us incorporate into our conception of scientific knowledge the part which *we ourselves necessarily contribute* in shaping such knowledge."

POLANYI AND PROSCH[3]

Introduction

"If cause succeed not cause from everlasting,
Whence this free will for creatures o'er the lands,
Whence is it wrested from the fates,– this will
Whereby we step right forward where desire
Leads each man on?"

LUCRETIUS, ON THE NATURE OF THINGS[1]

"How, therefore, we must ask, is it possible for us to distinguish the living from the lifeless if we can describe both conceptually by the motion of inorganic corpuscles?"

KARL PEARSON [2]

Let me set the stage for what is to follow by putting Darwin's theory in the context of a new vision of the world that has been emerging over the last one hundred and fifty years, and with which Neo-Darwinism is quite out of step. I will then say why a new logic, a new way of thinking, must be found that is appropriate to this new way of seeing the world, a logic that I shall develop in chapter 5. This logic, the logic of life and creativity, will incorporate yet go beyond what is generally known as classical or Aristotelian logic. I shall use, both as a justification and as a starting point for this logic, the principle of complementarity proposed by the quantum physicist Neils Bohr.

The main thrust of what I have to say is that neo-Darwinism is too limited to account for the evolution of human nature, and its claim to be able to do so is probably the main reason so many people either reject it outright, or only accept it with considerable reservations. I am not alone in seeking an entirely new way to understand how we, with all our loves and hates, wisdom and foolishness, creativity and destructiveness, have come to be, and I will be drawing on the writings of many others in support of what I have to say.

Darwin and a new view of the world

Darwin did not simply introduce a theory of species evolution. The clash between Christian fundamentalism and Darwinism is not simply a clash between a religious and a scientific view. Darwin broke from a static, space oriented, monolithic worldview to a dynamic, time oriented, and diverse worldview. He saw life as a dynamic flow, a continuous creation with species coming into and going out of existence. By contrast Creationists maintain a static, monolithic, reactionary view of life, in which species are God given absolutes, isolated from each other, fixed and unchangeable. In their view God is absolute, a supreme being, a Supreme entity.

Darwin's theory arose as part of a general awakening to a new view of the world that has been emerging since the mid nineteenth century and is still making itself known.[3] Freud gave us a dynamic view of the personality in place of a static soul; Marx saw history as a flow arising out of a dialectic process rather than the maintenance of the myth of the monarchy. This same movement from static to dynamic was evident in Maxwell's field theory, Einstein's theory of relativity, and in the recognition that mass can also be energy. This same trend away from static absolutes was carried on in sub-atomic physics and eventually into quantum physics where the fixed 'atom' became a probability wave, and where indeterminacy and uncertainty are the rule and no longer unwelcome exceptions. Systems, chaos, and complexity theories continued the trend. This awakening saw what Oswald Spengler in his *Decline of the West* called the transition from Apollonian man to Faustian man.

Darwin was one of the more celebrated prophets of this movement, from a static, hierarchic worldview anchored in a past Eden and given credibility and authority by Christian scripture, to a worldview based on progress, looking forward to a Utopian future, and given authority and credibility by empirical truths. This shift from structure orientation to a process orientation is still going on, and even the Utopias have given way to a more uncertain and open-ended future.

Dennett called Darwin's theory a 'dangerous idea' because, like a universal acid, nothing can contain it, and it will eventually eat its way through all structures, all containers. He seems to be justified in saying this because theorists have used evolution as an explanatory idea for evolutionary epistemology, economics, anthropology and sociology, and for many other disciplines. Scientists even say that the universe is evolving. I will show how evolution itself is evolving.

A new way of thinking

In view of the change from the static to the dynamic, to find that classical logic still holds sway is ironic. The irony is that the monolithic, static, worldview was not only justified by classical logic, but was a direct result of it. The keystone of this logic is the principle of identity. This is normally stated as A = A. Everything is what it is. According to this principle the world is filled with *things* that have their own static self-identity, their own self-being or eternal, unchanging essence. A chair is a chair; it is not a table. One can easily see how this principle could lead to the view that a specie is a specie, and to the belief that a specie has its own self-identity, its own essence — and so, being whole and complete it could not have evolved, it had to have been created by God.

The new view sees change as basic and things, including species, as temporary outcomes. From this view, that change is basic, the question, "How do things change?" cannot arise because as Henri Bergson said, "Things are change." Although those who cling to classical logic admit that change is possible, they find it difficult to explain logically how one thing turns into another. The Greek philosopher Zeno first showed the difficulty when he pointed out that an arrow could never get to its target. To do so it would have to pass through half the distance to the target. To reach the point halfway to the target, it has to pass through half the distance to that point, and so on.

The principle of causation, another offshoot of classical logic, presents similar difficulties. Some of these have long since been dealt with. Newton and Leibniz have shown with calculus how we can think logically, or at least mathematically, about change through time, and modern logic has critiqued and refined our understanding of cause. Nevertheless neo-Darwinism, the prevailing theory of evolution, still works from the belief that classical logic and the principle of causation are not simply ways of seeing and thinking about the world, but that they portray the way the world actually is. Neo-Darwinism is based on the notion of 'things', and the basic 'thing' in life is now thought to be the *gene*. Mutations in the gene, according to theory, cause changes to occur in the structure of an organism, which is another 'thing'.[4]

Science, as well as the logic on which it has been based, has been made by human beings and can be changed by human beings. What we know as science came into being in the seventeenth century to help us understand the workings of the material world. At that time the human questions — of human destiny and worth, of meaning and values, even of our origin and composition — were already taken care of by the Church, and could be conveniently left to the Church. Science was at that time under the thrall of Descartes, the scion of logical reasoning and the clear and distinct idea. He separated out the subject from the object, gave over the subject to the care of the Church, leaving science, and classical logic, to rule over the objective world.

The world has changed since then, and we live in a world of constant change, a dynamic world in which time dominates, and the importance of space is fast declining. In this world absolutes are rare. To live in this world of time and change, and have life sciences, including a psychology, which are still dominated by classical logic in which absolutes are the rule, is similar to driving a car with the hand brake on. The car goes along, but the stress on the system is enormous. Is it not time for another look at this logic?

Limitations of neo-Darwinian theory

Darwin's theory is immensely valuable because of its heuristic value. By this I mean that by using the idea we can integrate many other ideas, which, before, were separate and even in conflict. Our understanding of nature, of how life has evolved, and of the place of human beings in the scheme of things has been enhanced immeasurably by this theory. Even so, to look upon it *simply* as a 'scientific' theory is a mistake. The ongoing debate it has generated — not only between Creationists and neo-Darwinians, but also between interested lay people, within the Church and other religious organizations, within and between University disciplines — shows that the theory is more than just an explanation of the evolution of the species. It calls into question the very meaning of life, the place of human beings in the ecology of Being, the role of God, the possibility of a spiritual life and much more.

This criticism of the modern version of Darwin's theory, the neo-Darwinian theory, is particularly apt when we consider Evolutionary Psychology. Psychology, presumably, is the study of the *psyche*. The meaning of the original Greek work *psyche* was 'breath', then 'life principle', and then 'soul'. More recently we have come to see the psyche as 'mind' and 'personality'. Evolutionary psychology "is an *approach* to psychology, in which knowledge and principles from evolutionary biology are put to use in research on the structure of the human mind. . . . In this view, the mind is a set of information-processing machines that were designed by natural selection to solve adaptive problems faced by our hunter-gatherer ancestors. This way of thinking about the brain, mind, and behavior is changing how scientists approach old topics, and opening up new ones."[5]

Thus Evolutionary Psychology, based as it is upon the limitations of the neo-Darwinist, effectively banishes mind, consciousness, intention and allied subjects, as they were originally understood, from consideration in the same way that Behaviorism, its intellectual predecessor, also banished them from the domain of science. It makes more sense to change the name from Evolutionary Psychology to The Science of Some Aspects of Human Behavior, and so leave the field open for a genuine Evolutionary Psychology. Seeing the human mind, as well as the body, as having evolved from more primitive states, has great intellectual value. Indeed, I shall show, during the course of this book, how it has been possible for this evolution to have occurred, and so lay the foundation for a true Evolutionary Psychology. But those primitive states must, in some primitive way, have included mind.

I offered an earlier version of this manuscript to the editor of a respected scientific publishing house. He refused it saying that he doubted whether scientists interested in the theory of evolution would be persuaded by philosophical or religious arguments. However the wish to say, "this is scientific", "that is not scientific", comes from the same kind of thinking that I have just been criticizing. It suggests that science is some*thing*, that it has its own being, its own essence. Our thinking is segmented, fragmented, divided into territories upon which trespassers stray at their peril. Classical logic is the chief culprit in this process by which scientists are becoming alienated from other scientists, from philosophers and religious thinkers. While it is true that many universities and Think Tanks encourage inter-disciplinary dialogue, nevertheless this dialogue has only cosmetic value as long as the discussions are based upon an either/or way of thinking in which we have "this or that", "this is this and cannot be that".

Rather than worry about whether an idea is scientific or not, and into which intellectual niche it should be put, should we not look into the value of the idea? Some ideas are valuable because they can be proven, that is communicated in such a way that others can reproduce the results of the idea in their own laboratories. We can call them scientific, but why bother? Others are valuable because of their heuristic value. In pure mathematics heuristic value is a criterion by which a new theory is judged. New ideas can only enter an open mind; classical logic has the tendency to close the mind, it tends to set up artificial boundaries, and closures.

When the neo-Darwinian barricades are broken down, when we acknowledge that we cannot wall the theory of evolution into a biological ivory tower, that we must bring it out into the streets to answer to the needs of human beings in general, and not simply human beings acting within a very limited role as scientist, then we must admit that the neo-Darwinian theory is very limited, and even dangerous in a way not conceived of by Dennett.

Neo-Darwinism debases human beings

The last hundred years have been a hundred years of death. In the 1939–45 conflicts alone, more than forty million people were killed. Add to that some ten million killed in the 1914 war, as well as the toll from the many conflicts since, and the cost of human folly becomes staggering. Not only have armies clashing with armies been responsible for this carnage — the studied, deliberate and, in some cases, bureaucratic slaughter of human beings has added even more bloodshed. By bureaucratic slaughter I mean the systematic and 'legal' murders committed to clean the world of unnecessary objects: yids, wogs, slopes, nips, kulaks, and so on.

A well-known maxim states, "How one thinks, so one is." How we think about others and ourselves will determine how we behave towards them. This was starkly emphasized in the early part of the twentieth century when Social Darwinism and its offspring, eugenics, held sway and justified the excesses of Fascism, Nazism and their attendant atrocities. To change the behavior of others one must change their perception, and perception is not just a question of what is seen with the eyes, it also involves the judgments and choices that we make, and the logic that we use in making those judgments and choices. The horrible assaults on the Jews in Nazi Germany were made possible by years of anti-Semitic propaganda, years of educating one part of a nation to see the other part as sub-human. In South Africa, during the 1950s and 60s, the white population took for granted that their black compatriots were little more than animals, and for years the same outlook pervaded the southern United States.

Why mention this at the beginning of a book on evolution? Because some scientists, and they are the most vociferous, are perpetrating the same dehumanizing process this very moment. Scientists, nurtured and developed in the walls of the illustrious universities, of the world including Harvard University in America and Cambridge University in Great Britain, preach anti-humanism; these individuals are not political ideologues, they are not crackpots seeking to poison our minds, but scientists devoted to the explanation of human nature. Furthermore, not one or other segment of the human race is being dehumanized; but the human race itself. Nor are we simply being told that we are inferior. Our humanity itself is being stripped from us, and all in the name of science.[6]

For example, some leading scientists say that we are lumbering robots in the service of genes.[7] "You, your joys and your sorrows, your memories and your ambitions, your sense of personal identity and freewill are in fact no more than . . . a pack of neurons";[8] "if you believe in a soul then it's time you grew up and became an adult";[9] "we are pure accidents that might well never have been";[10] "we are but complicated computers destined to be surpassed by other more complicated computers";[11] "when we die we die and that's the end of us."[12] The irony is that this science, can only, by its very nature, embrace at best half the available facts about human beings. The half that is rejected is the most important if we are to have a science of the evolution of human nature.

I am not saying that this kind of ideology will cause another holocaust. But it will do nothing to prevent one, and may well, in time, be used to justify one. After all, do not these same scientists tell us that we're hard-wired for violence, and that ethics and morality are but quirks on the evolutionary trail,[13] or else, according to mathematicians like Hamilton, mathematically impossible.

In the past human integrity held some of our excesses in check. Integrity comes from a perception of the whole, of which each of us forms an integral part. A perception of the whole is the basis of ethics from which our morality, mores and laws are derived. This perception has led us to believe in the sanctity of the individual and the dignity of being human. But this perception of the whole is now scorned, and Nobel Prize winner Steven Weinberg assures us, "the reductionist worldview is chilling and impersonal." But, he says, though we may be appalled by these theories, and feel diminished by them, even so, "It has to be accepted as it is, not because we like it, but because that is the way the world works." [14]

It has no place for what is most typically human

Psychology means the study of the mind and no doubt many readers, like me, have at one time or other during their lives looked eagerly to it to tell us something about ourselves. In the last one hundred and fifty years, Darwin's theory of evolution has come to the forefront of scientific endeavor, and biological sciences have replaced physics as the leading science and now dominate the field of psychology as well. Darwin's theory of evolution proposes nothing less than an account of how you and I arrived on the scene. One would hope that it might have developed in the many years since Darwin first proposed it, and that we would have some scientific basis for understanding ourselves and our psyche and some answers to the question of where we fit in.

But alas! Neo-Darwinism tells us that we do not fit in. That is, if one understands 'we' to include our selves, our minds, spirits, and not simply our bodies. Scientists have validated Darwin's theory, it seems, beyond doubt, by the discovery of the DNA code. This discovery has confirmed that characteristics are transmitted only by way of the genes. With the recent success in mapping the human genome, and of genetic engineering generally, scientists now take it for granted that only a material solution holds promise of resolving the enigmas of the mind and of human existence. Cloning, stem cell research, organ transplants, cyborgs, genetic engineering — in fact all of modern technology — seem to have created a world in which we as selves no longer have a place. I am told that that I am a machine, that I have no special place in the world. I am an accident, something that need never have been. Heaven is imagination only, and God is long dead. As I have said, Dawkins has claimed that life no longer presents a mystery because Darwin and Watson have solved it.[15] But have they?

It takes away meaning and generates despair

The immediate effect of reading these diatribes is despair. Who, after having read a book by someone like Dennett or Dawkins, two materialist hard-liners, has not felt that numbing sense of futility? Despair mixed with outrage is the only response to being told that our lives are meaningless. Victor Frankl, who spent time in Auschwitz concentration camp, an unwilling witness to senseless slaughter, made the case that meaning is most valuable to a human being. He said that those who were most likely to survive the depredations of Nazi bestiality were those who had some reason to go on living, "Psychological observations of the prisoners have shown that only those who allowed their inner hold on their moral and spiritual selves to subside eventually fell victim to the camp's degenerating influences."[16]

But now we are told that we don't have a moral and inner self, that we are indeed no-where for no reason. One is not surprised to read that B. F. Skinner's daughter is said to have committed suicide after being brought up in a Skinner's box by her father, though the verity of this reported incident is disputed. Skinner, in the name of Behaviorism, an intellectual forebear of neo-Darwinism, and Evolutionary Psychology, made up his mind that it was time for human beings to let go of outmoded notions such as freedom and dignity.[17] Andrew Brown tells of a mathematician George Price. Price studied William Hamilton's equations. Hamilton was the originator of the myth of the selfish gene, a myth that Richard Dawkins has taken over and popularized. As Brown says,[18] "When Price had first found [the equations] he was so shocked that he set himself to do the work again, sure that there must be a flaw. He ended up reformulating them more generally and more powerfully; when this work was completed, *he went mad*" (my emphasis).

It is based on a faulty assumption

Apart from all this, neo-Darwinism stands condemned for failing to fulfill the original heuristic promise of Darwin's *The Origin of Species* and

The Descent of Man. It is based upon two faulty assumptions: the first, because a materialist basis enabled science to work near miracles in technology, the same materialist basis can work marvels for the life and psychological sciences;[19] and the second, classical logic is adequate as a logic of life. Classical logic is a logic of analysis and conflict; we need a logic of evolution through creativity.

An alternative view is possible

Although neo-Darwinism is the theory that most biologists and many evolutionary psychologists accept, nevertheless a great deal is happening that counters this mechanistic/materialistic trend. This happening is an additional reason why we should open up the theory of evolution to a wider set of disciplines than simply the biological. Quantum physicists, far from banishing consciousness from the universe, now recognize that it is an intrinsic part of it.[20] The notion of cause so beloved by the mechanist is hardly used in the new science. Writers such as physicists David Bohm and Roger Penrose, philosopher Karl Popper, physicist turned biologist Howard Pattee,[21] Edgar Morin, and many others have contributed to a completely new way of looking at nature and our place in it. All of this gives us reason to believe that the future may well see a new science of life and of psychology, based upon life's full meaning, and not as it is seen through the distorting mirror of materialism and mechanism. But to attain to this view we must change *the very way we think.*

1 | On Darwin's Theory

"Darwin and evolution stand astride us, whatever the mutterings of creation scientists. But is the view right? Better, is it adequate? I believe it is not that Darwin is wrong, but that he got hold of only part of the truth."

STUART KAUFMANN[1]

How have you and I come into being, what evolutionary forces have made us possible? By evolution I mean a continuous, creative process. No additional elements may be introduced later into the evolutionary process to explain the appearance of new forms or qualities. That I have written this book and you are reading it shows that you and I are conscious, creative, intelligent, and have volition. (I am taking it that you are reading it because you want to). If so, then, as evolution is a continuous process, these elements — consciousness, creativity and volition — must have been there right from the start of the evolutionary process. What I have to do then, in this book, is to show that indeed they have been there all the time. This will show that evolution is itself intelligent and so has been able to produce intelligent beings like you and me.

Most scientists, who have thought about and worked with Darwin's theory, in particular those working with the prevailing neo-Darwinian version, would contest what I will say if they do not simply reject it without further consideration. I therefore have to be very clear about what I mean when I use words like consciousness, creativity, intelligence, and volition. This will not be easy, not because I will be introducing new ideas that need a great deal of background for their development, but because what I shall be talking about is so very obvious that every one takes it for granted and so overlooks it. Instead of talking about consciousness, which is a word loaded by a variety of meanings and arcane theories, I shall talk about *knowing*. In a way it is absurd that I shall have to spend so much time talking about knowing. Everything that I will say about it will be perfectly obvious and transparent. But, and this is the paradox, what I say will seem abstract.

First, though, let me show that my introducing creativity, intelligence and intention into the theory of evolution is not contrary to Darwin's theory. Indeed, neo-Darwinism, by rejecting these, has negated half Darwin's theory. Darwin, when writing about the struggle for survival, distinguishes between two kinds of struggle; one of these I will call 'active' struggle and the other 'metaphorical' struggle. The qualities necessary for active struggle, I will show, increasingly modify the natural selection process and so evolution itself evolves. These qualities include consciousness, creativity, and intelligence. Moreover, actively struggling to survive obviously implies an intention to survive, and so intention, which has been rejected by evolutionary theorists up until now, must become a legitimate part of the theory of evolution.

What is Darwin's theory?

Darwin's theory has the elegance of all first-rate theories. It says that organisms have evolved. The changes leading to evolution have arisen through chance and random mutation. Through natural selection, some of these changes have allowed some organisms to become better adapted than others to their environment. Those organisms that are better adapted have tended to survive in greater numbers. Those that survive will likely transmit their characteristics to the next generation.

We must remember that Darwin's original theory made way for influences other than natural selection to be a means of species modification. He protested, in the last edition of *The Origin of Species*, "I place in a most conspicuous position — namely at the close of the introduction — the following words: 'I am convinced that natural selection has been the main but not the exclusive means of modification.' This has been of no avail. Great is the power of steady misrepresentation."[2]

More recently, neo-Darwinism has theorized that the vehicles for the transmission of these changes are the genes. It has also replaced Darwin's liberal open-minded approach with a rigid materialistic-mechanistic point of view, sometimes going so far as to state that the only purpose in life is the propagation of genes.

The struggle for existence

The key to Darwin's theory of evolution is the word *struggle* but this word 'struggle' is not as innocuous as it may seem. On the contrary, Darwin uses it in a very ambiguous way. As the consequences of this ambiguity are important to all that follows, I will quote him at length.

In Chapter 3 of his book *The Origin of Species* he writes about the struggle for existence. The first paragraph is quite clear and unambiguous: it stresses the importance of the idea expressed in the phrase 'the struggle for existence'.

> "All organic beings are exposed to severe competition. . . . Nothing is easier than to admit in words the truth of the universal struggle for life, or more difficult — at least I have found it so — than constantly to bear this conclusion in mind. Yet unless it be thoroughly engrained in the mind, I am convinced that the whole economy of nature, with every fact on distribution, rarity, abundance, extinction, and variation, will be dimly seen or quite misunderstood."[3]

This is a very clear, unambiguous statement about the importance of the idea 'struggle for existence'. But he then goes on, "I should premise that I use the term 'struggle for existence' *in a large and metaphorical sense,* including dependence of one being on another, and including (which is more important) not only the life of the individual, but success in leaving progeny."[4] I have emphasized 'in a large and metaphorical sense' because this part of Darwin's statement has been ignored by almost everyone who has written anything about the theory. Lewontin protests, "Modern biology has become completely committed to the view that organisms are nothing but the battle grounds between the outside forces and the inside forces. *Organisms are the passive consequences of external and internal activities beyond their control*" (my emphasis).[5] In a fictional letter to Darwin, Gabriel Dover, in his book *Dear Mr. Darwin,* says, "As you [Darwin] know, natural selection is not an 'active process' like artificial selection. The disproportionate increase of some genes at the expense of others . . . is a passive outcome of the particular interactions between prevailing ecological conditions and a particular set of genetically unique individuals."[6]

Yet, it is obvious that Darwin did not know this at all but knew something quite different. A metaphor says that something both is and is not the case. For example, Shakespeare said metaphorically, "All the world's a stage." Yet, obviously, the world is not a stage but something quite different. By using the word struggle in a metaphoric sense, Darwin says life is a struggle, and that it is not a struggle. He does this in the following way.

He says, "Two canine animals in a time of dearth, *may be truly said* to struggle with each other which will get food and live. But a plant on the edge of a desert is said to struggle for life against the drought, though *more properly* it should be said to be dependent on the moisture."[7] I have emphasized two phrases: 'may be truly said', and 'more properly'.

The struggle for survival is the keystone to his whole theory. Yet, in spite of the beauty of his prose and clarity of thought, he is ambiguous. He says that he will use the term 'struggle for existence' 'in a large and metaphorical sense'. It is a struggle because two dogs 'may be truly said to struggle'; it is not a struggle because 'more properly' it should be said that a plant is dependent on the moisture. In other words he conflates two *entirely different* meanings under the one term: struggle.

Darwin is convinced that, unless the struggle for existence "be thoroughly engrained in the mind . . . the whole economy of nature . . . will be dimly seen or quite misunderstood." Only the metaphorical struggle to survive has been thoroughly ingrained in the mind of the neo-Darwinians, and so they have only "dimly seen or quite misunderstood . . . the whole economy of nature, with every fact on distribution, rarity, abundance, extinction, and variation."

Metaphorical struggle

To explore this confusion, let us liken natural selection to a sieve. Those organisms that stay in the sieve survive; those that pass through die out. Let us suppose that size is a deciding factor. Organisms are put into the sieve, it is shaken, and after a while some have passed through the sieve and others remain in it. Some organisms survive and others do not. We find that the ones that survive are uniformly bigger than those that do not.

I call this *metaphorical* struggle. The organisms did nothing of themselves to survive. They just happened to be the right size and so stayed in the sieve. We can pass the surviving organisms through another sieve — this time for color, only green organisms will survive. We now find that surviving organisms are all big and green. Let us now sieve them for roundness. And so it goes on. Gradually the organisms become more and more modified over millions of years, which mean millions of sieves operating in sequence and in parallel.

An earthquake strikes a city and thousands die: the survivors mostly do nothing to survive. They just happen to be in the right place. A severe drought occurs. Some plants happen to be fortunate and are rooted near an underground well. The rest die of thirst. This is the neo-Darwinian idea of the struggle to survive. As Dover said above, "Evolution is not an 'active process' like artificial selection . . . it is a passive outcome of the particular interactions between prevailing ecological conditions and a particular set of genetically unique individuals."

Active struggle

Darwin used a fight between two dogs to show what he truly meant by the expression 'struggle to survive'. One of the chief characteristics of this struggle is the determination to win. The drive to dominate, to be the alpha male, is a feature of wild life, and the struggle is not simply a struggle for food but is an expression of what Nietzsche called the 'will to power'. Will to power, the will to dominate, is a driving force at all levels of life and makes the true struggle for existence possible.

This means that another form of struggle that I am calling active struggle, quite different from metaphorical struggle, is possible. We could call it 'intelligent struggle'. A gestalt ethologist, Kohler, performed the following very well known experiment on a chimpanzee. He put some bananas outside her cage and just out of her reach. He put a stick that she could reach close by the cage. When the chimp became hungry she saw the bananas and struggled to reach them by stretching her arm through the bars of the cage. She could not get them. After some frustrating moments she was able to perceive the gestalt,[8] bananas-distance-stick-hunger. She pulled the bananas to herself with a stick.

This is an example of intelligent struggle. The conclusion that has been drawn from this, and accepted by much of the scientific community, is that the chimp perceived a gestalt, the sudden appearance of whole: hunger-bananas-distance-stick-satisfied hunger. The perception of a gestalt in a field that is apparently disconnected and random is, as I shall show later, a creative and intelligent act. The chimpanzee used intelligence and creativity. This means that intelligence and creativity, as well as volition, may contribute to making active struggle possible.

Active struggle as part of the evolutionary sieve

We no longer simply have an organism being modified by the environmental sieve. We now have intelligent, creative and dynamic organisms that are part of, *and so modify*, the evolutionary sieve. Ernst Jantsch says in his book *The Self-Evolving Universe* "Evolution is open not only with respect to its products, but also to the rules of the game it develops. The result of this openness is the self-transcendence of evolution in a 'metaevolution', the evolution of evolutionary mechanisms and principles."[9]

When two dogs fight to determine who is to survive, the qualities that enabled the dog to be victorious now form part of the sieve and so the evolutionary mechanisms evolve. The qualities of the victorious dog 'sieved out' the defeated dog. The victorious dog won by strength, agility, speed and sharp teeth, all of which may have been evolved through successive metaphorical struggles. But also greater determination, stealth, cunning, intelligence were involved. These are now part of the sieve that the beaten dog passed through to extinction. Cunning, stealth, intelligence, these are all creative; determination is the opposite of passivity. Kohler's chimp used cunning and intelligence when getting the bananas. Future animals when pitted against animals of superior determination, intelligence, creativity, cunning, or stealth will have to pass the test of determination, intelligence, creativity, cunning or stealth to survive. But, because the more determined and intelligent will survive in greater numbers than the less determined and less intelligent, those that survive will raise the determination and intelligence threshold of the sieve. As the determination, intelligence, creativity and other such qualities of animals evolve, the sieve will evolve also, it will become ever more demanding, requiring higher and higher levels of determination and intelligence to survive.

Now that determination, intelligence, creativity, cunning and stealth are part of the evolutionary sieve, evolution is no longer the result of blind chance alone. Determination, intelligence, and the other qualities, now guide evolution as well as blind chance. That this is so, that the influence of intelligence becomes more important as the organism becomes more evolved, runs counter to most modern theories of evolution. To return once more to Dover's quote, he says, "Natural selection is not an 'active process' like artificial selection."[10] Yet, on the contrary, active struggle is very similar to artificial selection. Because determination, creativity, intelligence, and judgment, are all parts of the evolutionary sieve, evolution itself becomes active and intelligent.

Theories of evolution have the concept of the 'arms race'. For example, as prey become more swift of foot, so their swiftness selects out the less swift predators for extinction. These are unable to keep up with the prey and so starve. This means that the swiftness of the prey selectively breeds fast predators. But fast predators selectively breed fast prey. The evolution of creative intelligence is the basic arms race, and eventually, with the advent of human beings, becomes the most important element in the evolutionary sieve. Creative intelligence is the most essential ingredient in both prey (to avoid the predator) and predator (to capture the prey). Intelligent and creative prey breed intelligent and creative predators and intelligent and creative predators breed intelligent and creative prey.

Let us remember what Darwin said about active struggle: "two dogs fighting over food in time of dearth", may be *truly* said to be a struggle, but that metaphorical struggle, "a plant on the edge of a desert", is not so much a struggle and should more properly be said to be a *dependency* on the moisture. He exhorts us to remember the struggle to exist as a vital factor in evolution. My view is that, in general, scientists have only kept in mind metaphorical struggle, which is not truly a struggle, and have ignored active struggle. They do this because the notion of metaphorical struggle supports a mechanistic theory of evolution, while the notion of active struggle negates such a theory. I invite the reader to keep active struggle in mind while reading what I have to say, because this active, creative struggle is key to my thought. I will in the course of this book show what I mean by creativity and by intelligence and show

how, in a very attenuated form, these are present in all sentient life. I will also show that active struggle is *intentional* struggle. Intention, not causation or accident, powers this kind of struggle.

Intelligence is not arbitrary; it has to wait until the right circumstances are present. While the tree of evolution may branch out and modifications of species or new species arise, this is not because of foresight or because designs or decisions were made in advance; it is because the situation comes to demand it. Only very recently, and only in some modern art, has creativity come to be regarded as the expression of the arbitrary, the 'original', the different, and idiosyncratic.

If evolution is no more than a series of chance occurrences modified by an indifferent natural selection, then one does not need to ask why the dogs struggle. Metaphorical struggle means that the struggle just happens according to a chain of cause and effect. No because or purpose need be invoked; life begins by chance and goes on by chance. If, on the contrary, the dogs actively struggle, then one is inclined to ask why, why does life strive so hard to continue to exist? What follows will be an exploration of that why.

Darwin's theory is incomplete

Chance and random mutation alone cannot account for evolution. At least some of the changes that have resulted in evolution have been *created*. Further, I suggest that creativity and evolution differ only in timescale; evolution is slow motion creativity. Let me hasten to add that I am not a creationist and do not invoke a creator, conscious design, or Lamarckian intention.

The belief that Darwin's theory is incomplete is by no means new. It has been with us ever since the theory was first proposed in 1859. One of the most interesting alternatives to Darwin's theory that arose at the beginning of the twentieth century, and which attracted a great deal of attention, was Henri Bergson's theory of *Creative Evolution*. Many similarities will be found between what Bergson had to say and what I am saying, although I am not putting Bergson into modern dress. What I have to say was developed quite independently of his philosophy. Other critics who feel that the neo-Darwinian theory is incomplete include R. C. Lewontin, Jay Gould, Erich Jansch, Howard Pattee, as well as those developing the theory of intelligent design, and others developing the theory of complexity. Teilhard de Chardin and Arthur Young can also be added to the list.

Indeed, the dissatisfaction with Darwin's theory is so widespread that a 2004 Gallup Poll showed that although about half of America accepts that human beings have evolved gradually over millions of years, only 12 percent accept that natural selection, unguided, can account for the evolution of the human mind. Most think that the mind's evolution must have been guided by some intelligent force, some active designer. The neo-Darwinian Richard Dawkins bemoans, "For some reasons that are not clear to me, Darwinism seems more in need of advocacy than similarly established truths in other branches of science. . . . It almost seems as if the human brain were specifically designed to misunderstand Darwinism and find it hard to believe."[11] Among the reasons that the human brain finds it hard to accept the Darwin theory is because the theory is just not complete.

Although others have suggested that Darwin's theory is not complete, nevertheless the approach that I shall be taking is quite new. The neo-Darwinian theory in particular does not take into account the effect that subjectivity and intention — ingredients of creativity — have on evolution. I appreciate that vitalism, Bergson's *élan vital,* Lamarck's theories, as well as the theory of the Omega Point of Teillard de Chardin, have been either discredited or have dropped out of fashion. Nevertheless *active struggle to survive* implies *intention to survive* although, as will be seen, I use the word intention in a rather special way. Although Bergson may have dropped out of fashion, fashion is not an arbiter of truth and we must now try to find some alternative to the neo-Darwinian dogma.

2 | On Subjectivity and Objectivity

"The ideal of physics is to eliminate the subjective observer completely. It turned out that at the quantum level this is a fundamental impossibility, but that has not changed the ideal."

HOWARD PATTEE[1]

Our question is: what factors in evolution have made the evolution of human nature possible. When we think of *human nature* we do not simply think of our body. We think also of our mind. Intelligence, creativity, judgment and even intentionality, all imply mind and consciousness, and all of these can be seen to be elements in the evolutionary sieve. The evolution of the mind must therefore be included in any theory of the evolution of human beings. The next two chapters will lay the groundwork for an understanding of how this evolution is possible.

The concepts 'mind' and 'consciousness' are very complex and not easy to define. If some kind of rudimentary consciousness exists in very primitive organisms it must exist in a very simple, elementary way. We need, in other words, to find the very essence of consciousness, an essence that, over time, can evolve into the human mind. In the following chapter such an essence will be discussed. This chapter will discuss an essential feature of mind and consciousness — *subjectivity* — that neo-Darwinians as well as many other life scientists would like to reject or deny altogether.

However a scientist just cannot do this. *He* decides to study this phenomenon rather than that, *he* decides to do the study in this way rather than that. His research is based upon a number of theories that *he* has accepted as being valid. *He* decides what data is acceptable and how it must be interpreted. By 'he' I mean he the subject; the above decisions, and many more that he makes and that I have not listed, are all subjective decisions. Subjectivity therefore cannot be either rejected or denied.

On theory as a way of looking at the world

We must be quite clear about what we mean by a 'scientific theory' as this will help me show what I mean by the word subjective. But first, what is a theory? The word *theory* is based upon the word *theoreo*, a Greek word that means 'to look'. A theory is *a way of looking at the world. Someone* looks at the world. The belief that science is completely objective comes from ignoring that 'someone'. Whenever there is looking there is a subject that looks. Furthermore, a *scientific* theory, and this includes Darwin's, does not come from someone simply looking at the world. It comes from someone looking at the world in a way that is conditioned by a specific set of rules, and, as we saw in the Preface, conditioned by a set of assumptions.

We must not believe that, because the world seems to have certain characteristics when we look at it in a way conditioned by a set of rules and assumptions, it only has these characteristics. A botanist, an ethologist, a geologist look at an area of land in a very selective but, in many respects, quite different ways. To use an extreme example, if I look at the world through rose-colored glasses, I cannot conclude that the whole world is colored pink, that the characteristic pink is a property of the world. The rose-colored glasses condition my looking.

David Bohm says much the same in his book *Wholeness and the Implicate Order* when he states that "man has always been seeking wholeness — mental, physical, social, and individual." "Yet," he says, "over the ages, he has generally lived in fragmentation." Fragmentation is brought about, Bohm explains, "by the almost universal habit of taking the content of our thought for 'a description of the world as it is'."[2] We see the world as a collection of separate, isolated things, and, forgetting that this comes from the way we are looking at the world, we conclude that the world is simply a collection of things.

Science looks at the world through 'objective glasses'; it insists that the objective point of view alone is acceptable. It then concludes, because we only ever see the objective world when we look through these objective glasses, that this is the only world; an objective and material world is all there is. The subjective world is then disregarded or denied altogether. The subjective point of view, though, as I shall show shortly, is equally valid.

Should we not therefore, widen the scope of science, to include the subjective? Bohm advocated widening the scope of science saying that in this way, "We can . . . free scientific research from irrelevant restrictions which tend to result from . . . the supposition that a particular set of general properties, qualities and laws must be the correct ones to use in all possible contexts and conditions."[3]

On the meaning of the words subjective and objective

One of the reasons for the scientist rejecting the subjective is that the word has several meanings. Most people think that they know what the word 'subjectivity' means. They would say that it means our private world: the world of our fantasies, wishes, thoughts and feelings. But the word subjective is ambiguous; it has at least two other, more specific, meanings. Subjective information can mean information influenced and biased by our wishes, emotions, desires, prejudices and theories, and these include our assumptions. Whenever a scientist works with unexamined assumptions of the kind that I set out in the preface, believing that they are the way things have to be, he is acting subjectively. When in future I write about this kind of subjectivity I will use a lower case 's'.

Subjectivity can also mean direct, unmediated knowing, without reason or cause; alternatively it could be called direct *knowing*. I will spend the next chapter exploring the meaning of this subjectivity. Paradoxically, although this is most intimate and obvious, it will be very difficult to talk about, but let me say a very few words by way of introduction. I said just now that whenever there is looking there is a subject that looks. This is capital 'S' Subjectivity.

The word objective has two meanings as well. I will use a small 'o' to speak of the first. Information that is not biased by our personal wishes, emotions, prejudices and theories is objective. The word objective can also refer to knowledge based on information gained initially by the senses (or extensions of the senses through instruments). Information that we get through this kind of Objectivity, with a capital 'O', is what is normally thought to be scientific information.

The two meanings of both of these words are often confused. For example, we say a scientist is Objective, and we tend to think it means that emotions, egoism, jealousy, bias do not enter into his mind as he performs his experiments and draws his conclusions. Nobel prizewinner James Watson, in his book *The Double Helix*,[4] in which he recounts the driving competitiveness, the jealously, wrangling, enmities and debate that was involved in, and came out of, the research into the structure of the genes, dispels any such illusion. A scientist can be as subjective as any new age devotee.

Over the years scientists have gradually come to see that by using the Objective worldview alone we get greater control over the physical world. Because of this they gradually developed, not always consciously, the rules of science. Then, because of the overwhelming technological success that this Objective worldview has given, they tend to claim that this is the only true worldview.

Recent developments in quantum physics have shown that the Subjective, as the observer, is as essential as the Objective, what is observed, for something to happen.[5] Quantum physicist Max Born, in a paper called *Symbol and Reality* recalls his own shock as a young student when it dawned on him that all our perception and mental imagery, "everything without exception", is entirely [S]ubjective, and that only by the use of symbols can we communicate any objective components of our [S]ubjective, private experiences.[6]

If we want to understand how human nature, of which the Subjective is an essential component, can possibly have evolved we obviously cannot reject or overlook the Subjective. The irony is that when the neo-Darwinist insists that only the Objective data is permissible he is being subjective, with a small 's'.

In the West the idealist philosophies of Bishop Berkeley expressed the Subjective worldview. More recently idealism — usually under the name of anti-realism — has become even more respectable with work that is being done in quantum mechanics. The physicist Euan Squires, in his book *The Mystery of Quantum Reality* said, "There are [some scientists] who would claim that observation is all there is and that the idea of an external reality is simply an illusion."[7] Nick Herbert in his book

Quantum Reality writes, "Far from being a crank or minority position, 'there is no deep reality' represents the prevailing doctrine of establishment physics."[8] This is similar to the position of idealism of Bishop Berkeley, the view that the world is an outcome of the mind. This has been a philosophy in the East ever since human beings began to reflect on the meaning of existence. It is at the basis of much of the philosophy of the Vedanta from which come the *Upanishads*.

The conflict between the naïve realists, who believe the world exists independently of being perceived, and the idealists, who believe that the existence of the world is dependent upon being perceived, does not mean that half the world is stupid and the other half wisdom incarnate. Rather, we can see the world *Objectively* as a set of material forces, or we can see the world *Subjectively* as a set of ideas. These two views are independent of each other and have equal status. Our choice to adopt one or the other will depend, not on logic, experiment or scientific reason, but on faith alone. Our choice will be made in accordance with our own temperament.

Although neither worldview is complete in itself, each worldview, in its own way, encompasses the whole of the experience of whoever adopts it. Each of us holds our worldview with utter faith in its ultimate rightness, and each acts as though that worldview is *the* world. Although a materialist can learn about the spiritual way, nevertheless, for him, this learning is second hand and lacks the immediacy and certainty of his own way that is based on his native, Objective worldview. A materialist may intellectually accept or reject the spiritual way, but cannot completely understand it, if understanding is considered to include emotional acceptance.

On Faith

Faith is Subjective, that is *knowing* without recourse to understanding, reason or logic. I contrast faith with *belief*. The word 'belief' has a variety of meanings. In this context I use the word to mean knowing mediated by unexamined assumptions. Belief is therefore subjective. The faith that underlies both science and religion comes out of Subjectivity. Faith is absolute, although its consequences may change. Faith makes beliefs and assumptions possible; it is not a result of them.

When I say that faith is absolute I do not mean that the way that it is expressed cannot be changed. I mean that faith cannot be had in greater or lesser degree. If I know the world to be so, then for me that is the case. The world I know to be thereby forms for me a stable background against which beliefs, opinions and theories come or go. This background is taken for granted, and only after intense spiritual work can it be questioned, and its origins in knowing made clear. Science therefore is not scientific; only the methods and theories of science are scientific. The edifice of science is built on the foundation of faith. Faith is the light that shines, indeed burns, through the scientific worldview.

Faith and uncertainty in scientific research

A scientist rarely begins at the beginning, but most often finds himself in the middle, 'on the way', so to speak. He does not start from firm ground and continue along firm ground. The ideal of Descartes of starting and continuing with clear and distinct ideas is only possible if we deal with nature in the abstract. Each step on the way of an empirical science, such as the science of evolution, is a provisional, tentative step. The great number of different opinions and theories within any given scientific discipline, some in direct conflict with others, shows that each and all of them must be both provisional and tentative. For example theoretical physicists have at least eight different ways of answering the question, "What is quantum reality?"[9]

Because scientists have to start in the middle, and also because the theories they rely upon to do research are but the best available at the moment, the only truly firm ground that a scientist can find is within himself. As Karl Popper tells us, "Scientific discovery is impossible without faith in ideas which are of a purely speculative kind, and sometimes even quite hazy; a faith which is completely unwarranted from the point of view of science, and which, to that extent, is 'metaphysical'."[10] No scientific theory or law can take the place of this faith, nor prove its validity. Faith is the foundation upon which proof and the edifice of science are built. The faith to wander in the haze of uncertainly both sustains the great scientist and separates him from his peers. In other words, true science has no place for the dogmatic and evangelical approach shown by some modern biologists. Faith and uncertainty form the basis of all creativity.

What all this means is that notwithstanding the immense success of the physical sciences and technology, the scientist requires faith to sustain him no less than the Christian does. The faith of the scientist is expressed in his adherence to the rules of science in the same way that the faith of the Christian is expressed through the ritual and ceremonies of the Church.

On unity in life and thought

Unity lies beyond the Subjective and the Objective and plays a determining role in any theory. Monotheism, One God, is basic to the three Western religions of Christianity, Judaism, and Islam. The basis of most mystical experiences, out of which religions have grown, is a profound encounter with a basic unity. Most of the rules of science imply unity, and are based on faith in the idea that the world is one unbroken whole. The principle of identity of classical logic, the principle that everything is equal to itself, comes directly from unity. This principle of identity, in turn, gives rise to 'things', that is to say, *units* — or 'ones' — in the world. Occam's Razor, often wielded in science, is an application of the principle of simplicity, and is also based upon the faith that the world is one. The word 'simplicity' comes from a root word *sem*, which means One. The rule of completeness, another rule sometimes called upon in science, is also based upon the same faith: that the universe is a unity, that basically everything is related to everything else.

The intuition of unity makes the scientist instinctively cling to monism and to reject dualism as a possibility. This means that when faced with the alternatives, 'either idealism or materialism', or 'either Subjectivity or Objectivity', this same intuition of unity inclines the scientist to accept materialism and reject idealism, to accept Objectivity and reject Subjectivity. No scientific theory or law can take the place of this intuition of unity, nor prove its validity. When Einstein said that God does not play dice, when the astrophysicist draws conclusions about the most distant galaxy using theories developed on earth, or when Dawkins says, "A good case can be made that Darwinism is true, not just on this planet but all over the universe wherever life may be found,"[11] they are all, rightly or wrongly, relying on this intuition of unity.

The unknowable

The world that can be understood is the knowable world; but the knowable and explainable world exists as an island in the sea of the *unknowable*. As Robert Pollack, a professor of biology at Columbia University, points out, "The unknowable as a notion does not come easily to the scientifically minded. . . . As soon as the notion of the unknowable as distinct from the unknown placed itself before me, the shock changed both my career and the way I see the world." He had already said something that we must bear in mind throughout this book, "Dealing with the unknowable is a project full of paradox, requiring that one talk about the unutterable and anatomize the unmeasurable."[12]

Unknowable should not be construed to mean non-existent, nor does it necessarily mean mystical. One of the principal themes of this book is the influence and importance of the unknowable not only in evolution but also in our everyday, mundane life. As we shall see life and its evolution come from the interplay of the knowable and the unknowable.

3 | 'Knowing', the Basis of Experience

"That which knows all things, and is known by none, is the subject. Accordingly it is the support of the world, is the condition (that is universal and always presupposed) of all phenomena, of all object; for whatever exists, exists only for the subject. Everyone finds himself to be this subject, but only in so far as he knows, not in so far as he is the object of knowing."

ARTHUR SCHOPENHAUER[1]

We are enquiring into how it is possible that you and I have come to be. What, in the evolutionary process, has made it possible that I can sit here typing this book and you can sit there reading it? What has made possible the evolution of human nature, and ushered in the vast panoply of human creativity with all its great civilizations, religions, sciences, philosophies and arts that have paraded down through the millennia? The Bible tells us "man [or woman] does not live by bread alone." To tell just the story of the evolution of teeth and stomach is not enough. During the past one hundred and fifty years millions of men and women have devoted their lives, directly or indirectly, to the question of how the body has evolved. The full power of human creativity, ingenuity and intelligence has been beamed on to this question. To have excluded this same creativity, ingenuity and intelligence from the research, and even, as some scientists have done, to have relegated them to some accidental by-product of the activity of matter, would seem to an impartial observer a kind of perversity to say the least!

What are you? Not your body but you? What am I? This question, not in the form of philosophical musing, but as the stimulus for energetic, constant and systematic enquiry, is as old as humankind. The

Ancient Egyptians, Hindus, Buddhists, Sufis and early Christians, all developed methodologies and practices for making this enquiry systematic, meaningful and productive. Men and women have devoted their whole lives to this one question, "What am I?" and, by extension, "What is a human being?" A vast corpus of literature and a profound store of proven ways of investigation exist in the Far East, some of which is now streaming through to the West. When Hellenic and Arabic influences penetrated into Europe in the 15th and 16th centuries they ushered in a spiritual and scientific rebirth that brought in its wake the Renaissance and Enlightenment. So, in a similar fashion, the influx of Buddhist, Hindu and Sufi thought can bring about a new spiritual awakening, a new view, new for the West that is, on this question, "What is a human being: how have we evolved?"

Anyone who is prepared to admit information other than that accessible through the senses could say for himself or herself, *I am* and *I am conscious*. In this chapter let us explore the implications these two statements have for our study. The scientist Max Delbrück said, "A new conceptual language has to be developed to embrace this situation."[2] The situation he referred to was quantum physics, but the same is true for the study of the evolution of human nature. A new conceptual language has to be developed to embrace this study also. The word 'consciousness', which many people consider to be a *sine qua non* of human nature, is a difficult word to define. Different thinkers have different definitions, and in any case consciousness is complex. Instead of trying to define consciousness let us ask what is its essential characteristic? If even the most primitive organism is alive, consciousness is one of the characteristics of this aliveness. But the consciousness of this organism cannot be the same as ours, which includes memory, thoughts, images, concepts and much else besides.

I am suggesting that awareness or *knowing*[3] is the most essential aspect of consciousness. Knowing is the basis of all experience. For the time being let us leave aside the question, "what is this 'I' that knows?" and let us just concentrate on knowing. I will return to the question of 'I' in a short while after the word *being* has also been clarified. The meaning of *intention*, another basic ingredient of human nature, will be the subject of chapters 6, 7, and 8. All three — 'knowing', 'being', and 'intention'— will be part of the conceptual language that I must clarify. They are the basis of human nature, and the possibility of the evolution of human nature is dependent on their evolution. Thus we shall have to be able to demonstrate that they arise from very primitive organisms. Then, in chapter 13, after having laid a firm foundation, I will take up the discussion of consciousness.

Knowing, being, and volition — particularly in the guise of 'free will' — have been the subjects of a vast amount of philosophical speculation. I shall not, though, be using the words in a philosophical way, but in a very simple, demonstrable, and pragmatic way. The philosopher, John Locke, said words are tokens for the wise and money for fools. Let us use words as tokens, as pointers.

Two views of the world are possible, each is a whole view, but each excludes the other. I called the first 'Subjective' and the second 'Objective'. Above these lies a higher level, the *transcendental*[4] level, from which they are derived. Among scientists the term transcendental is virtually a term of abuse. At best they see it as referring to a general, abstract realm derived from conceptual arguments alone, and having no observable connection with the physical world. At worst they see it as a quasi-mystical domain that cannot be substantiated. I use the term transcendental simply to mean *beyond experience*. Although the transcendent level is beyond experience, nevertheless it is real; it is the reality from which experience, the physical universe and life are derived. Furthermore the truth of the reality of the transcendent can be demonstrated.

'Knowing' makes the Subjective worldview possible; 'being' makes the Objective worldview possible. By the word 'being' I simply mean that something *is*. The book that you are reading and the chair that you are sitting on both 'are'. Matter, energy, fields, waves and subatomic particles all 'are'.

Up to the advent of relativity theory, and the theory of quantum mechanics, physical scientists ignored the role of knowing in the universe. They simply relegated it to philosophy. Because many biologists, psychologists, social scientists — and, of course, scientists engaged in research into the evolution of life forms — try to model their sciences on the physical sciences, they pretend that they too can safely ignore knowing.

I hope to show the meaning of the words *knowing* and *being* in such a way as to awaken the reader to their meaning in an immediate way, not through definitions, theory or reference to other writers. Later, I shall talk about *intention* and then show how intention, knowing and being together constitute creativity and *are basic to all life.*

On what *I know* and that *I know*[5]

Someone might ask, "What is the weather doing?" I go outside, return and say, "It is raining." Strictly speaking, when I say this I should say, "I *know* that it is raining." The 'I know' is so obvious and so taken for granted that, in the interests of simplicity, we do not say it. The 'I know', or, knowing, is taken for granted. We take it for granted because 'knowing' *is unremitting, invariable and intrinsic to all experience.* We only report on what can come and go, vary, or on what is different.

I can say, "the car needs gas", or, "It is Thursday", or, "this is a good book". Yet, any statement about any experience that I can have, whether about the world, thought, feeling, or sensation, whether a precise scientific theory or an observation just made in passing, is always preceded, implicitly at least, by 'I know'. One can readily prove this by trying to find an experience that does not have knowing as its basis. One must surely find this impossible to do.

This simple example partly illustrates what I mean by the transcendental. 'Knowing' is a *transcendental* aspect of all experience. The transcendental has two other aspects — being and intention — and I shall return to these later.

When I say, "I know it is raining" the fact that it is raining could be looked upon as *the content* of my experience; 'I know' is the *transcendental* aspect. The content of experience, what is 'physical', is *what* I know. *That* I know it is raining is not part of that content; it is not part of what I know. Because *that I know* is not part of experience, and to the extent that understanding is arranging *what* I know in an orderly fashion, *that*[6] I know, or just simply knowing, *lies beyond all possible experience and comprehension,* and is therefore transcendental in the way that I am using the word.[7] *That* I know (the transcendental) and *what* I know (the experience) are quite different.[8] *What* I know is rooted in, and is dependent on, the brain. *That* I know is not so dependent. *That* I know cannot be reduced to *what* I know, even though the two cannot be separated.[9] They are like the mirror and the reflections in the mirror: they are not the same but cannot be separated.

The importance of 'I know'

When I report that it is raining, I ignore the 'I know'. Because I do this, and because everyone else does the same, we come to believe 'that I know' is unimportant or even meaningless. Even so, while it may well be unimportant for me to *say* that I know, the *truth* 'that I know' is very important and must not be ignored. It must not be ignored because, while 'that I know' cannot be experienced, it is intrinsic to, and makes possible, all experience. The belief that 'knowing' is unimportant, and can be ignored by hard science,[10] is made plausible because 'knowing' is quite inaccessible to experience. Knowing is inaccessible because it is *transcendental*; it is beyond experience.

To make the word 'beyond' easier to understand, let me use a metaphor. A movie is the outcome of the interaction of a projector, a film and a screen. When we go to a cinema we go to enjoy the drama, which has a different order of reality to the projector, screen and film. By 'different order' I mean that as far as the drama is concerned these three are beyond it and play no part in it. Now we must remember that science is based upon the assumption that everything in principle is knowable. Yet, as I shall show, knowing, intention, being — which transcend experience and so have a *different order of reality* to experience — cannot be known.

Someone may well say that he does not agree that 'knowing' is inaccessible. He might well say, "But I know that I know." He may do this for one of two reasons. Either he is saying, "I am aware of being aware", or he has an *idea* of what knowing means. I will have to leave the implication of being aware of being aware until chapter 13. However, to say, "I know *that I know*" transforms the italicized *'that I know'* into *'what I know'*, because it transforms *'that* I know' into the *idea* 'I know'. The *idea*-of-knowing and knowing are quite different, just as the idea of a meal is quite different from a meal. Because of this I cannot, strictly speaking, talk about knowing; I can only talk about the *idea*-of-knowing. We can now see why 'knowing' has been banished from the domain of science, which deals only with Objective facts. How can one research what is only Subjective?

Another objection yet could be made to what I am saying. "You say we cannot talk about knowing, yet what are you doing at the moment?" This is the paradox that Pollack spoke of when he said that we "talk of the unutterable." I say that I know it is raining. Yet if you were to ask me, "What do you mean by knowing?" or, "How do you know that you know?" or, "Is knowing a reality?" I have to say that I could not answer any of those questions. If you ask me to prove that I know, I have to admit that I could not do so. If you said that the 'I know' of the statement "I know that it is raining" is redundant, and that the statement "It is raining" is enough, I would agree with you. I just cannot know knowing because knowing has no content. *What* I know is the content.

Although 'I know' is redundant in the sentence, "I know that it is raining", and in spite of the caveats that I have given in the last paragraph, 'I know' is not a meaningless statement, even though I cannot say what the meaning is.

On not being able to define knowing

Because knowing is prior to all ideas, we cannot define it. I can, nevertheless use analogies to illustrate what I mean by 'knowing'. Knowing is often likened to light. If you look around the room you will see all kinds of things: chairs, table, carpet, walls, window, ceiling, and so on. Scientists tell us that what you are seeing is just light, light reflected from things. Normally, though, as far as you are concerned you see things. Similarly chairs, table carpet, walls, window, and ceiling, indeed all that you see, is knowing. Normally, though, as far as you are concerned you see things.[11]

Another aspect of knowing can be illustrated with the metaphor of light. A lamp 'illuminates itself' when illuminating the room. The lamp does not need another lamp in order to be seen. But everything else in the room does need a lamp to be seen. Knowing has no cause; it illuminates itself.

We must awaken[12] to the truth that *that* I know and *what* I know are quite different, and when awakening comes in this way, it comes as a surprise. I mentioned Max Born's surprise when it dawned on him that all our perception and mental imagery, "everything without exception", is entirely Subjective. In the epigraph to this chapter I quoted Schopenhauer as saying, "that which knows all things, and is known by none, is the subject." He too had awakened to the truth that the whole world is suspended in 'my' knowing. As he says, "Whatever exists, exists only for the subject. Everyone finds himself to be this subject, but only in so far as he knows, not in so far as he is the object of knowing."

Knowing and being

The transcendental is not just 'knowing'. The transcendental is also 'being'. Heidegger in his book, *Being and Time* makes the distinction between the ontological and the ontic, which is a similar distinction to the one I make between the transcendental and the physical. He quoted[13] Plato for the epigraph to his book, "For manifestly you have long been aware of what you mean when you use the expression 'being'. We, however, who used to think we understood it, have now become perplexed."[14]

The perplexity arises because when we try to talk about *being* we encounter the same difficulties that we had when trying to talk about knowing. We cannot talk about being. Words are abstractions; what is abstracted by using them when we talk about being is the very 'being' that we want to talk about.[15] The *idea* of being is not 'being' any more than the idea of knowing is 'knowing'. Even so we have no doubt that the room we are sitting in 'is'. The walls are; the floor is. Of this we have no doubt. We even emphasize this truth by saying that the room is 'real', or the wall and floor are real. Even so, *that* it is, its reality, must forever escape our intellectual grasp and our conceptual understanding.

That this is so is shown in the following way. If I were to ask someone, "Why do you say the world is?" he would probably say something like, "Well, I know that it is." But by appealing to knowing to confirm that the world is he resorts to idealism: the being of the world is a function of my idea. Dr. Samuel Johnson pointed this out in a very demonstrative way by striking the table to show the fallacy of idealism. By striking the table in this way, he also demonstrated that we cannot talk about being.

Even so, we cannot appeal to our senses to validate *that* the world is, because they can only tell us *what* the world is. Just as 'that I know' and 'what I know' are different, so 'that it is' and 'what it is' are also different. To say the world is hard, impenetrable, colored, extended, and makes a noise when you hit it, or to say that the world is made up of houses, cars,

roads, and trees, tells us *what* the world is. *That* it is escapes these observations. *That* the world is, is transcendental; *what* it is, is physical.
Being, however, is not some kind of substratum, a basic substance of
which everything is made. Conjuring up a substratum is just another
way of trying to make being knowable.

I am

Knowing and being come together as *I am,* the Subject: that which
knows all things, and is known by none. Just as I say the world is, so I
say 'I am', and I have no doubt that I am. No one, who can forego prejudice and preconception, can have doubts that he, or she, is real and not
simply some idea such as "I am the movement of molecules." As Subject,
knowing and 'I am' imply each other.

If I were to ask someone, "Are you?" The reply would most likely be,
"Yes, I am the body", or, "I am a person", or, "I am a woman", or, "I am
a man". The neurologist would say, "I am the brain." A priest might
well say, "I am the soul." Yet another person might say, "I do not know
what I am, but I am surely something." All of these are talking about
their *idea* of what they are, and furthermore, about their idea that they
are *something.* Just as 'that I know' and 'what I know' are quite different,
so 'that I am' and 'what I am' are also quite different.

Can I prove to another that I am? No, I cannot possibly prove this.
Can I describe to another what I mean when I say, 'I am'? No, I cannot
even do that. If I am not demonstrable, explicable or communicable,
what is the point of my saying that I am? What is demonstrable, explicable and communicable belongs to the realm of *what I am.* That I am
does not belong to that realm. It cannot be judged by the criteria derived
from another, different, realm.

Even so, using the word 'objective' to mean unbiased by my own
desires, wishes, and hopes, the statement 'I am' is quite objective, and
so should be acceptable as a scientific fact. Furthermore, what is known
by a scientist obviously depends on 'I am' of the scientist, that is the
scientist as Subject. What is known includes all possible experience,
including all the laws of science. By this I do not mean the laws of science
are dependent on the scientist as Subject for their truth, but for the fact
that she or he knows them.

Cogito ergo sum

The kind of confusion that 'I am' can create is shown by the famous *cogito ergo sum*, "I think therefore I am", of the philosopher René Descartes. Descartes doubted everything, until he realized, "I think, therefore I am." He felt that he had reached a bedrock certainty. He said, "I am, I exist, I exist is necessarily true each time that I pronounce it or mentally conceive it."[16] He said later on in the same Meditation, "But what then am I? A thing that thinks."[17]

Unfortunately, as has been pointed out through the ages, he said too much. Studies of the brain show that both consciousness and 'I am a thing', are constructs. To say, "I am a thing" is saying *what* I am. The essential certainty that Descartes found has been lost because all that he should have said with certainty is, "if there is doubting, there is knowing." By saying, "I am a thing", he opened the way for his insight to be reduced over the years to a ghost in the machine, and then, more recently, exorcised altogether. Unfortunately the truth that knowing is fundamental, which could well have been what he meant, has been exorcised also.

A note on the meaning of 'beyond'

As the notion of 'beyond', the transcendental, is so important in all that I am saying let me use the metaphor of a cinema once more. When you go to the cinema you see all kinds of situations: a man and a woman falling in love, a war, perhaps a volcano erupting. After the film is over, all that is left on the screen is a white light. Yet all that you saw were modifications of that white light. You did not see the light because it was beyond all that you were seeing. All experience whether religious, scientific or everyday experience, and this includes sleep and memory, is a modification of the light of knowing and being (I am). With this metaphor in mind, I say that knowing, being and 'I am' cannot be experienced and so cannot be described or defined, because they lie beyond experience.

Knowing and scientific requirements

Because knowing, being and 'I am' lie beyond experience they cannot be subjects of scientific investigation, as we know it in the West. Only *what* is known to be can be investigated. Karl Popper[18] gave three requirements for an empirical theoretical system. First, it must be *synthetic,* so that it may represent a non-contradictory, a *possible* world. Secondly, it must satisfy the criterion of demarcation *i.e.* it must not be metaphysical, but must represent a world of possible *experience.* Thirdly, it must be a system distinguished in some way from other such systems as the one that represents *our* world of experience (my emphasis).

Although knowing, being and 'I am' satisfy none of these requirements, without them there is no science.

Knowing and sleep

The reader may ask what happens to knowing and 'I am' when we sleep, believing that when we sleep 'I am' and knowing disappear. If this were the case then 'I am' and knowing would be dependent upon being awake, which implies some brain activity. This in turn would mean that knowing and 'I am' are products of brain activity.

When we sleep we are no longer *conscious.*[19] Human consciousness as I shall show is a structure, and is intimately tied in with language, memory, remembering and also self-reflection. Because, when we sleep, we no longer remember, and because self-reflection is absent (except in part when we dream), we do not remember knowing, nor are we aware of being. Only *what* I am and *what* I know can be remembered.

Everyone must have had the feeling of having 'slept', or having been absent, or absent minded, during some period of the day.[20] If sleeping were to be an absence of 'knowing' and of 'I am', then during these times when we are absent-minded we could not have accomplished anything at all. Yet we spend much of our lives in this absent condition. Normally we say that we were unconscious while asleep, or during the day we say that we acted unconsciously. The word 'unconscious' is a misnomer because during sleep, and when we act unconsciously, we enter another mode of awareness other than consciousness.

Sleep shows that *knowing without content is possible;* in sleep the distinction between 'that I know' and 'what I know' drops away. This does not mean that I know nothing; knowing nothing is still knowing an idea, or having a concept, of nothing. Simply knowing, other than during sleep, is possible only after long and difficult spiritual training but, even so, sleep gives us an intimation of this possibility. Knowing, without knowing anything in particular, is called 'samadhi' in Zen.[21]

Let me repeat once more, knowing is the basis of consciousness but knowing is possible without being conscious. Consciousness only arrives on the scene after a long evolution. This means that very primitive organisms, even though they may not be conscious, may well know.

Is knowing the outcome of complexity?

Many scientists take it for granted that "I *know* that it is raining" is *caused* by brain activity. Scientists normally explain the existence of knowing by saying that when a certain degree of complexity of matter arises knowing also arises. Knowing, in this case, is an epiphenomenon of the complexity of brain activity, in the same way that heat is an epiphenomenon of caloric activity. I do not doubt that "I know *the rain is falling*" can be demonstrated to be connected with brain activity and to a certain complexity of the brain, even though 'that I know' is not.

Even so, to be connected with and to be caused by are not the same. I know *it is raining* arises through a *correlation* of brain activity and knowing. I use the word 'correlation' to mean having mutual relations. When I know it is raining, knowing and brain activity are brought into mutual relation, or correlated, by the perception of the falling rain. We must keep clearly in mind the *mutual.* The truth is not that the physical occurs and the mental (knowing) follows, nor the other way around. Another way of explaining what I mean when I say that the brain is correlated with mental activity is that although both the brain and mind are *necessary* for knowing 'It is raining', neither by itself is *sufficient* to know this.

On the proof of knowing

I say 'I know' even though I cannot prove this to you. *You can nevertheless, prove this for yourself.* You can do this by simply asking, "Do I know that I am reading this book?" You do not have to say what the word 'know' means when you say, "I *know* that I am reading this book", you do not have to justify it, nor do you have to prove to another that you know. You simply refer to your own immediate, Subjective, knowing. You must do this experiment in the concrete and not in the abstract. Do not ask, "But how do I know that all of this is not simply brain activity." If you do you are slipping away from the concrete back into argument and the abstract.

If someone were to ask me to prove that knowing is not dependent upon brain activity, would I not be as justified in asking that person to prove that things exist, or for proof that the brain is not just an idea in my mind. At some point we simply have to say: this is how it is: things *are*; I *know*. So, when I say you can prove for yourself that you know, I mean that you can return to your origins, that is you can return to knowing and being without the intervention of understanding or thought; *you can return to the faith in which your whole life is lived.*

The world as a dream

All that we know has knowing as well as being as its basis. This knowing has been referred to as the 'light that shines by itself', or the 'eye that never sleeps'. Knowing, as Subjectivity, is the source of the faith that I referred to earlier, the faith that supports the worldview of the scientist and priest alike. Like a light that shines by itself, knowing has no prior cause and it is the final arbiter of the truth of what is. When I identify *that* I know with *what* I know, I sleep even with eyes wide open. I no longer say, "I know it is raining" but "It is raining!"

Summary

I have spent some considerable time defending the view that the mind (knowing) is not an epiphenomenon, not an outcome of the complexity of matter (being) but that knowing and being, the mind and the brain, have equal status. I have done this in spite of the problem of duality that arises as long as we remain within the confines of classical logic. This lengthy defense has been necessary because the prevailing view in science is that the mind can be understood entirely if one understands the neural correlates. Later I shall show how the problem of duality of mind and matter can be quite simply sidestepped.

4 | Knowing and Evolution

"There is grandeur in this view of life, with its several powers, having been originally breathed into a few forms or into one; and that, whilst this planet has gone cycling on according to the fixed law of gravity, from so simple a beginning endless forms most beautiful and most wonderful have been, and are being, evolved."

CHARLES DARWIN[1]

The affirmation of a continuous and unbroken evolution of life on earth makes sense in view of the fundamental intuition shared by scientists, philosophers, poets, mystics and theologians alike, that the world is one. The idea that all life gradually evolved from a common ancestry is like a beautiful symphony evolving from the simplest of themes. One cannot help thinking that because this idea is so beautiful, so utterly simple, it must be true. This belief in a continuous and unbroken evolution is a key element in my argument throughout this book. It means that if there is but one instance of knowing, even if only you or I know, then at least as far as that instance is concerned, the universe is not simply mechanical. Furthermore, if that instance of knowing appears at a later stage of evolution, say among humans, then, to some degree or another, however attenuated it might be, it must have been present at the very dawn of evolution.

When does knowing appear on the evolutionary scene?

That I know is a fact. Anyone can prove for himself that this is so even though each of us can only say with certainty 'I know.' I cannot say, 'You know' with the same certainty. The statements 'I *know* it is raining' and 'I know *it is raining*' are both meaningful, and so knowing and being participate equally in the experience 'it is raining.' Thus the possibility of our having evolved depends upon knowing having evolved as well as being, or, in other words, on mind having evolved as well as matter.

If we can accept that I know, then we must ask, "Was the universe mindless matter until I appeared on the scene?" If in the unlikely event this were so, when I appeared, it would mean that an entirely novel property — knowing — has suddenly appeared in the universe; a sudden, miraculous transformation of unknowing matter into knowing matter has occurred. This would negate assumption No.10 (see page xii) and would deal the gradualist theory of evolution a mortal blow. In the same way those who believe that consciousness is only present in human beings, or that it is the result of complexity, do in fact suggest that a sudden, miraculous transformation of unknowing matter into knowing matter occurs. Bearing in mind what Darwin said in the epigraph to this chapter — that evolution is a gradual and continuous process — they should justify doing this. But they do not do so; they just take it for granted that what they say is so.

If knowing did not appear with me, or with you the reader, when did it appear? When does knowing first appear in the Universe? With human beings? Most evolutionary theorists deny that human beings have any special trait that sets them apart from the rest of nature. And primates? Frans de Waal, the celebrated primatologist, has shown that primates have a range of activities that corresponds very closely to human behavior, and which most of us attribute, in part at least, to intelligence. Knowing is surely an important ingredient in intelligence. So we have to say primates also have a Subjective world. We cannot, though, stop at the level of primates because if we do we will have again introduced a hiatus, a break in continuous and gradual evolution.

So did knowing appear with vertebrates, with invertebrates? With cells, with molecules, with atoms? Why stop? A scientist has stated, "Life is a partial, continuous, progressive, multiform and conditionally interactive self realization of the potentialities of atomic electronic states."[2] It has even been suggested, in face of the two-slit experiment,[*]

---

[*] This is an experiment that shows that an electron has the ambiguous nature of being potentially both wave and particle.

that electrons are intelligent. Let me say very quickly that I am not saying that atoms are conscious. Consciousness is very complex and has evolved from knowing and is only present in human beings. Knowing on the other hand, because it has no content, is simplicity itself.

Knowing and genes

An alternative question to asking, "When did knowing first appear in the universe?" might be, "When did knowing first appear in me?" To answer this question we have to trace back through the embryo, through the fetus, through the fertilized ovum and ultimately to the genes. Do genes know? If not we again have a hiatus in the gradual development of life, which could only be bridged by some kind of specific miracle similar to the creation of the soul. According to the Catholic Church the soul is put into the organism at some time after conception. From the point of view of evolution, this is unsatisfactory because it implies a miraculous hiatus. Both the creation of the soul and the sudden emergence of knowing should be unacceptable from a scientific point of view. To avoid this unacceptable conclusion I must say that *if I know then at least in some way genes also know.*[3] To be more precise still we should say knowing and being are correlated in the phenomenon we know as a gene.

I shall come back to this question of whether genes know in some way in a later chapter. Let me just mention for the moment that David Deutsch, an Oxford University researcher in quantum computation, in his book *The Fabric of Reality*[4] says something that is tantalizing in this regard. He points out that some DNA sequences are genes and that others, even though they have the same molecular sequence as the genes, are nevertheless not genes. After some discussion he comes to the following conclusion: "We can see that the ancient idea that living matter has special physical properties was almost true: it is not living matter but *knowledge-bearing* matter that is physically special."[5] Just in case anyone might want to accuse him of heresy he hastily adds, "So knowledge is a fundamental physical quantity after all, and the phenomenon of life is only slightly less so." Even so, to any impartial observer who can look at things objectively, does not the word knowledge in 'knowledge-bearing' imply, somewhere, somehow, knowing? That knowing is involved in some way in the developing organism is suggested by Sean Carroll: "Fate maps reveal that, by some point in development, cells 'know' where they are in an embryo and to what tissues or structures they belong."[6]

A new branch of biology, Evo Devo, or evolutionary developmental biology, shows how truly marvelous evolution has been. Anyone reading Sean Carroll's book *Endless Forms Most Beautiful* must be filled with wonder and awe. Somehow one cannot help feeling while reading this book that such a very complex affair — at the same time so wonderfully simple — requires some degree of communication, intelligence and perception to make it possible. This, inevitably, has led some to conclude that an Intelligent Designer, or God, created it all. But, introducing God is a direct violation of the 10th assumption (see page xii).

On the other hand, when I say that knowing and being, mind and matter, are basic to the universe I am staying within the requirements of assumption No. 10. I will also show that this is a more reasonable way of looking at things than to say the world is simply matter, or that an Intelligent Designer is responsible. However most evolutionary scientists will reject what I say, some will do so with considerable aggression. Why is that?

One of the main reasons for the reluctance of scientists to accept that knowing and being have equal status is that they will have to accept an implacable dualism, and most scientists are not prepared to do this. They cannot accept dualism because it violates the most basic of all intuitions to which I have already referred, the intuition of *unity*. Most scientists, when faced with this dilemma, invoke Occam's razor — the explanation of any phenomenon should include as few assumptions as possible — and say that, by introducing knowing an unnecessary assumption has been introduced. In this way they eliminate one horn — knowing — of the knowing-being dilemma and so rediscover unity. They then claim that an explanation of the origin of species, and of human nature, can be made without invoking knowing. Their explanation, they would say, is simpler than the one that I am offering, which seems to be more complex and requires we accept a dualism — being *and* knowing — and this is unacceptable.

I say, 'I know'. One might think that this is too flimsy a basis to make a sweeping change in the theory of the evolution of the species. Yet, let it be remembered that classical physics was upset by the smallest of discrepancies in the spectrum of light. No doubt there was more than one physicist who would have wanted to sweep Plank's quantum under the carpet. After all it was such a stupid little anomaly. As well as Occam's rule of simplicity another equally important although contradictory rule of science is that *a theory must be complete*. A theory that knowingly leaves out data that is pertinent to the theory is a simplistic theory, not a simple one. Many scientists inadvertently overlooked the discrepancy that was so important to Plank. Yet no scientist worth his salt is going to say, once it has been pointed out, let us dismiss some evidence because it will wreak havoc with my theory. A scientist must have integrity.

The correlation of knowing and being

If we accept that knowing coexists with matter, or, as David Bohm says,[7] "everything has a mental side", then we see that at each step in evolution, the evolution of knowing is correlated with the evolution of matter. This means that if matter had not evolved, the evolution of knowing could not have evolved into consciousness. The evolution of cars can be used as an analogy. Without a corresponding evolution in roads, the modern car could not have come into existence. Even so, the evolution of matter did not *cause* the evolution of knowing, any more than the evolution of roads caused the evolution of cars.

I cannot help wondering whether the converse is true? If matter were not correlated with knowing, would matter have failed to evolve into organisms? Is knowing a kind of catalyst that is necessary for matter to evolve? I cannot also help wondering the following: although the evolution of roads made the evolution of the modern car possible, the evolution of cars made the evolution of roads necessary. Is it possible that the evolution of matter made the evolution of mind possible, but the evolution of mind made the evolution of matter necessary?

However the objection remains. We do have the intuition of oneness; how then can we accept duality? Indeed I am going to show that unity, dynamic unity, is the basic drive of life. In the next chapter therefore I will show how we can have both unity and duality.

A 'One Hand Clapping' interlude

The awakening to 'that I know' is an important step in the practice of Rinzai Buddhism and can be known as the Great Mirror Knowing.[8] Many koans, the enigmatic stories that are used in the practice of Zen, point to this knowing. They owe their enigmatic quality to the fact that they refer to that which transcends or goes beyond experience and conceptual description. The most famous of these koans is 'the Sound of One Hand Clapping.' The full koan reads, "You know the sound of two hands clapping. What is the sound of One hand clapping?" The sound of two hands clapping is *what* we know; the sound of one hand clapping is *that* we know. However, the student would not dare to give such a conceptual explanation. He would be required to show unequivocally without words what the koan is pointing to.

5 | On a New Way of Thinking

"Einstein threw out the classical concept of time; Bohr throws out the classical concept of truth. *Our classical ideas of logic are simply wrong in a basic practical way.* The next step is to learn to think in the right way, to learn to think quantum logically" (my emphasis).

DAVID FINKLESTEIN[1]

Our study is the study of human nature. How is it possible that you and I have come to be? I have spent some time preparing the groundwork for saying that that knowing (mind) and being (matter) are both basic ingredients of the world. The neo-Darwinian theory, because it takes no note of the influence of mind on evolution, is deficient. Neuro-scientists also generally ignore this influence.

An important reason for this neglect is that we all have a basic intuition that the world is one. The central logical principle, the principle of identity, draws its power from this intuition of unity. Occam's razor, the search for the simplest explanation, as well the requirement that a theory be complete and data not arbitrarily excluded from it's reckoning, are also the result of this intuition of unity.

If we are going to accept that mind is equal in status to matter we are forced into either an unacceptable dualism, or else into the need to revise our logic; but our intuition of unity makes us loath to do either. This same dilemma has pervaded philosophy with the idealist and realist, as well as, more recently, the realist and anti-realist arguments. Our logic allows only one of these — either mind or matter, either idealism or realism, either realism or anti-realism — to be true, and so we have to throw out, ignore or reduce in status one or other horn of the dilemma. Rather than doing this, as has most often been the case, let us take a look at the logic we use to see whether we can use another logic, *the logic of ambiguity*, which will include but go beyond classical logic. With its help we may be able to break the chokehold that materialism has on the life sciences.

Professor Lewontin sums up very well indeed the materialist-realist position and so I will quote him at length.

> "We take the side of science in spite of the patent absurdity of some of its constructs, in spite of its failure to fulfill many of its extravagant promises of health and life, in spite of the tolerance of the scientific community for unsubstantiated just-so stories, because we have a prior commitment, a commitment to materialism . . . we are forced by our *a priori* adherence to material causes to create an apparatus of investigation and a set of concepts that produce material explanations, no matter how counter-intuitive, no matter how mystifying to the uninitiated. Moreover, that materialism is absolute, for we cannot allow a Divine Foot in the door."[2]

The Divine foot that cannot be allowed in the door is not only God, but mind and volition also.

Physicist Amrit Goswami holds firmly to the opposite point of view, the mind-idealist position, and says, "everything (including matter) exists in and is manipulated from consciousness . . . the reality of matter is secondary to that of consciousness, which itself is the ground of all being — including matter."[3]

As we see from these two quotations, unity, through the medium of classical logic, presents us with a dilemma. We are forced to choose one over the other, although both have equal claim to being true.

The German philosopher Arthur Schopenhauer presents this dilemma in an interesting way in his book *The World as Will and Idea*.[4] He has 'subject' and 'matter' debate which one of them is real, and which one is derived from the other. He could just have well used the names 'idealism' and 'realism' or 'knowing' and 'being' instead of 'subject' and 'matter'. I have given the full debate in Appendix II. Schopenhauer concludes the debate by saying, "*At bottom it is one being that perceives itself and is perceived by itself, but whose being-in-itself cannot consist either in perceiving or in being perceived, since these functions are apportioned separately between the two of us.*"[5]

I have italicized this last section because, as I shall show, this is a crucial conclusion.

On classical logic

Classical logic is based upon three principles: x is either A or not A; x cannot both be A and not A; x is x. The principle of excluded middle (either A or not A) prohibits us from accepting knowing and being as equals. The history of the conflict between religion and science, between materialism and idealism, bears witness to this prohibition. Some say matter, or, being, is the whole of reality; others say mind, or knowing, is. Logically the dilemma is irresolvable.

Another debate that breaks out now and again is the debate between the monists and the dualists. The monists say that Unity is basic; the dualists say that dualism is basic. According to classical logic, one or other has to be true and the other false. This is why we must examine the logic at our disposal and not eliminate half the data. We do this in the face of some considerable opposition. For example, although the philosopher Quine recognized that "that certain developments in quantum physics may turn out to force revisions to the 'laws of thought' supposedly enshrined in classical logic",[6] he denies that, "we could ever, in principle, have rational grounds for preferring such a drastic response in the face of recalcitrant . . . evidence. Rather, we should suspect that there must be some problem with the evidence, some alternative (logic preserving) construal of it."[7]

Realism and anti-realism

Werner Heisenberg wrote, "Since physicists are not obliged to confront epistemological problems in everyday applications of quantum theory, they could easily ignore philosophical questions that seem to lie outside the conduct of normal science."[8] Many biologists, neuro-scientists and neo-Darwinians, have felt that they too could ignore philosophical questions. To show that this dilemma is not simply a philosophical one, and that it is of vital importance to biology in general and the theory of evolution in particular, let me say a little about the realism/anti-realism debate that, in spite of the wish of many scientists to ignore it, nevertheless rages in theoretical physics, for long considered to be the paragon of the sciences.

The theories of relativity and quantum mechanics have shown many scientists that the mind/matter dilemma, although previously ignored by them, cannot be dismissed. That this is so is shown by the fact that Einstein and Bohr had a long debate during which they tried unsuccessfully to tackle this very dilemma. As the philosopher Christopher Norris said, "there is clearly a marked tension (if not perhaps a downright inescapable conflict) between the orthodox [Bohr's] interpretation of quantum mechanics and Einsteinian relativity theory."[9] This debate has been continued after their deaths between realists, who by and large represent the opinions of Einstein, and the anti-realists who are mostly in Neils Bohr's camp.

The subject of the debate concerns whether saying, "I know *it is raining*" or "*I know* it is raining" best represents reality. Realists support the first assertion and they do so by ignoring the 'I know.' The anti-realists support the second. Realists say, "Whether I know it or not, the rain falls." Anti-realists say, "to say 'it is raining' is a statement that I make, and so it depends upon my knowing it to be the case." Both realists and anti-realists are equally able to muster a full arsenal of logic and reason to support their points of view, and the debate often ends with one assuming the other is either stupid or obdurate. The matter is made more interesting still because physics seems to have identified so many contradictions rooted in reality that defy classical, either/or, logic. One of the most well known of these is the wave/particle duality. Heisenberg posed the problem in this way: "Matter waves and particle pictures are of course mutually exclusive, because a certain thing cannot at the same time be a particle (i.e. substance confined to a very small volume) and a wave (i.e. a field spread out over a large space.)"[10] In quantum mechanics, for a particle to be that particle it has to be observed to be that particle. The scientist Von Neumann demonstrated that observation collapses the wave function. The physicist Goswami adds, "Separability is the result of collapse. Only after collapse are there independent objects."[11] If there are only independent objects after observation has collapsed the wave function, and if observation is a form of knowing, then knowing is necessary for the world to be as it is.

In the quantum world 'A' no longer always equals 'A', because 'A' only equals 'A' after the wave function has been collapsed, after separation has occurred, and objects have appeared. This is what prompted physicist David Finklestein to state, "*Our classical ideas of logic are simply wrong in a basic practical way*" (my emphasis).[12]

Modern theories of physics have introduced a number of other mutually exclusive antinomies. Robert Nadeau and Menas Kafatos, the former a historian of science, the latter a theoretical physicist, tell us, "In special relativity, mass and energy are constructs that displace one another in any single physical situation, and yet both are required for a complete understanding of the situation. In general relativity, space and time are revealed as profound complementaries . . . In quantum physics waves-particles, fields-quanta are also profound complementaries."[13] Many other similar anomalies could be given. David Bohm assures us, "Opposing and contradictory motions are the rule throughout the universe, and this is an essential aspect of the very mode of things."[14]

What is a scientific theory anyway? This question leads to another antinomy. Are the laws of nature *discovered* or are they *created*? There is a vast difference between a ten-dollar bill that I have discovered and a ten-dollar bill that I have created.

Alternatives to classical logic

One way, and the way that I am choosing to resolve the dilemma, is to change the rules; we must find a better logic.

I am not the first to attempt this. In the late 1930s Alfred Korzybski wrote *Science and Sanity*[15] in which he subjected the principle of identity, A = A, to thorough criticism. His insight was that the map is not the territory, nor is the word the thing. He had realized that our view of the world was *a view* of the world (I *know* that it is raining). He objected to the law of identity because it forces us to see existence as static. He pointed out that an apple at 8.00 a.m. and an apple at 5.00 p.m. are not the same apple. He wanted us to index words to indicate a changing and dynamic situation, which he felt to be nearer the truth than the static world forced on us by our logic. Thus an apple at 8.00 a.m. is apple $_{8.00\ am}$ and an apple at 5.00 p.m. would be apple $_{5.00\ pm}$.

Heidegger was another, more sophisticated, critic of the principle of identity. He came to question the principle through a contemplation of Parmenides' aphorism: *thought and being are the same.*[16] The relevance of this to our discussion becomes clear if we substitute the word 'knowing' for the word 'thought'. He asked, "What does this word 'same', or 'identity', mean?" Parmenides is saying the two aspects, 'I know' and 'it is raining,' are the same. Heidegger asks, what is this 'same'? As can be readily seen, Heidegger's question is the same as the one with which we are faced; we have one world, and yet that one world is either a Subjective or Objective world. But we cannot claim one or the other to be real and the other to be a product of it.

Another writer, André Lamouche,[17] has suggested a logic of simplicity. He felt that simplicity was not only a principle of logic but also a creative principle inherent in the world.

Hegel offered a logic of the dialectic. A thesis is always accompanied by an antithesis and demands a synthesis, which in turn becomes a new thesis calling for an antithesis and so on.

Stéphane Lupasco made another, more radical, challenge to classical logic.[18] Troubled by the anomalies of quantum theory he developed a new logic that questioned the principle of excluded middle. He introduced a third condition, that went beyond the principle of duality, that he called the T-estate. The T-estate is neither 'actual', nor 'potential' (categories replacing in Lupasco's language the 'true' or 'false' connectors of formal logic), but unifies the two. This logic is strikingly similar to the one that I am suggesting although the two were developed quite independently of each other.

Niels Bohr, the physicist, suggested a principle of complementarity to supplement classical logic to account for the wave/particle duality of quantum mechanics. Bohr uses the word *complementary* when referring to the relation of the two basic aspects of quantum reality: wave and particle. Both are necessary for a complete view of the situation, but the conditions for observation or measurement do not allow both aspects —wave and particle — to be present simultaneously. Nadeau and Kafatos, who elevated Bohr's principle of complementarity to a logic of complementarity explain, "Complementarity is . . . a logical framework for the acquisition and comprehension of scientific knowledge that discloses a new relationship between physical theory and physical reality."[19]

Bohr was a pragmatist and was not out to replace classical logic. He wanted to deal with practical problems in the simplest way. But we cannot, when we are faced with a contradiction while developing a scientific theory, use pragmatic expediency alone to decide whether to use complementarity rather than classical logic. We need firmer ground than expediency on which to stand. Nadeau and Kafatos, probably in order to avoid the apparent arbitrariness of its use, developed criteria that must be met if Bohr's principle of complementarity is to be both necessary and useful. These criteria are:[20] "(1) the theory consists of two individual and whole constructs, (2) the constructs preclude one another in a description of the unique physical phenomenon to which they both apply, (3) the complete situation cannot be reached through an addition of the two constructs.[21]

Unfortunately, these criteria show that Bohr's principle of complementarity, when elevated to a *logic* of complementarity in this way, is no longer adequate to account for the wave/particle ambiguity, the very ambiguity it was devised to resolve. As we shall see, all of the above alternatives, including classical logic, will find a place in the new logic that I am suggesting should be used.

Classical logic, duality and ambiguity

When we were very young we had to reach some basic conclusions about the world, and ourselves, and most of us opted for some dualistic understanding. Most often we act as if a world is 'out there', and I am 'in here'. Normally, most of us do not think about this very deeply, and we take it for granted that this dualist view represents how the world really is rather than how we perceive it to be. We then automatically adopt this incorrect view as reality. That is, instead of saying, "It is as though 'a world' is out there and an 'I' is in here", we say quite simply, "I am here and it is there".

This leads to confusion because we are also born with an intrinsic sense of unity. The very logic that we are considering, the logic of identity or unity, points to this intrinsic sense. The intuition of unity is expressed by all the great religions of the world; it is also a basic principle of art, architecture, literature and drama, classical music, as well as being the force driving the scientist to reject a dualist view of the world, a view that has mind and matter on an equal footing.

Generally speaking most people adopt a common sense attitude and are willing to live within this ambiguity of although we *experience* duality we can only *accept* unity as the truth. Sometimes though we feel compelled to seek this unity either out there or in here, because we believe it has to be one or the other. In order to help us, therefore, when we need to think more precisely, we, in the West, have enshrined an either/or way of thinking in a dogma of classical logic.

Although the rejection of ambiguity is basic to classical logic even so, as I have just pointed out, ambiguity is the very essence of life. *Situations arise which, looked at from one point of view are unambiguous (one,) looked at from another point of view are ambiguous (two). Life and its evolution, quantum reality and creativity are some such situations.* These situations cannot be understood using classical logic. When classical logic is used then inappropriate conclusions must inevitably be drawn.

The logic of ambiguity does not supplant classical logic, but shows the latter to be a subset of a more embracing logic. This is like the advance on classical physics made by quantum physics. Bohr said, "Classical mechanics is a subset of quantum mechanics."[22] He also said, "We can safely ignore quantum mechanical effects in dealing with macro level phenomena in most cases."[23] Similarly, for most problems that we meet with on a day-to-day basis we will go on using classical logic. We are either going out or we are not going out; either we'll eat at eight or we won't eat at eight.

What do I mean by ambiguity?

The etymology of the word *ambiguity* will help show the direction in which we shall be traveling. *Ambi* means 'two' as in *ambidextrous*, two handed, and *ambivalent*, two minded, so ambiguity will mean two-ness of some kind. When I use the word 'ambiguity' I do not mean vague and ill defined. On the contrary, the logic of ambiguity can be as reasonable and as clearly stated as classical logic. Instead of simply affirming, as does classical logic, *either* mind *or* matter, the logic of ambiguity will *also* affirm *both* mind and matter. This is very similar to what Lupasco has suggested.

Let me use the classical gestalt ambiguous figure oppostite to illustrate what I mean. Before we see it as a picture, this is a single black and white field that can be seen in two radically different ways: as a young woman and as an old woman. Both the young woman and the old woman are *whole* descriptions of the illustration. But neither is a *complete* description of it. This gestalt illustration conforms to the criteria given by Nadeau and Kafatos: (1) the illustration consists of two individual and whole constructs: these two are the young and the old woman. (2) The constructs preclude one another in a description of the complete picture to which they both apply: when you see the old woman you do not see the young woman. (3) The complete picture cannot be reached through an addition of the two constructs: to add the picture of the young woman to the old woman produces a mess. I will use this illustration as a guide throughout the following discussion.

Just as the statement 'I know it is raining' can be understood in two quite different ways — Subjectively, *"I know* it is raining", and Objectively, "I know *it is raining"* — so we can see the illustration in two quite different ways. This is similar to what we have already seen. When we see the old woman, the young woman is nowhere to be found. When we look at the world from an Objective, realist point of view, the Subjective is nowhere to be found; when we look at the world from a Subjective point of view, the Objective world is no more. Thus the illustration is a metaphor for the logic of ambiguity, ambiguity that has been strenuously rejected by philosophers and scientists alike.

Should we not stop looking at ambiguity as a fallacy? Is it not possible that ambiguity is an important part of life and consciousness?

Of course there might be ways out of the mind/matter dilemma. For example, someone may object to opposing mind and matter and say instead that a gradient exists between the two. But, this will reduce them to one substance and the question whether that substance is material or mental remains unanswered. The physicist David Bohm suggested this solution once in a conversation with Renée Weber: "Consciousness," he surmised, "is possibly a more subtle form of matter and movement."[24] Furthermore, referring back to the young and old woman, we can clearly see that no such gradient exists between them.

Instead of seeing consciousness and matter as extremes of a gradient scale, we could also alternate the two and act now as though the Objective were all-important, and now as though the Subjective were. In other words, we come back to our ordinary, every day point of view. However, when we are driven, as in science we so often are, to find a basic unity, to remain with our everyday point of view would leave us suspended between the two extremes in a condition of basic uncertainty and insecurity.

Another way out would be, on a pragmatic basis, to put the ghost back in the machine and claim a spirit or soul drives it. But, then do animals as well as humans have this ghost? Do cockroaches, plants or molecules have it? If not, how far back in evolution must we go before we no longer find the ghost?

Finally we could dismiss the whole question of the relation of mind and matter as of no account, interesting only to those who live in an ivory tower. But the question is important, probably more so now than at any other time in the history of the human being. How we respond to this question, the point of view that we adopt, determines the way we act, the way we regard each other and life itself. The philosopher Martin Heidegger pointed out that the very success of technological thinking — thinking, based upon classical logic and its consequence that the Objective viewpoint is the only one — must be feared because it "could so captivate, bewitch, dazzle and beguile man, that calculative thinking may some day come to be accepted and practiced *as the only* way of thinking . . . man would have denied and thrown away his special nature — that he is a meditative being . . . the issue is keeping meditative thinking alive."[25]

Why the principle of complementarity is unsatisfactory

Bohr's principle of complementarity, which Nadeau and Kafatos raised to the level of a logic, does not meet any of their criteria. The *Oxford English Reference Dictionary* defines the word 'complement' as "something that completes, one of a pair, one of two things that go together." A nut and bolt, when both are necessary to hold something in place, is an example of a complementary relation. For the complete situation, that is to say for them to function adequately, both are necessary. The nut is not 'whole' without the bolt. That is to say that without the bolt, a nut cannot serve its purpose. The same is true of the bolt; without the nut, the bolt cannot serve its purpose either.

In the gestalt picture, the complete picture is not the young plus the old young woman. Moreover, the young woman accounts for the whole picture and so does the old woman. Neither requires the other to be whole, but add them together and the result is a mess. A nut and a bolt are complements, they both need each other and complete each other, so neither is a whole situation. In the case of the nut and the bolt, the whole situation and the complete situation are the same. This means that the logic of complementarity does not meet the first criterion: that the situation must consist of two individual, whole constructs.

One does not say, "If a nut, not a bolt; if a bolt, not a nut" although in quantum mechanics, one does say, "If wave then not particle; if particle then not wave". The two ways of looking at subatomic objects are mutually exclusive, but a nut and a bolt are not. This means that the kind of relation that they represent does not comply with the second criterion: that the two constructs preclude one another. The nut and bolt do not preclude one another; quite the contrary, they demand one another.

Complementary logic does not fulfill the third criterion either, which says that the complete situation cannot be reached by adding the two together, because the nut and bolt must be added together to realize the complete situation.[26]

The one field as the third factor

Earlier I said that what we know as our world arises out of three transcendental factors. So far I have dealt with two: knowing and being. I must now say more about the third factor, *intention*. I shall do this by completing the description of the logic of ambiguity. We will see that the young woman/old woman illustration helps us in a very simple and elegant way to do this. In order to justify adequately introducing this third transcendental factor I must spend some time clearing the way. Although what follows may appear to be a detour, it will later be seen to be a necessary route.

Heisenberg introduces a third factor in addition to knowing and being by telling us, "Probability in mathematics or in statistical mechanics means a statement about our degree of knowledge of the actual situation. . . . The probability wave of Bohr, Kramers, Slater, however meant more than that; it meant a tendency for something. It was a quantitative version of the old concept of 'potentia' in Aristotelian philosophy. It introduced something standing in the middle between the idea of an event and the actual event."[27]

'The idea of an event' corresponds, roughly, to 'knowing', and the 'actual event' corresponds, also roughly, to 'being'. Heisenberg is saying that a third factor, *potentia*, stands between these two.

Later Heisenberg says we cannot say what happens between two observations, and that any attempt to describe what happens leads to contradictions. An old philosophical conundrum asks, "If a tree falls in the forest, and no one is around to hear it fall, does it make a noise?" As we saw in chapter 3, knowing has to be present before something that can be experienced and described, can happen. Thus the word 'happens' means what has been, or what is being, observed.[28] Because what happens is a physical event, (being) and observation (knowing) are necessary for what happens to happen, then, according to Heisenberg, both knowing and being are necessary for anything to happen. But, according to Heisenberg, and this is important for what I am saying in this book, beyond, or transcending, knowing and being lies a domain that cannot be described. This domain Heisenberg calls 'potentia.'

Each of the pictures, the young woman and the old woman, is a whole, but not a complete, description of the illustration. Let us for the moment say that the young woman represents idealism and the old woman represents materialism. Both idealism (knowing) and materialism (being) give a whole description of the world. Yet they do not give a complete picture. The complete picture is only given by what lies beyond knowing and being. Heisenberg gives the name of potentia to the *complete* picture. Furthermore he says that the complete picture is a 'tendency towards': it *is indescribable but real*, a reality that imagination tries to capture but is only able to do so in a vague way. All of the above could equally well be applied to intention, which, as I shall show, is beyond knowing and being, is indescribable but real, beyond imagination and *is a tendency towards.*

As well as seeing the illustration as the young and old woman one can see it as *a field of black and white forms.* This field is the *complete* picture. The young and old woman are *whole* ways of interpreting this black and white field. The black and white field is not only the complete picture: it is also, potentially, a tendency towards the young and/or old woman, in the same way that Heisenberg's potentia is a tendency towards a wave and a particle.

Unfortunately the illustration is static and unable to show the dynamism of this tendency towards. To extend the metaphor we could imagine that the illustration is projected on to a screen. As such we could still see the whole picture of the young or old woman on the screen, but the complete picture would be contained in the projection before it reaches the screen.

When we take the black and white shapes into consideration, another ambiguity is present in addition to the young/old woman ambiguity.* This ambiguity is "one black and white field/(young/old woman)." The one field both is and is not the young/old woman. This new ambiguity corresponds to the monism /dualism ambiguity that has dogged human thought through the ages. The black and white field we could say, stand for unity; the young and old woman stand for duality. One example of the unity/duality ambiguity is One God alone exists: and yet we have good and bad. Modern cosmology has a similar problem. Presumably, at the origin of the universe perfect symmetry (unity) reigned. How did asymmetry (dualism) enter the picture?

Thus the logic of ambiguity is necessary when *there is a condition, one aspect of which is without ambiguity while the other aspect is ambiguous.* I call this the 'logic of ambiguity' to distinguish it from classical logic and the logic of complementarity. To formulate the logic of ambiguity more precisely: *an ambiguity, one face of which (unity) says there is no ambiguity:*

* (I use [/] to indicate ambiguity).

the other face (duality) says there is ambiguity. Simply stated the logic of ambiguity is One/(yes/no) or (one/ two).

According to the logic of ambiguity, if we have two whole descriptions of a situation that we cannot add together to reach the complete situation, for example the wave and particle, then we can infer that the complete situation is a unity that lies beyond the two. This unity is neither one nor the other, nor both, nor not both, but beyond the two, just as the field of black and white is neither the young woman nor the old woman, nor both, nor not both, but beyond the two.

Let me recall what I said about the word 'beyond'. Throughout a movie you do not see the white light of the projector; you only see modifications of it. The light is *beyond* the film in the same way that the black and white shapes are beyond the young and the old woman.

I am suggesting that knowing/being (mind and matter) are to Unity as the young and old woman are to the field of black and white shapes. If we accept the logic of ambiguity, then, when we try to understand ourselves, or seek to develop a theory of human nature, unity must be a principal concern. This means that if I say that I am both body and mind then a unity lies beyond these two. Schopenhauer comes to the same conclusion in the dialogue between being and knowing: "At bottom it is *one* being that perceives itself [knowing] and is perceived by itself [being], but whose being-in-itself cannot consist either in perceiving or in being perceived, since these functions are apportioned separately between the two."[29] This is a crucial conclusion and this unity, what we know as our individuality and uniqueness expressed by 'I am', and immediately intuited by each of us, has its origin in neither matter nor mind nor both, but in a unity beyond them. Once we can see that knowing and being are manifestations of this unity, the problem of how the mind and body interact is no longer a problem. The interaction, instead of being a problem is an ambiguity. We could simplify this and put it in this way: I am Unity/(knowing/being) or Unity /(Mind/matter). Unity /(Mind/matter) is the anatomy of 'I am'.

The psychologist Carl G. Jung refers to this unity or oneness as the *unus mundus*. He says of this, "The idea of *unus mundus* is founded on the assumption that the multiplicity of the empirical world rests upon an underlying unity, and that not two or more fundamentally different worlds exist side by side . . . Causal connections exist between psyche and body which point to their underlying unitary nature."[30]

A complete definition of the logic of ambiguity

I must now complete the definition of the logic of ambiguity and by doing so will stress that unity is dynamic and at the same time *impossible* because unity itself is ambiguous.

On the one hand, we have a whole, a universe. Many people have had peak experiences in which the presence of unity and wholeness is paramount. The will to realize unity as wholeness is the drive behind religion as well as the drive towards the kind of unity sought by the scientist in the search for the theory of everything. This unity is *inclusive* unity and is given expression by the word 'universe', which etymologically means turning to the One.

But unity is ambiguous. Unity refers not only to original inclusive unity from which all arises, but also to the unity of the unit, the single one. The unit is expressed in classical logic in its formulation of the law of oneness or identity. A = A. The drive to unity that goes by way of classical logic also goes by way of analysis, which means cutting up, and by way of reductionism. This logic, through the use of 'either this or that', drives towards an *exclusive* unity. The search for the atom[31] is the search for that one, that unit, that cannot be divided. Such an atom can only truly be found in the dimensionless point. The word 'individual', that which cannot be divided, is the Latin translation of the Greek word *atom*. Each of us feels ourselves to be an individual: distinct, separate, and unique in the world.

Unity is then, at the same time, inclusive and exclusive, centrifugal and centripetal. As inclusive unity the tendency is from the center out to the periphery embracing more and more; as exclusive unity the tendency goes from the periphery to the center in a condition of increasing concentration. In both cases we are talking about *the same Unity*, One: a one that is two.[32] We can think and talk about two unities, but when we do so we think and talk about the idea of unity. In reality, beyond all ideas, two ones are impossible. This is why unity is dynamic and at the same time impossible.

Wholeness, unity, oneness, organic, all of this implies indivisibility, individuality, yet one is two. As we shall see creation arises out of the impossibility of divided unity. As Simone Weil says, "All true good carries with it conditions which are contradictory and as a consequence is impossible. He who keeps his attention really fixed on this impossibility and acts will do what is good . . . In the same way all truth contains a contradiction."[33] What she says of the true good could just as well be said of unity.

A complete statement of the logic of ambiguity now reads: the logic of ambiguity has one face that is ambiguous in principle but unambiguous in expression; in other words you see either the young or old woman. It has another face that is unambiguous in principle — unity, but ambiguous in expression — inclusive and exclusive unity. As a whole, the logic is one ambiguity in principle but, as we have just seen, two in expression. Seen in this way Unity is not simply a static container, or an abstract concept, but is intensely vibrant, dynamic and creative. Although I speak of Unity being this or that, I do not infer that unity 'is'. Unity is the categorical imperative that rules everything: it is the affirmation, 'Let there be One!' and is beyond being and knowing.

On the value of the logic of ambiguity

In the Middle Ages thinkers wrestled with such problems as: "How do celestial bodies differ from earthly ones?" "Why do some stars weave such an erratic course across the heavens?" "What gives the sun its power to run across the heavens?" These problems were never solved. They just dropped away with the understanding of a heliocentric world. In the same way, if we apply the logic of ambiguity, to the problems of how do body and mind interact, what is the 'I' or self, why do we laugh, what is the power of metaphor, what is creativity and decision making, these, and a whole host of other problems, drop away.[34]

A high price was demanded before the heliocentric world could be accepted. The earth — therefore the human beings who inhabited it — was no longer the center of the physical universe. Many were unable to pay that price and so clung to an outmoded worldview. In the same way the logic of ambiguity demands a high price. The law of identity, $A = A$, is no longer central. This means that, except in the abstract, we can no longer expect absolute certainty or security. We must wake up to a new uncertain, hazardous world in which absolutes have no place, where eternal peace is but a dream, where each solution is the start of new questions. In other words we must wake up to an evolving world in which not only species evolve but also the environment in which this evolution takes place, and even evolution itself evolves. This kind of evolving world makes the evolution of human nature possible.

6 On Intention

"This totality that encompasses the two is . . . the purely metaphysical, the thing-in-itself, which . . . we shall recognize as the will."

SCHOPENHAUER[1]

In the previous chapter I opened the way to introducing intention, the third transcendental factor. Many may find this factor very difficult to accept. The present trend in the life sciences generally, but in evolutionary science and in neuro-science in particular, is to see the human being as essentially a machine, and the brain as a complex computer. Intention has no place, it seems, in either machine or computer. Scientists may well throw up their hands in disgust when they hear talk of intention that is transcendent, metaphysical and unknowable. I will do my best in the following chapters to show that this may be a premature reaction.

In this chapter I muster support for the idea that intention is indeed the essential ingredient in the ecology of life. In the next chapter I will elaborate at length on the meaning that I give to the word intention, and in chapter 8 I will compare the explanation of behavior that intention affords with the explanation that mechanism affords by using the theory of *teleonomy* proposed by the biologist, Ernest Mayr. He offered this theory to sustain the mechanistic explanation of animal behavior.

I began this book by quoting Darwin on the 'struggle to survive'. I pointed out that this struggle is twofold: a metaphorical struggle, and an active one. If an earthquake were to strike a major city it would wipe out people indiscriminately, those who survive would do so by accident.

Strong or weak, intelligent or unintelligent, woman or man, it would make no difference. Natural disasters, such as a virulent virus, have wiped out most of a species. Those who survive do so without any struggle on the part of the organism. These are examples of metaphorical struggle. On the other hand, when two dogs fight and one defeats the other the struggle is an active one and the first dog survives because of its actions and not by accident. Instead of speaking of two kinds of struggle, we could speak of two kinds of survival: intentional and unintentional survival.

Is there a better way to describe the actions of animals in a fight, or an international soccer player scoring a goal in the world cup final, than to say their actions are intentional? On the other hand are there any reliable precedents in science, or even elsewhere, to justify using intention as an explanatory idea? Am I dealing with reality when I speak of unity or intention, or am I simply having recourse to words that sound big but mean nothing, products of an overheated imagination? Or, yet again, am I using these words much as the mathematician says, "Let x equal the unknown" with x remaining unknown?

These are some of the questions that I shall be tackling in this and later chapters. I will show why the third factor is real but unknowable, and also why one cannot say it is or it is not. To make this justification I call on traditional wisdom, on modern philosophy, and on quantum mechanics, in particular on the writings of the celebrated physicist David Bohm and the mathematician Roger Penrose. When I refer to unity I am not referring to a philosophical concept, but to what is as real as energy.

Intention as the third factor

Unity, that Schopenhauer calls will, is neither imaginary nor simply a conceptual idea made necessary by logic. Dynamic, directional[2] and purposeful, it is intelligent and creative. One cannot say 'it is', or 'it is not', but that it is *in potentia*. It is not something in particular, yet every 'something' is it. It is unknowable. It is the basis of all that is and all that is known; it is the third transcendental factor.

As we saw in the last chapter, quantum theory has its own formless, unknowable, reality, its own transcendental or metaphysical factor that

Heisenberg referred to as potentia. The philosopher Norris also indicates that, 'quantum reality' — potentia — is taken as belonging to "a noumenal realm that lies beyond reach of any concept we can frame concerning it." He assures us, "Whatever the notional reality 'behind'. . . . phenomena, it cannot be grasped, described or represented in conceptual-intuitive terms."[3]

Unity is unknowable, not unknown. The unknown may one day become known; the unknowable will always remain unknowable. The statement that unity is unknowable is not a theoretical one, nor do I expect to be able to prove logically what I say. Even so, I will show that unity, which manifests as intention in organisms, is real because it has identifiable effects in the world and in life.

Kant's noumenon: the third factor

Kant, the eighteenth-century philosopher, postulated a third, unknowable factor. He called it the *noumenon*. "All life is noumenal only . . . the whole world of sense is only a picture hovering before us, formed by our present mode of knowledge — a dream lacking any objective reality in itself."[4] On the Web[5] the following definition is given of the word noumenon. "In the philosophy of Immanuel Kant, a noumenon or thing in itself (German *Ding an sich*) is an unknowable, indescribable reality that, in some way, lies 'behind' observed phenomena." I prefer to say *beyond* observed phenomena.

If Kant were asked, is the statement 'It is raining' a statement about knowing or about being he would say that it is an amalgam of the two: an amalgam of sensory experience (being) and categories of the mind (knowing). If one asked him whether it still rains if no one is there to see it raining, that is to say, when the categories of the mind, (knowing) are not there, he would say that one couldn't answer the question.

The Vedic hymns and the third factor

The noumenon, potentia, will, or intention has been known of since the earliest of times. The Vedic hymns are some of the oldest extant religious texts whose origins go back many thousands of years. Even then the hymns stressed the importance of the third factor that lies beyond knowing and being. According to them, "Divine and human forms of expression reflect in [their] own way that transcendent, hidden, unified principle of harmony and order that supports and directs the movements of all things."[6]

In Sanskrit, this unified integrative principle is called *Rta*. This is a difficult word to translate into English, and expressions such as 'universal law', or 'cosmic order', that are normally used are unsatisfactory. William Mahoney in his book on the Vedas explains that, "*Rta* is that hidden structure on which the divine, physical and moral worlds are founded, through which they are inextricably connected and by which they are sustained."[7] He also says that the Vedic Hymns refer to it as 'One', 'the One Reality' or simply as 'It'.[8] *Rta* plays the same role in the Vedas that the word 'dharma', another meaningful but virtually untranslatable term, plays in Buddhism.

Tibetan Buddhism and the third factor

Tibetan Buddhism has a transformative philosophy designed not to bring one to a conceptual truth but to awakening. Many Western scholars now recognize that Tibetan Buddhism contains a wealth of valuable insights into the human condition. These insights have been compiled over hundreds of years by human beings researching the nature of consciousness, life and human nature through the medium of deep meditation and within the structure of Indian Buddhism. Although undoubtedly an abundance of superstition and fantasy has become mixed in with the more common interpretations, nevertheless to dismiss this treasure simply on that account is as foolish as to dismiss Christianity because of the excesses of fundamentalism.

Herbert Guenther before his recent death was a professor of Oriental studies at the University of Saskatchewan, and in his book *Wholeness Lost, Wholeness Regained*[9] gives an account of the third factor in the teaching of the *rDzogs-chen* school of Tibetan Buddhism. According to the *rDzogs-chen*, "the universe is not only intrinsically 'intelligent', but is also a self organizing whole of what superficially looks like a, or the, One (*nyag-gcig*)." This one or unity is not an entity or absolute but "the fusion of two contrary notions into a single dynamic one."

Another rDzogs-chen text[10] states that reality beyond form is, "That fundamental pervasive, unified, holistical process whose highly energized dynamics set up the variety of sub-processes and their associated structures." The name that is given to this dynamism is the Ground (*gzhi*), and it "is the ground and reason for everything . . . [it is] thoroughly dynamic . . . [and] responsible for the variety of structures, things, and experiences that are said to make up Reality." Guenther goes on to say that he will use the word Being instead of ground, but "It is crucial to avoid associating the term Being . . . with any determinate, isolatable, static essence or thing."

Zen Buddhism

Zen Buddhism too has a dynamic X, the noumenon. The late Yasutani, a contemporary Zen master, called it by its Japanese name *ku*, which, although unknowable, "is not mere emptiness. It is that which is living, dynamic, devoid of mass — the matrix of all phenomena." He goes on to say that the world of ku is "unfixed, devoid of mass, beyond individuality or personality — is outside the realm of imagination. Accordingly, the true substance of things . . . is *inconceivable and inscrutable*"[11] (emphasis added).[12]

The Sufi tradition and the third factor

The last tradition that I will refer to is the Sufi tradition. Ibn 'Arabi, a tenth-century Sufi saint and exponent of Sufism, also makes reference to the third factor beyond knowing and being. In Arabic this realm is called the *alam al-mithal*, which means the *intermediate* realm. It is intermediate between the 'spiritual and the corporeal state',[13] knowing and being. The intermediate realm is expressed through *himma*. Henri Corbin says, "Himma is an extremely complicated notion which perhaps cannot be translated by any one word. Many equivalents have been suggested: meditation, project, intention, desire, force of will . . . [and] the one aspect that encompasses all others, the creative power of the heart."[14] Himma is also "a hidden potency which is the cause of all movement and all change in the world."[15]

The third factor is universally accepted

Modern philosophy, represented by the works of Kant, and the traditional teachings, represented by the Vedic Hymns, Tibetan and Zen Buddhist and the Sufi traditions, all include the third factor as essential, indeed fundamental. Many other traditions, including Taoism, the teachings of Sankara, and the modern teacher Nisargadatta, all include the third factor as a basic ingredient of their teaching. Even Descartes, although he is best known as the first Westerner to formulate a dualist view of the world, also had a third factor, God. This is often overlooked. Heisenberg tells us, "If one uses the fundamental concepts of Descartes at all, it is essential that God is in the world and in the I and it is also essential that I cannot be really separated from the world . . . it is just this division that we have to criticize later from the development of physics in our time."[16] Heisenberg makes the point because he wanted to prepare the way for introducing the third factor — *potentia* — into quantum physics.

Ambiguity in quantum mechanics

As most of us now know, according to the theory of quantum mechanics photons are waves but they are also particles. This is something like saying that the sea is waves, but it is also, simultaneously, a block of ice. To say that the sea is now waves and later becomes a block of ice simply means the waves and the block of ice are complementary and this presents no difficulty. But, how can it be both waves and a block of ice simultaneously? The same question may be asked about waves and particles. A photon must be either a wave or a particle. But, experiments show that this is not so until after an observation has been made.

If we do one kind of experiment we get wave like properties; if we do another, we get particle like properties. One way to resolve the problem that this creates is to say that they are both properties of something else. This raises yet another question, "If the wave and particle are properties, what are they properties of? What *thing* has the property of being a wave and a particle?" Goswami elaborates on this by saying, "Quantum objects must be thought of as objects in potentia that define *a non-local domain of reality that transcends local space-time* and thus lies outside of the jurisdiction of Einsteinian speed limits"[17] (emphasis added).

Some physicists say that it does not make sense to ask what the wave and particle are properties of. It cannot be known. To quote the writer Nick Herbert, "since the nature of unmeasured reality is unobservable by definition, many physicists dismiss such questions as meaningless on pragmatic grounds."[18] What Herbert is calling the 'unmeasured reality', I am calling the transcendental.

Others are certain that the non-local domain is real and not just a useful concept. What Stephen Hawkins calls the 'mind of God', in different guises, and under different names, has been a reality for different religions throughout history. David Bohm called it *Undivided Wholeness in Flowing Movement*. He said, "Flow is, in some sense, prior to that of the 'things' that can be seen to form and dissolve in this flow."[19] He says further, "There is a universal flux that cannot be defined [known] explicitly but which can be known only implicitly."[20] In saying that flux cannot be known explicitly but only implicitly Bohm implies that flux transcends experience and so is transcendental according to the way that I am using the word. He adds, "Definable forms and shapes, some stable and some unstable, can be abstracted from the universal flux. In this flow, *mind and matter are not separate substances. Rather, they are different aspects of one whole and unbroken movement.*"[21] I have emphasized this last sentence because it corresponds exactly with what I am saying: Just as the young and old woman are different aspects of the black and white field, so mind and matter, knowing and being, are different aspects of the third force.

The mathematician Roger Penrose, in his book *The Large, the Small and the Human Mind,* also spoke of three aspects that he called mysteries: the 'Platonic' world, the 'mental' world and the 'physical' world. The Platonic world was, for Penrose, what the third factor is to my thesis. He introduced a feature into the third factor that was anticipated in the Vedic Hymns. He says that the third factor is responsible for structure, law, and order of a very precise nature. This factor is a world of Platonic absolutes.

On the question of the relation of knowing and being he said, "I suppose Bishop Berkeley [the idealist] would have thought that in some sense the physical world emerges out of our mental world, whereas the more usual scientific viewpoint is that somehow mentality is a feature of some kind of physical structure."[22] Penrose, too, sees two equally valid realities, a mental and a material reality, because he adds, "It seems to me that there is a fundamental problem with the idea that mentality arises out of physicality."[23]

Three scientists — Heisenberg, Bohm and Penrose — all highly respected scientists in their fields, have tried to imagine what the transcendental world beyond experience is like. All of them are thoroughly familiar with quantum theory and have offered very similar answers to different aspects of the question, "What is 'Reality without form?' " They conclude that it is a whole, a world in potentia, and beyond being and not being. It is implicit, and not explicit, dynamic, and includes both knowing and being. It has some affinity with the Platonic world, and is the source of the laws of nature.

To sum up: we have arrived by four separate and quite independent routes at the notion that a reality lies beyond experience. These routes are philosophy, traditional teaching, quantum theory and the logic of ambiguity. Because this reality is beyond experience, it must also be beyond the realm of form and knowledge. It is a third and unknowable, transcendental, factor.

The logic of ambiguity

Let me summarize what I have said so far.

The basic ambiguity has two faces: one is the face of unity or no ambiguity; the second is the face of ambiguity. This second face of ambiguity can be seen in two valid but mutually contradictory ways. We have been considering the mind/body ambiguity. In this case one way this second face can be seen is as mind, that is as knowing. In theoretical physics this face could be seen as the observer. This same face could also equally well be seen as matter: that is as being. In this case the theoretical physicist would see it as the experiment that he is conducting. I use the young and old woman in the gestalt picture as a metaphor. One sees either the face of the old woman or the face of the young; yet both are present simultaneously.

I likened the face of no ambiguity to the black and white field. The black and white field can be used as a metaphor for the non-local domain, for Kant's noumenon, for Heisenberg's potentia, for Bohm's Undivided

Wholeness in flowing movement or for Penrose's Platonic world. It is neither knowing nor being, or, to put it positively rather than negatively, it is One. This one is itself not unambiguous. It is both inclusive and exclusive, both centripetal — going to a dimensionless point at the center — and centrifugal — going towards the whole. I defined the logic of ambiguity by saying that *basic ambiguity has two faces: one is the face of ambiguity, the other face is a face of no ambiguity, but this face is not unambiguous.*

As we can now see, Unity, the One, as I am using the term, is not simply an abstract container waiting to be filled, but, as the third factor, it is the very source of creativity itself. Seeing that it is raining is not a passive condition wherein light waves come from the rain, enter the eye, travel along the optic nerve, enter the brain and are there transformed in some miraculous way into sight. Seeing it is raining is intensely active and creative. Furthermore this creativity does not come from either the observer, or the rain. It comes from the original complex one/(knowing /being) or creativity/(knowing/being).

Dynamic unity, when acting *as* a living organism, is intention. I have emphasized 'as' to ensure that one does not make the mistake of thinking intention acts in or through the organism like some *élan vital*. Schopenhauer makes a similar point when he talks about the One as 'will.' "The act of will and the movement of the body are not two different things objectively known, which the bond of causality unites; they do not stand in the relation of cause and effect; but they are one and the same."[24]

Neo-Darwinism takes no account of knowing or intention. The theory only takes into account the physical, 'being', and ignores the other two aspects. I devoted chapters 3 and 4 to giving reasons why knowing as well as being should be taken into account. Now I am saying that intention too has to be taken into account. Much more has yet to be said, but in this chapter I have given a further reason for questioning classical logic, and I have given a number of reasons for suggesting that a third factor, which, for want of a better word, I shall call *intention,* must be taken into account.

7 | Intention as a Dynamic Process

"Organization is more than mere order; order lacks end-directedness; organization is end-directed."

ERNST MAYR[1]

In chapter 2 I asked why two dogs fight for survival. Why do they struggle for dominance? But then, what powered Caesar, Napoleon, Alexander in their relentless striving for domination, what enables the Olympic athlete to suffer the pain and struggle of training in order to compete, what pushes mountaineers to climb Mt. Everest, swimmers to swim the English Channel, and explorers to venture into unknown lands and to put up with the privations and difficulties that this entailed? Is there not some common searching for, reaching after, yearning, in all of this? J. L. Mehta, in his article *Heidegger and the Vedanta,* asks, "Is it not precisely in this straining towards the impossible, the Absolute, that the very passion, the ecstasy, and the moving power of all great thinking lie, in this incessant, relentless pushing beyond its ever incomplete accomplishing?"[2] I am calling this power *dynamic unity* and, when it operates as organisms, *intention.*

Intention, knowing and being together are what we call life. We are so fixated upon the physical, on the body, that we take it quite for granted that the body (being) is fundamental, and that intention and knowing, if they exist at all, exist as attributes or functions of it. In the illustration of the young and old woman this would be tantamount to saying that the old woman is the real illustration and the young woman and the black and white forms are her attributes. Yet it would be truer to say that the black and white shapes are the reality and the young and old woman the attributes because they both 'come out of' the black and white shapes. In a similar way, dynamic unity is basic and knowing and being are ways by which it is manifested. This is why I emphasized in the last chapter that intention does not act in or through the organism but as the organism.

If I am a spectator at a sports event, at the beginning of a hundred meter sprint I see a group of athletes at the starter blocks, crouched, ready to take off the very moment the gun fires. That is to say that I see a set of bodies. I can see no awareness, no intention at all. Yet if I am one of the athletes I am just intention. My awareness is totally centered by intention. I am one-pointed, 'all ears' for the crack! of the gun, and I am aware of very little else. My body is poised precisely, with the intention to break away at the very instant the gun is fired. When the gun fires I am just movement. The cheering of the crowd scarcely penetrates through to me, the strain of the body is barely felt. As this is such an important point let me repeat Schopenhauer again. He says, "The act of will and the movement of the body are not two different things objectively known, which the bond of causality unites; they do not stand in the relation of cause and effect; but they are one and the same."[3] On the other hand, when I am enjoying a good movie, or deep into an interesting novel, I am 'lost to the world', lost in a mental world of my own. I am just knowing. How we look at the world: whether from outside or from within determines whether intention, knowing or being is the 'reality'. Because science only knows the Objective viewpoint, the only reality for scientists can be the body (being).

Objects are normally stationary until some outside cause puts them into action. A cause and effect explanation is sufficient to explain their activity. But this means that as long as we insist upon an Objective viewpoint to be the only true viewpoint, and so seek explanations that are suitable only for understanding machines, we can never understand life; life is not just an object (being) but intention, knowing and being. Scientists who work in the field have recognized this and accept, somewhat reluctantly, a teleological answer to the question, "Why do animals act as they do?"

For example, the primatologist Frans de Waal tells the following story. "When guests arrive at the Field Station of the Yerkes Primate Center, near Atlanta, where I work, they usually pay a visit to my chimpanzees. Often our favorite troublemaker, a female named Georgia, hurries to the spigot to collect a mouthful of water before they arrive. She then casually mingles with the rest of the colony behind the mesh fence of their compound, and not even the sharpest observer will notice anything unusual. If necessary, Georgia will wait minutes with closed lips until the visitors come near. Then there will be shrieks, laughs, jumps, and sometimes falls when she suddenly sprays them."[4] Most of us would say that Georgia collected the water in her mouth *in order that* at the opportune moment she could spray the visitors with it.

Let us recall for a moment what Darwin has to say, "Unless [the universal struggle for life] be thoroughly engrained in the mind, I am convinced that the whole economy of nature, with every fact on distribution, rarity, abundance, extinction, and variation, will be dimly seen or quite misunderstood." Let us also remember that the universal struggle for life includes active as well as metaphorical 'struggle'. Animals struggle *in order to* survive. To say they have a 'vigorous *intention* to survive', instead of saying 'they struggle to survive' would not distort Darwin's meaning at all. When discussing evolution and its variety of expressions, it is necessary to appreciate the significance of active struggle, the intention, determination or will to prevail, because, without taking it clearly into account, and recognizing how important it is, we shall never be able develop a true understanding of evolution.

Two theories seek to explain why animals struggle to prevail: causation and teleology, and these correspond to the metaphorical and active struggle to survive. The following two sentences illustrate two alternative ways of describing animal behavior: "Georgia filled her mouth *and* sprayed the visitors," and "Georgia filled her mouth with water *in order to* spray the visitors." The first describes Georgia's behavior as the outcome of cause and effect with no intention necessary, and bio-nuclear scientists, neuro-scientists, geneticists and neo Darwinians favor this explanation. The second implies that Georgia's behavior is teleological. Primatologists and ethologists, the people who go into the field to study animals directly, often construe the behavior of animals using, at least implicitly, this theory.

On cause

Mechanism and materialism are based on the belief that cause is the sole agent of change. Many scientists take it for granted that all life's processes, as well as the evolution of these processes, are the effect of prior causes, and the effects of these causes become causes in turn. If this is so, then an unbroken chain of cause and effect is adequate for our understanding and intention is unnecessary.

Most people take the principle of cause and effect for granted so that it remains unquestioned. As Howard Pattee writes, "Causation is so ingrained in both the syntax and semantics of our natural language that we usually feel that events are somehow causally explained by almost any grammatically correct declarative statement that relates a noun and a verb phrase to the event."[5] For example, 'The sun causes flowers to grow'. Yet he also doubts whether the concept of causation, "In any of its many forms, has ever played a necessary role in the discovery of the laws of nature."[6]

Quantum mechanics has shown that the cause and effect relation is not invariable and that at the quantum level it does not pertain. This has opened up possibilities of showing how another kind of influence may operate at that level. This, in turn, has created some considerable doubt about the view that the world is a vast machine.

Far from playing a necessary role, the principle of causation has severely impoverished our understanding. This is the opinion of evolutionary biologist, geneticist and social commentator R. C. Lewontin. He is a materialist and an advocate of the banishment of religion. As a scientist he holds the Alexander Agassiz chair in zoology at Harvard. Criticizing the human genome-sequencing project he says, "The impoverished notion of causation that characterizes modern biological ideology, a notion that confuses agents with causes, drives us in particular directions to find solutions for our problems."[7] He says that many intelligent scientists want to sequence the human genome because "they are so completely devoted to the ideology of simple unitary causes that they do not ask themselves more complicated questions." [8]

Causation and control

The impoverished notion of causation can be seen in the following example. Imagine that you find a man who has been shot to death and six feet away another man stands with a smoking gun in his hand. What 'caused' his death? The bullet? The gun? The man who pulled the trigger? The jealousy of the man who pulled the trigger? The dead man's folly in getting mixed up with another man's wife? The wife who seduced the dead man? The inventor of the gun? The man who sold the gun? The government that allowed guns to be sold? The genes of the killer? Each of these could be considered to be the cause of the man's death. A forensic scientist would say that the bullet caused the death; someone lobbying for gun control would say it was the gun and the ease with which guns can be obtained; a psychologist might say it was jealousy; people who feel our morals are too lax would say it was the wife's adultery; a socio-biologist might say it was the genes. Each of these interested parties sees the particular factor they are citing as the causative agent. The death of the man was the result of all these causes and more, but in saying that I have shown causation to have indefinite explanatory value.

On teleology

The doctrine of teleology says that all of nature, or at least all intentional agents in nature, are goal oriented, or functionally organized. For example, human beings can plan ahead, set goals and act in a way to achieve these goals. Aristotle believed that nature was teleological and that each thing or organism was constructed in such a way that it was able to reach its goal or *telos*. At one time it was believed that evolution was teleological and the goal of evolution was to create human beings. But then, according to the *Cambridge Dictionary of Philosophy*, "Darwin explained the teleological character of the world in a non-teleological way. The evolutionary process itself is not teleological but gives rise to functionally organized systems and intentional agents." Bertrand Russell writes of teleology in the following way: "Broadly, a teleological system is one in which purposes are realized, i.e., in which certain desires — those that are deeper or nobler or more fundamental or more universal or what not — are followed by their realization."[9]

Generally speaking the problem with teleology is that it involves, in some way, conscious agents who have goals and purposes along with designs and plans to achieve the goals. The ultimate conscious agent is God.

Examples of mechanistic and teleological explanations

Suppose I were to ask why the engine of a car is running. The mechanistic answer would be that someone had turned on the ignition. This caused a connection to be made between the battery and the starter motor. This causes a flow of electricity to turn the starter-motor. This caused the motor to turn the engine. This caused the pistons to go up and down. This caused gas to enter the cylinder . . . etc.

Supposed the same question, why is the car running were answered in a teleological way. I might say I started the car because I want to go into town. I want to go into town to visit a shop. I want to visit the shop to buy food.

> I get into the car *and* go into town, or
> I get into the car *in order* to go into town.

The mechanistic explanation is correct because each part of a machine is made to perform a specific function. This in effect means that a machine is programmed to run in the way that it does. The mechanist theory says that just as human beings produce the parts of a machine so natural selection produces the parts of an organism. An organism just like the machine is programmed by natural selection to run the way it does.

A teleological explanation is based upon the idea of separate but nested goals. The final goal is to buy food. Nested in that goal is the goal of going into the shop. Nested in that is the goal of going to town and so on. Both approaches are premised on the belief that, to understand a situation one must segment it. This is the way the analytical process works. One identifies the elements and then assumes what relationship they have to each other. In the case of mechanism the elements are the functional parts; in the case of teleology the elements are the goals.

Cause, intention and time

If we think about cause and effect we always think that cause comes first and effect comes later. Looking at something that is happening now we assume that something in the past caused it to happen. On the other hand, when we think teleologically we assume that something we want to do or have in the future determines what is going on in the present.

I am turning on the car's ignition now because I want to go to town in the future.

The difference between the two is that causation exerts its influence from the past to the present; teleology exerts its influence from the future to the present. *The Cambridge Dictionary of Philosophy* [10] has a disparaging comment on teleology, saying that it implies, "a future state that does not yet exist exerts an influence on the present behavior of a system." A similar comment could be made about causation. A cause in the past that no longer exists exerts an influence on the present.

We cannot say that one or the other of these two explanations is the right one; either is right depending on the point of view that one adopts. The one advocating the theory of causation adopt the Objective point of view; the one advocating the teleological point of view adopt the Subjective point of view. They are manifestly both right and yet incompatible. In this case two ways of looking at the one 'influence' are possible: as causal or as teleological — and these two stand in an ambiguous relation similar to the young and old woman. We can only understand them by using the logic of ambiguity. They are both ways of talking about the ongoingness of life.

On intention

This ongoingness is intention. Intention too is oriented towards the future, but not necessarily towards a known and preconceived goal that lies in the future. Just as we see causation acting from the past to the present, so we see intention acting from the present to the future. Intention is nevertheless dependent upon the past, although not caused by it. Beethoven's ninth symphony could not have been written had there not been an evolution of musical theory, musical instruments and audience appreciation, but the 9th symphony still required Beethoven's intention embedded in his creative genius. Similarly, each step of evolution is dependent upon the past, but this does not necessarily mean it has been caused by it. In writing the 9th symphony Beethoven was forward looking. Intention carried him along towards the future, towards completing the symphony. Even so, the agony that he endured in his creations arose not because he had a design that he was trying to realize — he did not have the 9th symphony in mind and struggled to find a way to write it down in note form. The symphony emerged slowly, according to new conflicts that were generated as he resolved earlier ones.

Intention and energy

At one point in his book *The Blind Watchmaker* Dawkins makes a covert attack on Bergson's *élan vital*. He says that if he wants to understand how a steam engine works "I should definitely not be impressed if the engineer said it was propelled by *force locomotif.*"[11] Yet without doubt, he would be impressed if an engineer told him that the steam engine was propelled by energy. Energy is now an accepted word and explanation. Even so the word 'energy' as we know it today is relatively speaking a newcomer to our vocabulary. The use of the word energy "can only be traced in its modern sense to the mid 1800's."[12]

According to a dictionary of philosophy, energy is: "the power by which things act to change other things." "Potentiality in the physical." "The capacity to do work."[13] According to Webster's dictionary it is, "The capacity for being active or acting", "intellectual energy", "natural power vigorously exerted", "work with energy".[14] None of these definitions say what energy *is* but rather what it *does*. But for the dictionary's use of the word 'things', these same phrases define intention. Both energy and intention have the same source, the third force, and both are transcendental in the way that I am using this term.

Let me repeat, intention acts *as* the organism; intentional acts are not action *by* the organism. Intentional action *by* the organism is teleology; it implies that the organism, or some ghost in the organism, by some kind of design and forethought consciously applies intention to achieve a goal. It also implies that the organism is a 'thing'. To see the organism as a process, as intention, and not as a thing is in agreement with the trend in modern thought, which I spoke of in the introduction, away from the seeing the world as a collection of things to seeing the world as a dynamic process, or, to use Bohm's word, as a 'flow'. "Definable forms and shapes, some stable and some unstable, can be abstracted from the universal flux."[15]

Although intention and energy are not 'something', they are nevertheless real. Popper says, "We accept things as 'real' if they can causally act upon, or interact with, ordinary objects."[16] If we can accept that Georgia filled her mouth with water in order to later spray the visitors, in other words that intention guided her actions, then intention is real.

Intention, like energy, is unknowable in itself; both can only be known indirectly through their effects. One cannot even legitimately ask, "What is intention?" because the word 'is' refers to the Objective worldview of Being. Our language is ill equipped to speak of relationships and forces. This is why we have had to develop a special language, the language of mathematics to overcome this problem.

Adopting the top down method of investigation, if [I] know, then the universe has knowing as an aspect. In the same way, if [I] intend, then the universe has an intentional aspect also. As Heisenberg pointed out, the universe and I are one. I am not added to or a part of the universe. The universe is not one thing and I another thing. Because I am intelligent and one with the universe, then the universe also, to some degree, is one and intelligent: one/(knowing/being).

8 The 'Blind, Unconscious, Automatic' Process of Intention

"The force by virtue of which a stone falls to the ground, or one body repels another, is in essence no less strange and mysterious than that which produces the movement and growth of an animal."

SCHOPENHAUER[1]

How can we see intention in action? I gave an example of knowing when I said, "*I know* it is raining." A great deal of ink has been spilt over questions such as, "is the universe intentional?" "does it have a purpose?" Or "does chance alone rule?" Or, "is evolution simply the evolution of machines?" I can, to my own satisfaction, prove the contrary to this idea with a very simple experiment: [I] lift my hand.[2]

I have the same reservations about using the word 'I' here as I had when talking about 'I' know. This is why I put [ ] around the word 'I'. The way that most people use the word 'I' implies that 'I' am something, a soul, a spirit, a person, in short a ghost in the machine. In Chapter 3 I made the distinction between 'that I am' and 'what I am'. 'That I am' is the transcendent I am. To say I am a soul, body, spirit, or person, refers to 'what I am'. I say, "I raise my hand." Yet if someone were to ask me what muscles and nerves I use to raise my hand, 'I' just could not say. A moment's introspection will show that the hand rises quite without 'my' knowing how it happens. Most of us if we are challenged would say that we raise the hand 'unconsciously' or 'automatically'. This, though, is simply a way of saying that an unknown force beyond consciousness was responsible.

When I say that I raise my hand I am using 'I' because our language forces me to do so. I am not saying that 'I' have free will. Free will is most often associated with 'I', and, by letting go of the 'I' as an autonomous agent, the question of 'free-will or determinism' drops away. If 'I' is but a grammatical requirement, then 'I' cannot have or not have free will. Those who advocate free will claim that 'I' can do things; those who advocate determinism say 'I' cannot. Do away with the 'I am something' and both free will and determinism fall away. The question, as it has traditionally been posed, is meaningless.

Intention, the brain and faith

The intention in the experiment of raising my arm, of course, is to show that the world is intentional. But the question remains whether intention is just the result of neural activity of the brain. Or, to put the question slightly differently, are caloric and electrical/chemical energies the only motive powers: am I simply an elaborate machine, a robot?

Most scientists would reply, "Yes", because they are convinced that somewhere neural activity of the brain causes what we might want to call intentional activity. They would say that the brain only needs caloric and electrical/chemical energy. A stroke, they might well point out, could effectively do away with my ability to raise my hand. Would it, though, do away with the intention? While neural activity is obviously necessary for intention to be effective, must we infer also that physical forces cause intention? Is the brain both necessary and sufficient to create intention? Or is it just necessary? Suppose someone, who knows nothing about electricity, sees a lighted bulb break and the light go out. Would he be justified in thinking that the bulb was both necessary and sufficient to produce the light?

We are at the same impasse with intention as with knowing and are again at the level of faith. One must not believe that I just have *faith* that more than neural activity is necessary to lift my arm, whereas the scientist has scientific *certainty* that neural activity alone is sufficient. My faith that knowing and intention are necessary does not differ from the mechanist's faith that they are not. I am not talking about faith v science, but faith v faith. A mechanist may well be certain that I am mistaken, but that in no way changes the fact that he is talking from faith. My faith leads me to believe that the neural activity does not cause intention, although neural activity is necessary to execute the intention. This faith moreover is given credence by the fact that, as we shall see, intention has a greater explanatory power, or has a greater heuristic value, than cause and effect when explaining the behavior of organisms.

Intention /(knowing /being), or intention/(mind/brain), is an irreducible whole and we cannot, except conceptually, subdivide it into components, nor say that in the ecology of life one component is more important than the other. One must not look upon intention as some ghost in the machine. Intention is the 'machine' in the same way that being and knowing are the 'machine', and in the same way that the black and white shapes, the young and the old woman, are each the Gestalt illustration.

The blind, unconscious, automatic process of intention

In order to clarify in greater detail what the word 'intention' means let me use the mechanist's version of evolution. Dawkins says that evolution is a "blind, unconscious, automatic process." Let us reflect on each of these words to see them in relation to the theory that intention is necessary for evolution.

On the notion of 'unconscious'

Intention too is 'unconscious'. When I raise my hand I am at quite a loss to say how I do it.[3] Intention does not arise from consciousness, nor is it even dependent upon knowing or awareness. On the contrary, knowing is one of the ways that intention is manifest. On the other hand, intention is not mechanical — not just the outcome of 'the blind forces of physics'.[4]

On the notion of 'blind'

Is intention blind? Richard Dawkins says that evolution is blind. By this I think he means that evolution is reactive, and dependent solely on chance and what is past. But 'blind' could also mean that evolution is intentional, but the outcome of the intention is not known in advance. Intention does not have any purpose or design. To have a purpose and design means envisioning some specific outcome that one wants to attain. If one uses this meaning of intention then evolutionists are justified in rejecting it. Furthermore to have a purpose and design implies that some knowing-being, some self, person or God, or an entity of some kind, knowingly modifies nature according to a preconceived plan. This is the argument put forward by the Intelligent Design theory. The belief in a design and in a designer may be far subtler than I have expressed, but even so it implies a knowing or conscious element that projects a force, an *élan vital*, in a direction towards some known result. This explanation with its need for beings, designs, and goals, seems to be too inelegant to be true in a world that is essentially elegant. One of the most important outcomes of Darwin's theory is that it does not need a creator. Intention is not a Creator; but, as I shall show, it is the essence of creativity. [5.]

Purposes and designs are dependent upon consciousness, but intention is not. Intention may be said to be purposeful but it does not have a purpose. If we use the word blind in a metaphorical rather than a literal way and, because intention does not imply design, forethought or purpose, it could be called 'blind'.

On the notion of 'automatic'

Dawkins says also that evolution is automatic. One could say my raising the arm is an *automatic* activity. The expression 'automatic activity' can mean either of two things. [6] It can mean an action that is not dependent on external influences, cause, control, or operator. Raising my hand, if one uses this definition, is automatic, although I prefer to use the term *spontaneous.* The expression 'automatic activity' could also mean 'acting without intention'; I use the term *mechanical* for this kind of activity. Dawkins no doubt uses the word automatic in this way. A spontaneous action and a mechanical reaction are quite differently. The difference is what I am calling 'intention'.

Intention as the drive towards simplicity

So what 'is' intention? *Intention is activity with a direction, and the direction, the telos, towards which it is going is towards the One.* Earlier I said that dynamic unity is a categorical imperative, "Let there be One!" The similarity of this imperative with my definition of intention is hardly a surprise as intention is dynamic unity in action as organisms. Because intention has a direction it is future oriented, but this is not a future in time but a future 'in order'. Intention has no specific future towards which it is directed. Intention creates the future in time.

The former chief naval architect of the French navy, André Lamouche,[7] devoted a good part of his life to promoting the idea that *simplicity* is not only a principle of reason, but also a force in nature. Nature is essentially dynamic; the drive towards simplicity is the motive power behind this dynamism, and, in organisms, intention the source.

When I refer to the 'simple' it should be kept in mind that I am also talking about the One, the face of no ambiguity. The drive to simplicity is the drive to One. *Sem*, the etymological root for the word 'simple', means 'one'. Simple and one are, at root, two words with very similar meanings. Lamouche, in his three-volume work on simplicity, gave detailed and convincing proof of the power of the drive to simplicity both in nature and in human reason.

Earlier in the book we saw how unity drives the human being. The monistic stance of science, its rules, particularly Occam's razor, the rule of completeness and the faith of scientists that scientific laws are universal, all come from this drive. Classical logic, and in particular the law of identity, attests to our need for unity. In religion unity is basic. The Jewish prayer tells of it, "Hear, oh hear! Oh Israel, the Lord our God, the Lord is One." The Muslim tradition is "If not Unity then no Divinity." Plato, Plotinus, and Parmenides, the German Idealists were all imbued with the One. Unity, moreover, is a regulatory principle in art, music, drama, philosophy and theology.

My very intuition of myself as an 'individual', that which cannot be divided, of the world as a 'universe' (meaning turning to the One,) as well as our search for the atom, the indivisible unit, all attest to the importance of unity. All the manifold forms of competition including sport, politics, business and office politics among others, are all driven by the categorical imperative: "Let there be One!" Unity is important to us because we are one/(knowing/being) made manifest. The drive to unity and the drive to simplicity are both the drive of dynamic unity, which I am also calling intention.

However, just as unity is not unambiguous, being both inclusive and exclusive, so simplicity is not simple.

Non-composed simplicity

Lamouche showed that simplicity manifests in two different and contradictory ways: *non-composed* and *non-complex*. When we think about simplicity we usually think of *non-composed simplicity*. The principle of Occam's razor is derived directly from this drive to unity via non-composed simplicity. One extreme form of non-composed simplicity is the number one, another is the atom: that which cannot be divided. The drive towards this kind of simplicity prompts scientists to reject intention saying that it is unnecessary as all behavior can be explained without it. The reductionist works towards reducing complex phenomena to the interplay of simple, standard and specialized *units*: ones that are not composed of parts and so cannot be further divided. In physics scientists have looked for non-composed simplicity as atoms, then as particles, now as vibrating strings. If Superstring[8] theory proves to be acceptable, then all matter will be understood to be modifications of one simple indivisible element: a vibrating string. The ultimate, non-composed simplicity is the dimensionless point.

Non-complex simplicity

Simplicity is also *non-complex* simplicity. This simplicity addresses the relations between the elements in a system; to achieve this simplicity one reduces the number of unknown relations. The rule of completeness is derived from this form of simplicity. This is the rule that evolutionary scientists ignore when they reject intention.

In industry, during the 1920s and 30s, a form of work simplification was introduced called *Taylorism*. Taylor identified, and then simplified, units of work and this made way for the production line and mass production. He based his simplicity upon the standardization, specialization and simplification of units of operations in a work situation. Industrial engineers, Frank and Lillian Gilbreth, likewise analyzed work into individual and discrete units of activity called *therbligs* [9] and then eliminated those they felt were unnecessary.

This kind of work simplification went toward non-composed

simplicity by reducing the variety and number of elements. By contrast, contemporary work simplification consists mainly of setting up work-flow patterns, job descriptions, PERT charts, organization charts, and so on. All these enable the occupants of roles in the company [the elements] to know their relation to the other roles and to the whole. This is going towards non-complex simplicity.

System and simplicity

The mathematician and philosopher J. G. Bennett defined the word 'system' as *a set of independent elements that are mutually related*. For example, the solar system, the nervous system, a corporation, a car's electrical system, all have elements in mutual relation. A system is a non-complex simplicity, and is the opposite of a random set of unrelated elements. We get to know the relations in a system by intuition and we find the elements by analysis. When we *analyze* a system we reduce it to its elements by ignoring the relations; when we *understand* a system we see the elements in relation. Any thinking process obviously uses, with different emphasis, both intuition and analysis. Intuition is a non-computational way of using the mind and so cannot be simulated by a computer.

We can approach non-composed simplicity through smaller and smaller units towards the dimensionless point. We can go from a cell to its elements, molecules, and from there to the elements of molecules, which are atoms, from atoms to their elements, which are particles, and now its seems that further reduction is possible to go from particles to vibrating strings. This is the way of reductionism. We can go in the opposite direction towards non-complex simplicity through more inclusive systems to the whole universe. We then go from vibrating strings through particles and atoms up to molecules and beyond to cells to organisms, worlds and galaxies. None of these levels is the *real* level from which all other levels are derived. The real level is the one that is most appropriate, and this depends upon my needs. For the physicist the particle or the atom may be the real level, for the chemical engineer it would be the molecule, for the micro biologist it is probably the cell, or the primatologist it is the animal, or even the tribe in its environment.

Intention as a field under tension

The drive towards non-composed simplicity is going in the opposite direction to the drive towards non-complex simplicity. The drive to non-composed simplicity is a drive towards the center: it is centripetal. The drive towards non-complex simplicity is the drive towards the periphery, and is centrifugal. These two contrary drives together create a dynamic field having both centrifugal and centripetal force. The word intention, as well as allied words such as 'attention', and 'tension', are derived from the Latin word *tendere*, which means 'to stretch'. *In future I will be referring to this dynamic field when I use the word intention.*[10]

Wholeness, unity oneness, organic, organism, all this implies indivisibility, individuality; unity is fundamental. Yet unity itself is divided against itself. I will show that creation arises out of the 'impossibility' of this divided unity.

9 | On Causation and Programming

"Biologists don't talk about intentions and emotions."

FRANS DE WAAL[1]

The teleological response

Mayr describes the dilemma existing in the biological community: "There are numerous and weighty objections to the use of teleological language yet biologists have insisted that they would lose a great deal, methodologically and heuristically, if they were prevented from using the language."[2] He uses the two sentences that I modified in the previous chapter to illustrate what he means: "A turtle came ashore *in order to* lay her eggs," and the statement "A turtle came ashore *and* laid her eggs." He sees the problem the mechanist faces to be how to say that a turtle came ashore with intention of laying her eggs, without committing the sin of teleology.

Frans de Waal, the primatologist, gives another example of behavior that calls for more than a simple mechanistic explanation in the following. He first explains that getting a good look at a newborn ape is difficult, as it is really no more than a little dark blob against a mother's tummy. But, he was eager to see the baby, which had been born the day before, of an ape named Lolita. He called Lolita from out of the group and pointed to her belly. "Lolita looked up at me, sat down, and took the infant's right hand in her right hand and its left hand in her left hand. This sounds simple, but given that the baby was clinging to her she had to cross her arms to do so. The movement resembled that of people crossing their arms when grabbing a T-shirt by its hems in order to take it off. She then slowly lifted the baby into the air while turning it around on its axis, unfolding it in front of me. Suspended from its mother's hands, the baby now faced me instead of her."[3] De Waal points out, "With this elegant little motion Lolita demonstrated that she realized that I would find the face of her new born more interesting than its back."[4] Many biologists have puzzled over how to account for this kind of behavior and have offered many conflicting conclusions and criticisms of these conclusions.

Objections to teleology

Biologists object to teleology for several different reasons. As we have seen, teleological statements and explanations very often include purpose, design, or goals. Teleology, furthermore, has often been combined with theological beliefs. A Christian hymn expresses this combination well:

"God is working his purpose out,
As year succeeds to year."

Another objection yet is that teleology involves an assumption that future effects can be the cause of present behavior, and this conflicts with the principle of causality, which is based upon the notion that present effects require a past cause. To say Lolita turned the baby around *in order that* de Waal could see its face, means that enabling de Waal to see the face is the cause of the action. But, when Lolita first starts to turn the baby around, the fact that de Waal will see the baby's face is in the future. So, it seems that the future causes an action in the present.

Possibly the most serious objection of all is that teleology breaks the continuity from inanimate to animate nature. As Mayr says, "The aim of many biologists is to show that life is simply a continuation of the physical world, and that it therefore obeys the same laws as the physical world."[5] One of the most basic of these laws in the minds of neo-Darwinians is the law of cause and effect.

Mayr's solution

Mayr tried to build a bridge across the gap of the two worldviews, mechanism and vitalism, and uses programmed or *teleonomic* processes as the bridge. Many biologists were critical of Mayr for even introducing the concept of *teleonomic* processes, in spite of the high regard they had for him. Teleonomic processes, they felt, are too similar to teleological, or goal seeking processes. Even so, Mayr claimed that his argument is still based upon cause and effect and so is completely mechanistic. As he says, "Teleonomic explanations are strictly causal and mechanistic. They give no comfort to adherents of vitalistic concepts."[6]

We must remember the esteem with which Mayr was regarded among biologists and must see his argument as one of the better attempts made by a biologist to justify the mechanistic approach while bearing in mind that we have to explain Lolita turning the baby around *in order that* de Waal could see its face.

Excluding human behavior

When Mayr, to avoid the sin of teleology, enlarges upon the biological term teleonomy, he excludes human behavior from what he is talking about. He said, "Intentional, purposeful human behavior is, almost by definition, teleological. Yet I shall exclude it from further discussion because use of the words *intentional* or *consciously premeditated,* which are usually employed in connection with such behavior, runs the risk of getting us involved in complex controversies over psychological theory."[7]

This exclusion is strange for a number of reasons. Biologists such as Jacques Monod and Stephen Jay Gould specifically, and most neo-Darwinians generally, are adamant that human beings do not occupy any special place in nature. Furthermore, by excluding human behavior from teleonomic explanations, Mayr is failing to do what he has said is the aim of many biologists: "To show that life is simply a continuation of the physical world, and that it therefore obeys the same laws as the physical world." This is all the more important bearing in mind that we are using the 'top down' approach. This approach specifically includes human behavior because it starts with it. How has the evolution of human behavior been possible? That behavior above all must include the very intentional activity that Mayr wants to exclude.

What are teleonomic processes?

I would like to discuss in some detail the route that Mayr takes when explaining causally and mechanistically why Lolita turned the baby around. He will say that she is programmed by evolution to do so. The idea of 'programming' is used with increasing frequency in the life sciences to explain the mystery of life, and Mayr can help us appreciate something of what is involved in this kind of explanation.

Teleonomic processes or behaviors — that is programmed behavior — he says, have the following characteristics: they are directed towards attaining a goal, and they owe this goal-directness to the operation of a program.[8] They imply a dynamic process rather than a static condition.[9] This dynamic process has two components: a program to guide it, and *some end point or goal, which is foreseen in the program that regulates the behavior*[10] (italics added). Natural selection produces, and variations adjust, each particular program in ways beneficial to the survival of the organism. But then he says, "a program is material, and it exists prior to the initiation of the teleonomic process. Furthermore it is consistent with a causal explanation."[11]

Mayr claims that though organisms have goal directed behavior, "a teleonomic explanation is in no way in conflict with the laws of physics and chemistry." He claims that a program is *material*, but defines a program as "coded or prearranged information that controls a process (or behavior) leading toward a given end."[12] Furthermore, the program that Mayr is suggesting contains both the blueprint and also instructions on how to use the information of the blueprint. This means that the program — in the guise of instructions on how to use the information of the blueprint — in some way 'reflects on itself', the blueprint. In short, the program reflects on the program. As Mayr insists that the program is matter this means that matter reflects upon matter.

He says that organisms are no different from man-made machines and he chose his definition of a program deliberately to show the mechanistic nature of organisms. "One might overlook the mechanistic nature if one were to make a distinction between what seems to be 'purposive' behavior in organisms from man made machines."[13] The truly characteristic aspect of goal seeking behavior according to Mayr is not "*that mechanisms exist which improve the precision with which a goal is reached, but rather that mechanisms exist which initiate, i.e. cause this goal seeking behavior*"[14] (italics added by Mayr).

A critique of Mayr's teleonomic process

The following critique, although made about Mayr's teleonomic process, is nevertheless also a critique of the prevailing theories of 'programming' that are proliferating to explain animal and human behavior.

Mayr tells us that teleonomic processes are based upon 'programs'. All too often we hear that we are 'programmed' to do this or that, or that the genes are 'programmed'. If we are not programmed then we are 'hard wired'. The mind we are told is the 'software' and the brain the 'hardware' and between them they produce behavior without the intercession of intention or creativity. These ideas are used too often because, although they are simply metaphors, they are often used as facts. Mayr is using a metaphor when he says that teleonomic processes are based on programs, in the same way the geneticist uses a metaphor when he says that DNA is a 'program'.

A metaphor says, 'this is like that'. Her cheeks are rosy, is a shortened version of 'her cheeks are like roses'. We should not be surprised to learn that during the time when clocks were first invented the world was seen to be a machine. Nor is it surprising when steam engines came into existence that Freud should see the unconscious as a head of steam being built up under pressure needing safety valves and explosions to relieve it. In an age when we have a love affair with computers, they will, of course, be a natural metaphor for life and the mind.

When I said that 'her cheeks are like roses' is an extended version of 'her cheeks are rosy' I missed a very important point. The metaphor says, 'her cheeks *are* roses', just as the advocates of artificial intelligence say, 'the mind is a computer'. But, a metaphor also says, simultaneously with 'her cheeks are roses', that 'her cheeks are *not* roses'.[15] That her cheeks are not roses is overlooked at one's peril. It would indeed be a fool who watered his beloved's cheeks and fed them with fertilizer to keep them fresh and young. The metaphor is powerful because it contains the conflict 'it is/it is not'.[16] The metaphor, 'the mind is a computer', is a powerful one, as are the metaphors, 'the world is a machine', and 'the

teleonomic process is a program'. But only a fool would take these as
literal statements.

More specific criticisms

But the problem is not just that Mayr uses programs as metaphors
while acting as though they are not. He says that programs are
material, and in this way he emphasizes his belief that organisms are
elaborate machines. By saying that a program is material and an organism is a machine, Mayr tries to make both programs and machines
consistent with a material, causal explanation. He wants to make the
programs consistent with the principle of causation because he says
that one cannot draw a line and say organisms are purposeful and
machines are mechanistic.

But a program has two parts: the material on which it is inscribed
and the program's code. When I buy a program I buy a DVD; not long
ago I bought a CD. Before that the program was put on a floppy disc;
and before it was put on to any of these the programmer most likely
wrote the program on paper. DVD, CD, floppy or paper, all are material.
In this way the program is material, and material that obeys the laws of
physics and has had its own evolution. But, the program is also a code,
and a code is not material. As far as the code in which the program is
written is concerned, it does not matter what kind of material is used on
which to inscribe it. The code is not material; it is 'mental'. The
language in which the code is written is an offshoot of written language,
which in turn is an offshoot of spoken language, and so has its own long
evolution that is quite distinct from the material on which it is written.

Geneticists also conflate the material and the mental, and reduce
them both to the material. The DNA code is 'written' on molecules,
which are matter. Even so, just as the computer program is written on
material things but is not material, so the DNA code is written on
molecules, but it isn't the molecules. Molecules *are what the code is
recorded on*.

The CD, floppy, and molecules obey physical laws. These must be
thought about in one way; the program is subject to semiotic controls
and these must be thought about in another way. Semiotics is the study
of how meaning is made and understood. But Mayr is saying that the

code is subject to the same physical laws as the material on which it is inscribed.

Mayr's programs, moreover, are blatantly teleological. He says that teleonomic processes are directed towards attaining a goal, *which is foreseen in the program that guides them*. Whether a 'mind' or a 'program' foresees the goal, and directs the organism to attaining it, the result is still teleological. Mayr moreover says a mechanism exists which initiates goal-seeking behavior. A program, neither its material aspect nor its semiotic, does not, and cannot, initiate goal-seeking behavior. Programs are tools that may improve the precision, speed, or accuracy by which a goal is realized, but intention, not tools, gives rise to what could be described as 'goal seeking' behavior. No amount of research into programming is going to change that fact.

A program and intention

A program is an extension of the programmer's intention. For example, he writes a program 'with the intention that', when he presses a button on the computer, a printer in the next room *will* begin to print. If he does not have that intention he will not write that program. Furthermore the intention guides the programmer in everything he does including checking whether it functions as it should. If it does not, the programmer will trouble shoot the program, and this trouble shooting will be guided by his intention and, if necessary, he will write another program and this again will be guided by his intention.

One can say that getting the printer to print is the 'goal' of the programmer, if one likes. But this is just a way of talking. In the description that I gave of what happened I did not feel that it was necessary to use the word 'goal'. The word intention means goal oriented but that does not mean the intention and the goal are two and separate. When a composer writes a piece of music he may write a melody. But the melody is not the goal of writing the music. The programmer does not have a goal of writing the program nor does he need to have an image of a printer being turned on as he writes the program. Moreover a 'goal' has no bearing on the way either the program or the printer will operate. The programmer's intention on the other hand does determine the way the program, and so the printer, *will* operate. I have emphasized the word 'will' because the 'goal', that is the outcome of the intention, is in the future. But this future is not the future in time, but the future in sequence: first this, then that. Nothing *lies* in the future. *The intention creates the future.*

The programmer could just as well go through to the next room, press a button on the printer with the intention that the printer should begin to print. By doing this he simply bypasses the program. The program just makes it easier for the programmer to carry out his intention. Whether he does by-pass the program or whether he writes the program makes no difference to the intention; it remains the same.

After the program has been written and installed anyone can come along and press the same button and print a page. Someone might prefer to say that the printing is 'automatic', meaning mechanical. This is true of the activity of the printer; it is entirely mechanical: this wheel turns and lifts that lever which turns on that circuit and so on. Another person might want to say that the program prints the page. Yet it is the programmer's intention that does the printing, coded as the program, and inscribed on the DVD though it may be.

The hardware of the computer and the printer is necessary, but it too operates according to the intention of those who designed and manufactured it. Even so one would not examine either the machinery of the printer for the intention of the engineer who designed it, or the CD of the program in the hope of finding the programmer's intention lurking in it like some ghost in the machine. But, without the intentions of the programmer, and the printer's designer the printer, will not print.

Artificial Intelligence

Recently scientists have written computer programs to simulate evolution. Their intention has been to show how, within a few parameters built into a program, forms or structures evolve, compete with others, mate and procreate. The success of the programs have led these scientists to claim they have demonstrated that the evolution of life forms involves no *deus ex machina*, no *élan vital*, no purpose or intention. Evolution 'just happens' once the preliminary and simple limits have been imposed.

The irony is, however, that these programs demonstrate quite the opposite.

The claim that evolution does not need a *deus ex machina* is refuted by the presence of the programmer. The programmer is the *deus ex machina* and chooses among a vast variety of highly sophisticated mathematical formulae in order to find the appropriate one to establish the necessary initial parameters.

The claim that intention or purpose is not necessary is refuted by the scientist's own purpose which is to simulate a purposeless evolution. Whitehead points out the irony of this when he says, "Scientists animated by the purpose of proving they are purposeless, constitute an interesting subject for study."[17] If a particular formula for proving that evolution is possible without purpose does not give the desired result it is refined, improved upon or rejected and another is sought. Thus, built into the program, is the scientist's purpose. By 'built in' I do not mean that one will find it in the binary logic of the program, but that the sequence and pattern of this program embodies the scientist's purpose.

The claim that *élan* vital is not necessary in the simulated evolution of species is refuted by the fact that if a power failure occurs the evolution stops and, unless an automatic 'save' has been installed into the program, all evolution would be lost. In other words the electric current flowing from positive to negative gives the thrust to the simulated evolution. Another way of putting this is that time, or *durée*, or a dynamic unity is given by the current, which makes evolution possible.

Finally the simulated evolution of the species does not proceed 'ex nihilo'. On the contrary the computer itself simulates a highly sophisticated cosmic gel or cosmic soup in which the new 'life forms' crystallize out. One only has to touch the innards of a computer inadvertently and again evolution crashes to halt. This inadvertent touch is perhaps a metaphor for a slight change in the environment within which life forms arise and within which they can be destroyed.

Thus far from proving what he sets out to prove, that the evolution of life forms is a purely materialistic, purposeless and valueless affair, the scientist, by creating his ingenious programs, proves just the opposite. Furthermore the forms generated are not material forms at all, but purely symbolic forms, animated mathematical formulae with interesting graphics. Just as chess playing programs do not understand, in an intuitive way, the strategies they use as a chess master does, so, within the working of these evolutionary programs, no creativity is involved.

Perhaps, after all, evolution does not require creativity, and perhaps the chess master does not need to understand the moves he make in an intuitive way, but these programs can do nothing to resolve the question, all that they can do is to pose it in a newer and more interesting way. Indeed from what we have been saying it would seem that a kind of Gödel's law could be proposed: one cannot consciously and intentionally prove the nonexistence of consciousness and intention.

Intention and machines

A car is also 'programmed'. The parts of a car are assembled in a certain way *in order that* when a key is turned in the ignition the engine of the car will start to run. The structure of a car and its program are the same. A computer differs from a car because although it too is programmed in a certain way so that when a key is turned or button pressed the computer begins to run, a program other than its structure is necessary.

One could say that a clock is programmed to tell the time. Telling the time is the purpose of the clock. But, of course, the clock does not tell the time, nor does the clock have the purpose; the person who uses the clock, has the purpose and tells the time. Whoever invented the clock did so because he intended to tell the time, or he intended that when other people intended to do so they could look at his clock. The purpose of a computer could be said to be to process information. But, again, the computer does not process information; the person using the computer does so, but finds it expedient to use the computer to help in doing this. Even the computer in a guided missile does not process information; the programmer who programmed it does so. This is also true of programs that can learn as they go that are built into robots. The robot neither processes information nor is it intelligent. The programmer uses arcane mathematics that has taken millions of human beings working for millennia to develop, and more recently the programming language, with which he codes his intention so that a robot *appears* to be processing information and acting in an intelligent way.

The two behaviors, that of a machine and that of an organism, do not form a continuous gradient as Mayr would have us believe. But the break in continuity does not occur because the machine is mechanical and the organism intentional. A steam engine and an organism both use three 'energies' in their activities: caloric, electrical and intentional. The difference between them is that *intention is extrinsic to the engine and built into it by the designer, but intention is intrinsic to the organism*. The origin of the intention of a machine comes from outside the machine; it comes from the machine's designer. The origin of the intention of an organism is the organism itself.

Said slightly differently: a structure that has intention as one of its dimensions, (an organism)[18] is different to a structure which has the dimension of intention added to it (a machine). This distinction is very important and one that Mayr overlooks. The programmer's intention is essential for the creation of the program, no matter how sophisticated that program happens to be, although the intention cannot be found by examining the program. With an organism the intention is intrinsic to it: intention is one of its three aspects: intention/(knowing/being).

When he was describing the teleonomic process above, Mayr said, "A teleonomic process depends upon some end point or goal, which is foreseen in the program that regulates the behavior." In a program this end point or goal is not 'foreseen' in the intention of the programmer. 'Foreseeing' is a way of describing intention. In the same way, an organism does not have a fixed and determined goal that it foresees. The 'goal' changes constantly according to the changing circumstances of which the organism is a part. One could say that just as intention is purposeful without having any fixed purpose, so an organism is goal oriented without having a fixed goal.

In spite of all that he says, Mayr leaves the most important question of all unanswered: "How does a program direct a given teleonomic activity and how does it cause goal seeking behavior?" Mayr in truth replies, "Alas all the biologist can tell us is that the study of the operation of programs is the most difficult area of biology." One reason for this is "The number of qualitatively different cells in a higher organism almost surely exceeds a billion."[19] "Indeed", he also says, "it must be admitted that the concept of a program is so new that the diversity of meanings of the term has not yet been fully explored." [20]

Mayr is saying that he is not quite sure what a program is and how it does what it does, but nevertheless he is sure it does it.

10 | What is Creativity?

"Something new has happened, something that cannot be wholly explained by *anything that went before*. That, I believe, is what we mean by 'creation'."

T. S. Eliot[1]

Evolution is not mechanical. It is creative and intelligent, grand, subtle, complex and simple. Human creativity is a continuity of the creativity inherent in life. Out of this has grown magnificent civilizations, works of art, architecture, music, and dance, the scientific wonders of technology, and the intricate genius required by genetic engineering, and in gaining neurological insights. Human creativity is a fact as solid as any other scientific fact. How are we to account for it? Moreover a religious urge has powered the growth of ceremonies, rituals, prayers and meditations throughout the history of humankind. This urge comes from the sense of a perfection that transcends the senses, yet nevertheless for some people it is more real than the urge for sex or food. How can we account for this religious yearning, as well as for the evolution of the best and greatest in human beings, their capacity for love, their appreciation of beauty, their altruistic capability? As I have insisted throughout this book, we can invoke no new agents to explain the results of the evolutionary process; we cannot invoke God or the mysterious power of complexity. Only what is present at the beginning can appear at the end. No miraculous interventions, no special cases may be allowed.

Evolution is an ongoing, creative process made possible by intention/(knowing/being). The present chapter and chapter 11 are crucial in that I will lay the foundations to justify this statement. In these two chapters I will clarify what I mean by *creativity*, give an example of creativity and show that creativity, and therefore evolution, is possible without a creator. To do this I will have to explore at some length the 'unconscious' nature of creativity, the difference between creativity and choice, and also how chance, accident and creativity are different, yet, to an Objective observer, remarkably similar. I will then show why I say that life is a continuous, creative process, and, finally, I will offer a suggestion about the origin of living organisms.

Creativity can be understood in a number of different ways. I will use a definition proposed by Arthur Koestler.[2] He says that creativity arises when a *single* situation or idea is perceived in "two self consistent but habitually *incompatible* frames of reference."[3] James Beatty, an eighteenth-century English poet, gave a similar description of humor. He said that it arose "from the view of two or more inconsistent, unsuitable, or incongruous parts or circumstances, considered as united in one complex object or assemblage."[4] A point of interest is that, according to an ancient Hermetic text, the world was created by laughter.[5]

An American economist, Kenneth Boulding, when writing of conflict, defined it as, "A situation of competition in which the parties are *aware* of the incompatibility of potential future positions and in which each party *wishes* to occupy a position which is incompatible with the wishes of the other."[6] This definition fits the conflict between two dogs engaged in an active struggle for survival. Each wants the food but only one can have it. They are incompatible. This means that the struggle to survive and the struggle to create have the same basic structure. The definition is also strikingly similar to the definition of creativity. Both creativity and conflict have two incompatible frames of reference and one unifying idea.

The logic of ambiguity and life's rhythms

Few people have difficulty with the two incompatible faces of the young and old woman as most alternate between the two, now seeing one face, now the other. Because of this alternation, some feel that classical logic is sufficient to understand the phenomenon; the young woman, while you see her, is the young woman, $A = A$. Even so we need the logic of ambiguity to understand how alternation is possible.

According to the way we think when using classical logic, the picture of the young woman — or old woman — is a whole; it accounts for the complete situation. On the other hand, if we think according to the logic of ambiguity, the picture of the young woman is a whole but it does not account for the complete situation; we need the old woman as well to account for the complete situation. But we cannot add together the two — young and old woman — to make the complete picture, so an alternation takes place from the young to the old woman.

In order to breathe we must inhale. But, although inhalation is a whole movement, it is not enough. We also have to exhale. But we cannot exhale at the same time as we inhale. So an alternation has to occur. An out breath is a whole movement but as exhaling is not enough, we need to inhale and so another alternation takes place.

Rhythmic alternation is a feature of life; the beating heart, inhalation and exhalation of the breath, the peristalsis of the alimentary canal, the systolic and diastolic arterial pressure, and the alternations involved in locomotion of the snake and the quadruped alike, are but a few examples. Thus, in addition to creativity, humor and conflict, alternation is another example of life's activity that can be understood, if one uses the logic of ambiguity, in a different and more profound way.

The conditions for creativity

The conditions of creativity are twofold: a single, unifying idea, and at least two conflicting frames of reference, although more than two may be involved. In future, for convenience, I will call these contradictory frames of reference *dissonance*. Creativity, according to this description, transcends, but does not negate, the excluded middle of classical logic. If A and B are the incompatible frames of reference, then A is not B, B is not A, and, in this part of the definition of creativity, the principle of the excluded middle is not negated. The 'single idea', that is unity, demands that A *is* B; in this way creativity transcends the excluded middle.

Other factors may be involved in the creative process and I am not suggesting that Koestler has said the last word on this complex subject. Nevertheless, his description fits well what I have said so far. The *single* idea comes from intention and, as pointed out, intention is the drive to unity, a drive to the simple, to the single. Intention is also unknowable and so creativity always has an unknowable aspect. Many people who have conducted research into creativity have underlined the importance of this unknowable or 'unconscious' aspect of the creative process. Although creativity has this unknowable aspect nevertheless it can be known through its results: the result of the creative process is a simplification of what was previously a dissonant situation, bearing in mind that simple means both non-complex as well as non-composed.

In addition to the single, unifying idea, creativity requires at least two conflicting frames of reference. The frames of reference must be present simultaneously for dissonance to be possible, and therefore for creativity to occur. Knowing makes possible simultaneous presence, *and so makes possible incompatibility.* Only when we know simultaneously both the young and old woman do we realize the inherent conflict and impossibility of the gestalt illustration. Without the two incompatible frames of reference arising simultaneously, that is arising within knowing, the conflict necessary for creativity to occur could never arise. This means that knowing as well as intention is essential for creativity to occur. Naturally, in a creative situation, the frames of reference must *be* in some manner, and this indicates that the third factor of the basic ambiguity, *being*, must also be present.

The basic ambiguity intention/(knowing/being) *is the primordial creative process.* Knowing and being are two self-consistent but habitually incompatible frames of reference. The ongoing debate between realists and idealists is evidence of their incompatibility. Intention, the drive towards unity, represents the single idea in Koestler's definition. Putting the opening sentence of this paragraph in a slightly different way: intention/knowing/being are necessary *and* sufficient for creativity to occur. As I will show, this creativity is what we call life.

An example of creativity

During the renovations of a building that we were going to use as a meditation hall at the Montreal Zen Center we found that the staircase was illegal in its dimensions and we had to rebuild it. The law stated that the treads of the staircase had to be 10" and the risers 8". If we were to build the staircase to these specifications, then it would have to go through the facing wall, which obviously it could not do. If we did not build the staircase according to these specifications, the building inspector would not approve it. What could we do? The two self-consistent but mutually incompatible frames of reference were the dimensions of the space in which the staircase had to go, and the legal dimensions of the staircase. These were incompatible. This incompatibility generated dissonance.

Not being a builder or an architect it took a while before I came up with the answer: insert a landing at the necessary height from the floor to which the staircase had to climb. The insertion of this landing had the effect of lowering the floor. In this way we were able to build the staircase according to specifications.

The dimensions of the space available for the staircase, and those of the staircase, were given, or discovered. The solution was created, and was entirely novel (at least it was to me). I could not have discovered the solution in either of the two frames of reference. Had it been possible for me to do so, then the solution would have been more properly the result of choice than of creativity.

What is apparent from this example is that the dissonant *elements* in nature, which are necessary for creativity to occur, are discovered. They already are. This means that creativity is not *ex nihilo;* it is dependent upon, but not caused by, pre-existing causes or conditions.

Another example of creativity

A fertilized ovum is a unicellular organism. It is a whole, yet it is not homogeneous. It consists of two incompatible sets of genes. They are incompatible because each set has its own specific, inherited characteristics, and so its own specific potential. This means that the ovum is an example of a creative situation: two incompatible frames of reference, and one uniting force: the ovum is one yet two. The result of this creative situation is the growth of the organism, which, basically, is accomplished by cell division. But when the ovum divides into two it is not simply two unicellular organisms; it is also one organism that has two cells. This produces yet another creative situation because each of the cells will have its quota of incompatible genes causing a further division. Furthermore, the two cells each being a whole, yet not the complete ovum, are two incompatible frames of reference within a single ovum thus bringing about another creative situation.

Organs of an organism emerge as the total organism grows. The emergence of the organs as wholes and the growth of the organism as a whole are not two occurrences. The organism is always one. It may grow into a deformed embryo. But it is still one deformed organism. The drive to unity still prevails.[7] In this way one could say that the organism is irreducibly complex. The organism can, however, be analyzed, or 'reduced', conceptually.

A metaphor for this is number. The number two is one whole, and yet it is made up of two units. The mathematician Poincaré pointed out that each number is a unique whole. Each "possesses its own kind of individuality, so to speak; each of them forms a kind of exception."[8] Von Franz in her book *Number and Time* said that this unique aspect of each number "appears to contain the mysterious factor that enables it to organize psyche and matter jointly."[9] This mysterious factor we know to be dynamic unity or intention.

Every number, like every cell, is One. The number four is one and so is the number 10 or 50. *Qualitatively* the number four is an indivisible, or irreducibly complex, whole.[10] For example, the four of the four angles of a square, or the four of the four points of the compass, is indivisible. Four, of the four corners of a square, is not simply three of the three angles of a triangle plus one angle. Nor is the four of the four points of the compass, the three of the three dimensions of space plus one. So the four of the four cells of the organism is not two plus two, or one multiplied by four, but an irreducible whole with an intrinsic quality.

At each stage of its growth, and of its evolution, the organism is always growing or evolving as an irreducible whole that has its own intrinsic quality. This is possible, not because God makes it so, but because creative evolution and organic growth are not the process of adding new units, but the process in which a whole becomes increasingly, but irreducibly, non-complex.[11] This means that although we can speak of the evolution of the eye, this is an abstraction from the reality. The reality is an evolving organism with the power of perception. We cannot say that the starfish has half an eye; the starfish has a whole eye but limited perception.

Protean behavior and creativity

Dissonance is basic to creativity; in the case of building the staircase, something did not fit, yet that something had to fit. Ethologists have used the concept of dissonance to explain the random behavior that animals use to escape from their enemies. The name that they give to this kind of behavior is *protean* behavior. Biologist Geoffrey Miller says that protean escape is probably the most widespread and successful adaptation against being eaten by predators, and is used by virtually all mobile animals on land, under the water and in the air.[12] He says further, "Proteanism depends upon the capacity for rapid, unpredictable generation of highly variable alternatives."[13] In order to survive, the prey must become more creative and, in order to be able to capture prey that is ever more creative in its ways of escape, the predators also have to be more creative; thereafter a kind of arms race develops. Miller concludes, "Creativity researchers agree that creativity depends on exactly this sort of mechanism . . . Donald Campbell insisted upon the importance of randomness in creativity. He saw an analogy between creative thought and genetic evolution: both work through an interplay between 'blind variation' and selective retention."[14]

The creative urge

The drive to unity through the resolution of randomness or dissonance is the basic motivation in a scientist or any thinker who develops a new way of looking at the world. The scientist sees that something does not fit, it does not add up. An existing theory, for example, may leave out some important elements that are in direct conflict with it. The dissonance nags at him until he comes up with a creative insight that resolves the nag. Dissonance creates, at some level, an irritation, a sense of profound dissatisfaction, a feeling of discomfort, which at times can become unbearable. The scientist will work to eradicate this feeling. The feeling is eradicated when a new unity, wholeness or harmony emerges. Many scientists, interestingly enough, rely on the beauty, the intrinsic harmony, of a new theory as one indication of its truth.

The mathematician Poincaré's creative moment is very well known as he documented it quite thoroughly. It bears repeating as it illustrates so well what I am saying. He saw that the arithmetic transformations of indeterminate ternary quadratic forms were identical with those of non-Euclidean geometry. That is, he saw that two frames of reference that ostensibly have nothing to do with one another were in fact describing the same thing. In his description of the experience he said that for fifteen days he had struggled with a mathematical problem without success. Then one evening, contrary to his usual work habits, he drank black coffee and could not sleep. He said:

"Ideas rose in crowds; I felt them *collide until pairs interlocked*, so to speak, making a stable combination. By the next morning I had established the existence of a class of Fuchsian functions, those which come from the hypergeometric series; I had only to write out the results, which took but a few hours."[15] I have italicized *collide until pairs interlocked* as the phrase is very suggestive of Koestler's definition.

About this time Poincaré went on a geological excursion. The change of routine and scenery made him forget his mathematical work. Then "having reached Coutances, we entered an omnibus to go some place or other. At the moment when I put my foot on the step the idea came to me, *without anything in my former thoughts seeming to have paved the way for it*."[16] This idea finally resolved the mathematical problem that had nagged at him for so long. He went on to say he did not verify the idea as he did not have the time but, instead, took his seat in the bus and went on with a conversation already commenced. Nevertheless he said that he felt perfectly certain of the truth of the idea. On his return to Caen, for conscience's sake, he verified the result.

This example shows all the elements of the creative process: the dissonance, the intellectual work necessary to clarify the nature of the dissonance, the 'unconscious, incubatory period' and the sudden burst of creative insight with the appearance of a new unity. Maria von Franz says, "Mathematical discovery has a numinous effect on the discoverer and leaves him with a feeling of absolute assurance." [17]

A German poet, Gottfried Benn, described the creative urge that comes out of the drive to unity as:

"A Bodiless childful of life in the gloom
Crying with frog voice, "What will I be?"[18]

T. S. Eliot, commenting on the drive to unity and on its being beyond consciousness, wrote, "The poet has something germinating in him for which he *must* find words [and] uses all his resources to express this obscure impulse . . . *He does not know what he wants to say until he has said it*"[19] (my emphasis).

The suddenness of the creative moment

While doing research a scientist may get a feeling that something does not fit the data that he is receiving. He feels uncomfortable. After being in this state of discomfort for a while the scientist has a hunch. This reduces the tension and he uses logic and experiment to see whether his hunch was correct. Often, if the hunch is completely correct, he will have a sense of the rightness, even the beauty of the resolution, and will know without logic or experimentation that it is right. The hunch is often expressed as the Aha! feeling.

The Aha! feeling is contradictory: it is both a feeling of surprise, even astonishment, and at the same time a feeling of the utterly familiar, the obvious. The act of creation brings into being the novel, the unexpected, something completely new but, at the same time, it reestablishes unity, and unity can never be absent and so is completely familiar. Creativity, moreover, is not gradual, but sudden; unity cannot appear little by little, but all at once or not at all. Sometimes the creative moment comes and one may spend years working out its implications. At other times one may work for years and suddenly the moment arrives. Preparation and working out the implications may be gradual, but the creative moment is not.

11 | Creative or Mechanical Evolution?

"When presented with two alternative equations both purporting to describe Nature, we always choose the one that appeals to our aesthetic sense."

A. ZEE[1]

I am making a case for saying that evolution is creative and not mechanical. I am also saying that the source of the creativity is transcendent, that is beyond experience. In order to show the difference between this view and the neo-Darwinian view of evolution, let me compare what I have said about creativity with what a mechanist like Richard Dawkins says about it. This will show the richness of the former explanation and the poverty of the latter. I will then justify further my saying that the source of creativity is transcendent. And finally I will end this chapter with a discussion of a possible explanation for the origin of life on earth.

Dawkins on creativity

Dawkins wrote a computer program based upon iterative equations that produced what he called *biomorphs*, diagrams that changed progressively. He was very excited about the result and wrote, "I cannot conceal from you my feelings of exultation as I first watched these exquisite creatures emerging before my eyes. . . . I distinctly heard the triumphal opening chords of *Also sprach Zarathustra* in my mind."[2] He obviously thought that he was watching the dawn of creation.[3] Yet, "Technically all that we are doing," he goes on to say, "when we play the computer biomorph game, is *finding* animals that, in a mathematical sense, are waiting to be found. What it feels like is a process of artistic creation . . . Effective searching procedures become, when the search space is *sufficiently* large, indistinguishable from true creativity."[4]

While search procedures and creativity may be indistinguishable to an outside observer, and exultation confused with the radiance of the Aha! feeling, Dawkins' computer, by his own admission, is 'finding' or discovering existing elements. It is not creating. The program that he uses already prescribes all the forms that the computer produces and can produce. Furthermore, the computer does not *choose* the forms (which are certainly not animals as Dawkins claims) it simply produces them. Dawkins chooses them. Moreover, if the forms were not to his liking he would change the program to match his intention of simulating evolution.

Choice is always made from among already existing forms; creativity gives what is new, what, hitherto, has not existed. Choice is conscious; creativity, coming from intention, is not conscious. As I have pointed out creativity always contains an element of the impossible, the completely contradictory, but choice is the selection among alternatives and no contradiction exists between these alternatives. Naming the forms may be a limited creativity, but this limited creativity is no different from the creativity involved in looking at Rorschach inkblots. In any case naming the forms is different from producing them. Finally if, as Dawkins claims, creativity is simply dependent upon a wide search space, did Einstein really just find his famous equation by widening his search space?

Dawkins must equate creativity with choice, because if he does not do so, if, as I maintain, the outcome of creativity is a new departure from existing trends and cannot be explained mechanistically, then his whole theory of evolution based upon materialism and mechanism is thrown into jeopardy. His example of the biomorphs proves my point because, as I say, nothing new was produced by the program, the biomorphs were all already 'in' the equations that he used to write the program. Dawkins believes that creativity requires 'vision', 'foresight', 'purpose' and 'planning'. This is why he says, "Natural selection has no purpose in mind it does not plan for the future. It has no vision, no foresight, no sight at all." But, creativity has none of these either. As Eliot said, a poet is "haunted by a demon, a demon against which he feels powerless, because in its first manifestation it has no face, no name, nothing; and the words, the poem he makes, are a kind of form of exorcism of this demon."[5] The poet, according to Eliot, does not even know what he is going to say until he has said it.[6]

The Blind Watchmaker

Dawkins makes this remark about the need for creativity to have vision etc. during his refutation, in his book *The Blind Watchmaker*, of Reverend Paley's argument in favor of a Conscious Designer. Let us spend some time considering Paley's argument and Dawkins' rejection of it for it will bring us to the critical part of my thesis: to show how evolution is creative without introducing a creator. To do this I will spend some time discussing the transcendent source of creativity. This discussion of Dawkins' refutation of Reverend Paley will give me an opportunity to provide a firm foundation for saying that evolution is One/ (knowing/being): intentional, intelligent, and creative.

Paley was a nineteenth-century Anglican clergyman who wrote before Darwin's theory had emerged. He knew a good deal about the science of his day and made a case for creativity in evolution. According to Dawkins, Paley gives the best-known exposition of the 'argument from design,' and so by refuting Paley's argument Dawkins feels that he has refuted all and any idea of a Conscious Designer theory. Dawkins concluded that Paley was "wrong, gloriously wrong." In arguing against Dawkins I do not want to condemn him in such a manner. I would, though, like to rescue Paley from this damning rejection, and say that he, no less than Dawkins, is simply giving an incomplete account.

First, let us be sure of what Paley said. He begins his treatise, *Natural Theology* with a famous passage:

"In crossing a heath, suppose I pitched my foot against a stone, and were asked how the stone came to be there; I might possibly answer, that, for anything I knew to the contrary, it had lain there for ever: nor would it perhaps be very easy to show the absurdity of this answer. But suppose I had found a watch upon the ground, and it should be inquired how the watch happened to be in that place; I should hardly think of the answer which I had before given, that for anything I knew, the watch might have always been there."[7]

Paley comments on the precision with which the parts of the watch is made and concludes that it must have had a maker, "That there must have existed, at some time, and at some place or other, an artificer or artificers, who formed it for the purpose which we find it actually to answer; who comprehended its construction, and designed its use."[8]

Paley, unfortunately, insisted, "Nobody could reasonably dissent from this conclusion." I say 'unfortunately' because Dawkins, of course, does dissent and declares, "That is just what the atheist, in effect, does when he contemplates the works of nature."[9] I too disagree with the way Paley expresses himself, although not with the spirit that lies beneath this expression. If we wish to use the expression 'God' then I suggest that we understand God to be creativity rather than a creator. In other words, God would be the dynamic process of evolution rather than a static Being, who, as in Intelligent Design, tinkers now and again with the forms that arise in the evolutionary process. In the tenth assumption this tinkering was specifically declared inadmissible.

Be that as it may, Paley is saying that creativity, and not simply the blind forces of physics, is involved in producing both the watch and life forms, and he uses Christianity, the idiom of his day, with which to say it.

Paley draws an analogy between a telescope and the eye, saying that as the former had a creator so the latter also must have had a creator. Dawkins says that this analogy is false. Here is the crucial point, because he then says, and I quote him at length, "All appearances to the contrary, the only watchmaker in nature is the blind forces of physics, albeit deployed in a very special way. A true watchmaker has foresight: he designs his cogs and springs, and plans their interconnections, with a future purpose in his mind's eye. Natural selection, the blind, unconscious, automatic process which Darwin discovered, and which we now know is the explanation for the existence and apparently purposeful form of all life, has no purpose in mind. It has no mind and no mind's eye. It does not plan for the future. It has no vision, no foresight, no sight at all. If it can be said to play the role of watchmaker in nature, it is the blind watchmaker."[10]

That natural selection "has no purpose in mind does not plan for the future. It has no vision, no foresight, no sight at all", is the essence of the neo-Darwinian theory of evolution. It is now enshrined as a dogma because only the creationists and intelligent designers seem to be willing to challenge the notion, and their alternative demands such a high price that few are willing to pay it. The price is the loss of much of what science has painstakingly shown to be by the abrupt introduction of God into what otherwise is a very elegant and simple theory.

As demonstrated in chapters 7 & 8 an alternative is possible. Intention, even when involved in human creativity, is intrinsically purposeful, but it does not have a purpose in mind nor does it plan for the future. It has no vision, no foresight, no sight at all. I say that intention does not have a purpose because purpose is another way of talking about intention: intention is purposeful. Intention does not plan for the future, because, as I have also said, intention creates the future. If the turtle leaves the sea in order to lay its eggs, then, when leaving the sea, laying the eggs *is* the future for this turtle. No empty bag or box or space called the future lies waiting for the turtle to fill it with its eggs. The turtle does not need a plan or design or even image to leave the sea, any more than I need any plan, design or image to raise my hand.

One might well object and ask, "Did not Poincaré have a design, foresight vision, planning and so on when he worked on his mathematical problem?" Certainly one could describe what happened in this way. Yet close inspection of the event shows that what was crucial was the anomaly: two dissonant frames of reference. His recognition of this dissonance did not come from any foresight, vision or planning. It would have come as a nag, as a discomfort, as a 'childful of life crying'. His intellectual work would have been trying to find alternative ways to resolve the nag. He finally met with the impossibility of resolving the problem in this way and tried to forget the problem and go to sleep. Finally, the breakthrough came, again without foresight or even forewarning.

The transcendent source of creativity

When we speak we create, although, admittedly, to say, "Good morning" does not require much creativity. But trying to explain in words what creativity is, or what anything else is for that matter, does require creativity. I constantly have to reconcile what I am saying with the possibility of another person understanding. I also have to take into account objections and different points of view. Yet when I write I do not know in advance what I am going to write. You, the reader, could prove this for yourself. Do you know what you are going to say before you say it? Furthermore, do you know what you are going to decide before you decide it? Speaking is a creative act; it is not a conscious one, it does not involve vision, foresight or any sight at all, even though one is obviously conscious of speaking. David Bohm means something similar when he says, "I have an intention to speak at this moment, and it is implicit in what I am going to say; I don't know what I'm going to say exactly, but it comes out. Now the words are not chosen one by one, but are rather unfolded in some way."[11]

No doubt many would object even more strongly and say that speaking is not creative at all. In this case let us consider writing poetry. I quoted T. S. Eliot earlier who used Gottfied Benn's couplet to describe the creative urge of a poet:

"A Bodiless childful of life in the gloom
Crying with frog voice, 'What will I be?'"

An unknown, unknowable, urge pushes the poet to create. Eliot explains, "the poet has something germinating in him for which he *must find* words" (emphasis added). Anyone who has created anything, even painted the kitchen, knows how compelled one can be by the urge to create. Yet as Eliot goes on to say, "He [the poet] does not know what he wants to say until he has said it."[12]

When we speak, we know that we are doing so, but the creative impulse behind the speaking is intention. Intention is transcendent and unknowable. Stravinsky refers to this unknowable, creative urge, "the foretaste of the creative act accompanies the intuitive grasp of an unknown entity already possessed but not yet intelligible, an entity that will not take definite shape except by the action of a constantly vigilant technique."[13]

Technique, which is allied to discovery — a word that usually means 'to bring into consciousness' — through knowing makes the elements available and uncovers their dissonance; creativity integrates them into a new whole. I say discovery *usually* means to bring into consciousness because this is not always so. The problem, or dissonance, that the creativity resolves may not be consciously known until after the resolution. Gregory Bateson stated in his *Ecology of Mind,* "Sometimes — often in science and always in art — one does not know what the problems were till after they have been solved."[14]

Brewster Ghiselin makes the point about the unknowable in

creativity in the following: "The secret developments that we call unconscious because they complete themselves without our knowledge and the other spontaneous activities that go forward without foresight yet in full consciousness are induced and focused by intense conscious effort spent upon the material to be developed or in the area to be illuminated. . . . Then without warning the solution or the germinal insight may appear."[15]

In other words, in creating, conscious efforts and 'unconscious', or transcendent activities, are both necessary. We consciously select the problem or difficulty that needs to be resolved, and we consciously search for alternatives. After all alternatives have been explored and found wanting we then probe the contradiction, conflict or difficulty that is the problem. Then 'unconscious' activities and incubation bring forth the new creation.

Jacques Maritain also tells us, "We must recognize the existence of an unconscious or preconscious which pertains to the spiritual powers of the human soul and to the inner abyss of personal freedom, and of the personal thirst and striving for knowing and seeing, grasping and expressing: a spiritual or musical unconscious which is specifically different from the automatic or deaf unconscious."[16]

He is at great pains to distinguish this creative unknowing from the Freudian 'unconscious' — an important distinction if for no other reason than that people sometimes think that somehow this unconscious of Freud is an actual creative force. One of the ways that the art community adopted this theory was through some kind of automatism, a rejection of conscious control, rather than through a genuine opening to creativity. This kind of activity, as Maritain says, "separated from intellectual light, the automatic life of the unconscious is fundamentally unable to reveal anything really new."[17]

To quote Brewster Ghiselin once more, "To the creator . . . the earliest effort may seem to involve a commerce with disorder." The earliest efforts are entering into the dissonance. This dissonance is not chaos, but indeterminate, one cannot pin it down because as he says, "It is organic, dynamic, full of tension and tendency." This is a fine description of intention at work. Going on he says, "What is absent from it, except in the decisive act of creation, is determination, fixity, any commitment to one resolution or another of the whole complex of its tensions."[18] When we think logically we use the mind in quite a different way. The discriminating mind uses what Descartes called clear and distinct ideas. It fixes 'this' as this, and 'that' as that, and opposes the two. Clear and distinct ideas are quite the opposite of that 'indeterminate fullness and activity of the inner life' of which Ghiselin speaks.

Later Ghiselin goes on to say, "It is essential to remember that the creative end is never fully in sight at the beginning and is brought wholly into view only when the process of creativity is completed." Yet, as he has pointed out, to abandon determination, fixity, and commitment to one resolution, does not throw us into chaos and disorder. On the contrary in this way we enter into what he calls "the organic, dynamic, which is full of tension and tendency."

Spontaneity and the transcendent

Intention is spontaneous and spontaneity is transcendent. The meaning of spontaneity can be illustrated by Zen Buddhist practice and by the various arts that have been developed from this practice. In calligraphy and sume-i painting, for example, exquisite productions are created with single, continuous strokes of the brush on very porous paper. In the martial arts, some of which had their origins in Zen practice, spontaneity is essential. Premeditation and conscious deliberation brings hesitancy and openings for the opponent to thrust home. We must distinguish, however, between spontaneity and thoughtless impulsiveness.

D. T. Suzuki says the following about the spontaneity of the master swordsman. "His movements are like flashes of lightning or like the mirror reflecting images. There is not a hairbreadth interval between one movement and another."[19] Earlier he had written:

> "However well a man may be trained in the art, the swordsman can never be the master of his technical knowledge unless all his psychic hindrances are removed and he can keep the mind in a state of emptiness, even purged of whatever technique he has obtained . . . [his] body will move as if automatically, with no conscious effort on the part of the swordsman himself . . . All training is there, but the mind is utterly unconscious of it. The mind, it may be said, does not know where it is."[20]

This is a description of one/(knowing /being) before the arising of consciousness. Such an emptiness of mind should not be looked upon as absent-mindedness or having a blank mind. Quite the contrary, emptiness of mind is the emptiness of the mind that is fixed on method, purpose, design or goal. Intention is called 'the invisible spirit' symbolized by the Sword of Mystery: "this sword stands as symbol of the invisible spirit keeping the body, mind and limbs in full activity. But we can never locate it in any part of the body."[21] The Chinese know the invisible spirit that I have called intention as *ch'i* and the Japanese as *ki* as, for example, the *ki* in Aikido and *joriki*, the power of concentration in Zen. In China and Japan *ki* is not simply a human attribute but is the basic power in the universe: the power that creates the work of art, and also creates the artist.

Spontaneity, chance and accident

It is necessary to distinguish between spontaneity, chance and accident. Objectively, that is to say when we look from the 'outside', they are indistinguishable, and the words are often used more or less as synonyms. In particular the reductionist, in the interests of simplicity, tends to conflate all three and so surrounds them with a kind of simplistic, conceptual haze.

All three are 'uncaused' and are breaks in the continuity of cause and effect. All are unconscious, unexpected and unpredictable. Yet, although the spontaneous is unexpected, the unexpected may not be either spontaneous or chance or even an accident. Dawkins found that his biomorphs had shapes that, as far as he is concerned, were quite unexpected. However, someone more versed in programming and mathematics would not have found them at all unexpected: the program that he wrote pre-determined everything that occurred to the biomorphs. No spontaneity, chance or accident was involved.

Evolutionary theorists use a double standard to assess chance and creative spontaneity. One cannot say why chance or creative spontaneity bring about change, nor how or why chance or creative spontaneity occurs. Yet while one is allowed to say that mutation can occur by chance, the idea that wholes are created spontaneously is quite unacceptable, although both chance and creativity are ultimately inexplicable. Creation, chance and spontaneity fall outside the principle of cause and effect and logical explanation.

The words accident and chance are often used as synonyms. Yet, accidents do have a cause. Some accidents are closely associated in our minds with disaster: automobile accidents, plane accidents, accidentally losing one's wallet. Those that do not have a negative outcome are more often called 'luck' than accident: winning the lottery, finding one's wallet by chance. An accident is an event that is not foreseen yet it does not occur outside the realm of cause and effect. When the plane crashes, or when I cannot find my wallet, no 'accident' occurs. A plane crashes according to the laws of nature in the same way that it flies according to the laws of nature. When a plane crashes investigators seek the cause of the accident; what law of nature was violated? The wallet is not lost; it lies between the cushion and the back of the chair ever since it slipped there from my pocket, although it may lie there for the rest of my life and be 'lost' to me forever. So an accident depends upon one's viewpoint. The relatives of the person killed in the accident will consider it to have been an accident because they could not have foreseen it.

From structure to process

Intention, as the third factor, is a dynamic field and is the source of all that both is (being) and all that is known (knowing); so to understand a natural process such as evolution we must make a radical shift from a structure to a process orientation. We must see a system not as I said earlier as a set of *elements* in relation, but as a set of *processes* in relation, which may nevertheless manifest as elements. As Erich Jantsch comments, "The notion of system is no longer tied to a specific spatial or spatial temporal structure nor to a changing configuration or particular components, nor to a set of internal or external relations. Rather, a system now appears as a set of coherent, evolving, interactive processes which temporarily manifest in globally stable structures that have nothing to do with the equilibrium and the solidity of technological structures."[22]

The normal view of evolution is that forces acting externally, such as changes within the DNA code, cause changes within the cell structure. Some 'thing' acting on some 'thing' else is what we mean by cause and effect. With this new process oriented view, the structure arises from process, and, in turn, the structure modifies the process in a self-organizing, self-regulating way. The process that I am calling intention, moreover, is the dynamic flow in the direction of unity. Within this intentional dynamic flow, things, structures, appear. This is like whirlpools appearing in a stream. The whirlpools in turn modify the flow of water. This kind of process has been called *autopoiesis*. Furthermore, to quote Jantsch, "An autopoietic system is, in the first line, not concerned with the production of any output, but with its own self renewal in the same process structure."[23]

The origin of living organisms

What then is the most basic autopoietic structure? This is tantamount to asking how did living organisms begin? Dawkins dealt with this problem in his chapter *Origins and Miracles*. It all began, he said, with a miracle and "a miracle is a tremendous stroke of luck."[24]

Let us try again.

According to the traditional scientific theory the early atmosphere of earth evolved into primordial soup, which, with the aid of lightning, was spontaneously transformed into primitive life. A research student, Stanley Miller, working in the Chicago University laboratory, performed experiments to test the theory. He simulated the atmosphere of the earth and the composition of the oceans in a flask, and passed a spark through the mixture. He was rewarded with significant quantities of amino acids, the building blocks of protein. Miller's achievement was looked upon as a first step in the creation of life in the laboratory. The belief was widely accepted that, given time and a sufficiently large ocean, Miller's primordial soup should polymerize to form peptides and complex proteins, eventually yielding self-replicating molecules. It was believed also that further experiments would prove the truth of this theory. This has not yet happened; even though for fifty years numerous experiments have been conducted, no self-replicating molecules have been produced in a laboratory. One can only conclude that something is wrong with the theory, something vital has been overlooked.

Some scientists have indeed objected to the idea that the earth could produce primordial soup capable of producing self-replicating molecules. Some have believed that the origin of life occurred somewhere out in space. From there it was delivered to earth either by meteors or by intelligent beings seeding the universe. Crick, in his book *Life Itself: Its Origin and Nature*,[25] offered this theory which is called *panspermism*.

However, such an explanation does not solve the problem of the origin of organic forms; it simply transfers the problem elsewhere.

Howard Pattee criticizes the primitive soup theory on another level altogether. The origin and evolution of life, he says, is not simply an increase in the complexity of matter; it also involves — if for the moment we adopt a materialist's point of view — matter controlling matter. This, in turn, involves *self-reference* or *self-description* on the part of matter. Mayr said that the program regulating behavior contains not only the blueprint but also instructions on how to use the information of the blueprint. This is what Pattee is referring to as self-reference. He says, "Self describing means that the actual constructing mechanisms [self-replicating molecules] must be made out of parts which are described and which can read their own description. And that's too complicated, in my view, to arise under our present picture of primitive soup with random polymerization of amino acids perhaps and nucleotides."[26] In a paper titled *Evolving Self-Reference* he points out that self-reference has many meanings, which include ambiguity and introspection "and is often considered one aspect of consciousness."[27]

The idea of self-reference, according to Pattee, is necessary if we are to understand evolution, development, and learning at all levels of organization, from the origin of life to the mind itself. In a later chapter we shall see how self-reference is involved in the evolution and activity of consciousness. Instead of adopting a completely materialist point of view, Pattee suggested that two kinds of order are necessary: physical law and symbolic structures.[28] He looks upon these as complementary.

The two kinds of order are mutually exclusive because the laws of physics cannot be derived from symbolic structure or symbolic structure be derived from the laws of physics, yet both are unified as a living organism. The laws of physics correspond to what I refer to as 'being', and symbolic structure to what I have referred as 'knowing'. The unification arises out of intention. Pattee tells us that Von Neumann felt that origination of symbolic and material functions "is a miracle of the first magnitude." This, Pattee says, is the origin of life problem. He elaborates: "The most difficult problem when considering the origin of life and evolution is how material structures following physical laws with no function or significance were gradually harnessed by syntactical rules to provide function and significance as symbols."[29] I have suggested that we can only understand this problem by having recourse to intention/(knowing/being) that makes this 'miracle' possible.

He goes on to say, "A productive approach to the theories of life, evolution, and cognition must focus on the complementary contributions of non-selective law-based material, *self-organization* [emphasis added] and natural selection-based symbolic organization."[30] We see that here Pattee introduces a third factor: 'self-organization'. These three aspects — (1) self-organization, (2) symbolic organization and (3) law-based material — correspond to the three aspects of intention /(knowing /being), and these aspects are primordial. Pattee steers clear of using knowing or consciousness in his theories, although these are clearly implied by them.[31]

When and how did life appear? With the materialistic science this question is normally taken to mean 'when did lifeless matter first become living matter?' The criterion used for living matter is that matter is capable of self-replication. If matter alone is involved then we have to question whether knowing and intention appear later in the evolutionary process. If so, when and how? The alternative is to deny that these have ever appeared — a thesis that I show to be difficult to defend.

The question 'when did life appear?' suggests that life is a special non-recurring event, which I believe is questionable. A better question would be 'when did living organisms first appear?' Because their appearance seems to be inexplicable, the word 'miracle' is frequently used when considering their origins. Even Dawkins uses the word, though he hastily reduces miracle to accident. As just pointed out, if material self-replication were the only criterion then two further miracles would have to be invoked to account for the emergence in living organisms of knowing and of intention. This would add up to three miracles in all. And yet miracles are what materialism seeks to banish, and they certainly should have no place in a theory of natural evolution.

I am suggesting that the origin of living organisms was autopoietic, a spontaneous self-creation that occurred by way of intention/(knowing/being). In other words the question how did inert matter become living matter drops away. Living organisms came after matter (i.e. being) had already evolved to a certain point, possibly somewhat in the manner of Miller's primordial soup. Even so, the complex 'intention/(knowing/being)' is irreducible — one can only refer to one of them independently of the others in a conceptual, abstract way. In the concrete the complex 'intention/(knowing/being)' is indissoluble. This means that matter did not evolve by itself. Both knowing and intention were also necessary: knowing alone can make sense of symbolic organization; intention is necessary for there to be organization. This means that the whole complex 'intention/(knowing/being)' evolved. A gradual evolution occurred without having to invoke any miracles. When the ambiguity 'intention/(knowing/being)' became sufficiently complex, that is when it became sufficiently evolved, matter, with the help of knowing and intention, became self-replicating.

Why evolution?

Evolution is necessary for the following reason. Creativity is a response to dissonance. What has been created in resolving the dissonance gives rise to new dissonance, and the search for renewed simplicity — or non-complexity — begins again. Renewed simplicity is constantly attained and then lost again. For example, every new scientific discovery brings a new simplicity, but it also carries within it its own set of new problems. Adapting the Marxist dictum,[32] one could say that every answer carries the seeds of its own questions. From alternating simplicity and dissonance, order and disorder, life evolves through spontaneous re-creation. During this evolution life becomes increasingly complex and increasingly unstable, and so accident, hazard and randomness also generate the need for new creativity. Evolution is thus ongoing. The beginning of life, as we know it on Earth, was not the beginning of life itself, which has no beginning. What began were living forms. The universe is alive; we divide it into the sentient and insentient for the sake of convenience only.

The universe is alive. Like a hologram, the ambiguity — intention/(knowing/being) — forms each region of the whole, from particle through all sentient beings through to the universe itself. That the one is in the all, and the all is in the one, is the basis of the *Hwa Yen* School of Buddhism.[33] A beautiful way of describing this whole in the part and part as the whole is found in the parable of *Indra's net,* which is recorded in the *Avatamsaka* sutra, the basic sutra of the Hwa Yen. "Innumerable ornaments in the form of small crystal marbles . . . are interlaced in various patterns forming a great complex network. Because of the reflection of light, not only does each and every one of these marbles reflect the whole cosmos including the continents and oceans of the human world down below, but at the same time they reflect one another, including all the reflected images in each and every marble, without omission."[34] In order to appreciate the full significance of this metaphor one must be one of the crystal marbles in the net.

Because the basic ambiguity is ubiquitous throughout the universe it means that the whole universe is creative. It also means that evolution is the way that creativity is realized. The universe, not just life forms, is alive and evolving. Furthermore this creativity is not the work of a creator, is not conscious and does not require foresight, planning or design.

A note on Intelligent Design

The discussion that is raging at the moment about Intelligent Design is reminiscent of the discussion that took place during the twentieth century between the psychologists who advocated trial and error as a method of learning, and the Gestalt psychologists who advocated sudden insight. The trial and error theory states that an organism learns something new by performing a series of random actions one of which sooner or later is rewarded by success. This reward tends to bias the organism in favor of that action and increases the chances that it will be repeated sooner among a new set of random movements. Eventually the movement will become selected by being rewarded invariably.

The connection between this and the neo-Darwinian account of evolution is obvious. Both are dependent only upon chance and neither requires awareness or intelligence. Survival both of the action and the new organism is determined by an outside and indifferent source: natural selection on the one hand and success rewarded on the other.

Trial and error research was conducted within a materialist philosophy and according to certain assumptions. The first was that psychology is the science of behavior and not the science of mind. The second was that we do not need to refer to mental events or have recourse to internal psychological processes to describe behavior. The third rule was that behavior is the response to external, environmental stimuli.

Any mental terms or concepts that creep into descriptions or explanations of behavior should be replaced by behavioral concepts. The Gestalt psychologists changed the rules and introduced mind back into psychology and opened up a rich vein of scientific investigation.

Just as there are parallels between the theory and philosophy of trial and error and the theory and philosophy of neo-Darwinian evolution, so there are some parallels between Intelligent Design and the Gestalt psychologists' gestalt. Both challenge the theory that a sequence of events — cause and effect or stimulus response — are the only way that a new situation arises; both introduce creativity as the cause of a new situation. Both imply some kind of intelligence.

Michael Behe in chapter 11 of *Darwin's Black Box, Science, Philosophy and Religion*[35] criticizes the materialist bias of the life sciences and concludes the chapter and his book, by affirming, "The simplicity that was once expected to be to be the foundation of life has proven to be a phantom; instead systems of horrendous, irreducible complexity inhabit the cell. The resulting realization that life was designed by an intelligence is a shock to us in the twenty-first century who have gotten used to thinking of life as the result of simple natural laws."[36]

Behe tells us that he is a Catholic and so he concludes that the intelligence that designed the irreducible complexities was God. Yet he insisted earlier, "the separateness of the spheres of science versus philosophy and religion is as it should be."[37] Yet again one page later he states, "The philosophical argument . . . that science should avoid theories which smack of the supernatural is an artificial restriction on science."[38] Whereas the Gestalt therapists were willing to change the rules, Behe seems to be wanting to play by them. As we have seen with the debate about realism and anti-realism, scientists can no longer separate science and philosophy. Similarly in the life sciences the separation of science from religion is no longer feasible, provided that by religion one simply means being open to the transcendent. If however religion means adhering to one particular interpretation of the transcendent, or if science means being "forced by our *a priori* adherence to material causes to create an apparatus of investigation and a set of concepts that produce material explanations,"[39] then the separation, and conflict, is inevitable.

12 | The Evolution of Intelligence

"There is no fundamental difference between man and the higher mammals in their mental faculties . . . the lower animals, like man, manifestly feel pleasure and pain, happiness and misery . . . even insects play together, as has been described by that excellent observer, P. Huber, who saw ants chasing and pretending to bite each other like so many puppies."

CHARLES DARWIN[1]

The evolution of intelligence is a major theme of this book. For a long while human beings claimed that intelligence set us apart from other beings. In this chapter I will show that we are not alone in being intelligent nor is intelligence limited to the level of primates and above; it can be found at all levels of nature. Darwin[2] himself said, "I could show that none of these characters of instinct are universal. A little dose . . . of judgment or reason, often comes into play, even in animals very low in the scale of nature." I shall first say what I mean by intelligence and show the part that 'ideas' play in its development. To help in this I shall also introduce the term 'covariance' — a term used by Ken Richardson, formerly senior lecturer in the Center for Human Development and Learning at the Open University, UK, in his book *The Making of Intelligence*.

Before going on, let me be clear that I am not trying to develop a theory of intelligence. This would be too vast and complex a subject for the present study and in any case beyond my competence. All that I need do is to show that some intelligence can be found at the lowest levels of organisms, and, because it would become a factor in the arms race — and so a factor in natural selection — intelligence is inherent in evolution.

The relation a lion has to its environment, which includes its relation to the terrain in which it lives, to other lions, as well as to its prey, deer and zebra, is of course of prime concern in its struggle to survive. This relation is largely dependent upon perception. Perception is not simply a stimulus of eyes or ears; it involves active seeking. Perception occurs when attention and intention guide seeing. Perception is a mode of awareness-of and this in turn comes from intention. The more intense the attention and intention, the greater is the acuity of perception. Perception thus is not simply a function of the brain [being]; intention and the mind [knowing] are also involved.

Intelligence and perception are closely related. The word 'seeing'[3] can be both seeing with the intelligence, as in 'I see what you mean', or seeing with the senses; the second is the continuation of the first. Intelligence — that is to say interpretation, judgment and reason — is present in varying degrees with all perception. Interpretation integrates a given perception with past experience and future expectation. As the ratio of interpretation to seeing increases, so perception becomes increasingly intelligent. The neo-Darwinians say that the single cell organism and organisms such as the oyster are able to perceive; in this case, because of what I have just said about perception, they also have very rudimentary intelligence. According to Richardson, "Some recent speculation about the nature of intelligence has certainly included a more healthy emphasis on complexity, change, representation and the uncertain-futures problem." He quotes with approval another writer, Mark Johnson, who writes that intelligence "refers to a sophisticated capacity for representation that enables an animal to be especially flexible in applying what it has learned to novel situations." [4]

The connection that these observations have with Koestler's definition of creativity is fairly obvious: the first, complexity, change, representation and the uncertain-futures, refers to the dissonant frames of reference that must be present for creativity to occur; the second, speaking of 'sophisticated capacity for representation', has overtones of Koestler's 'single idea'. All this tends to suggest that perception and intelligence are modes of creativity.

Perception and co-variance

A very primitive form of perception is the perception of sameness and difference. As an example of what I mean by sameness and difference, we perceive apples, oranges and bananas to be the same when we perceive them as 'fruit'. We gather them together or intuit them within the same gestalt that we call 'fruit'. We would perceive some apples to be different from each other should we separate them, that is, analyze them, according to size or color. Sameness and difference are both functions of the intentional field, that is they are functions of the drive towards simplicity: 'sameness' goes toward an inclusive, non-complex simplicity; 'difference' goes toward an exclusive, non-composed simplicity. Most intelligence tests are designed to measure, among other things, an individual's ability to perceive sameness and difference.

Sameness and difference provides a very primitive way to perceive pattern in the world. All organisms that can perceive can also perceive pattern. Pattern, which could be seen as a system — a set of independent but mutually related elements — arises when perception relates, or joins together, several elements. As an example: the blinds covering the windows in the room in which I am sitting contain a pattern. The slats of the blind are all the same. They are interspersed by spaces, which are different from the slats.

For a relation to be perceived, the things in relation must be present at the same time or in sequence. The slats of the blind are an example of the first, and a piece of music is an example of the second. With sequential relation, memory is necessary. Memory enables a sequence of events to be present simultaneously, just as awareness enables things to be present simultaneously. We must distinguish between memory and remembering. Memory is a function of awareness-as; remembering is a function of awareness-of and comes when we focus upon specific aspects of memory.

Patterns and their relations, even those perceived by primitive organisms, are rarely simple, static patterns, but are highly complex, changing and deeply embedded patterns. Even so, being able to perceive pattern, primitive or otherwise, is scarcely any good on its own in the struggle to survive. The perception would have to have consequences. A perception must be accompanied by some kind of prediction or projection into the future to be of practical use. Being able to predict, as well as being able to perceive pattern, both of which are vital for survival, are aspects of intelligence. Perception, attention, prediction, projection, creativity and intelligence are all ways that intention makes itself known in the living world.

Ken Richardson calls complex, changing patterns, *covariance*. The simplest *covariance* is given in the 'if-then' formulation. If it rains then the ground will get wet, or Shakespeare's, "If winter comes [then] can spring be far behind?" and if lightning flashes, the sound of thunder will follow. An animal relies on the 'if-then' covariance to survive; if it hears a sound, then a predator is possibly near. A different example of a covariant system is a triangle. If one changes an angle or a line, the whole system changes accordingly. The angles and the length of the sides of a triangle may be varied continuously, but throughout the changes we still recognize it as a triangle.

Richardson makes the point that the capacity to perceive covariance is an important, if not the most important, aspect of intelligence. He says that an animal's ability to make sense of its world, to understand its meaning, "depends on inducing a representation, or dynamic model, of the covariation structure of objects and events as experienced in ever changing forms, rather than fixed cues." [5] Furthermore, he believes that if the overall covariance remains constant for a fairly long time, behavior that is appropriate to it becomes controlled by equally constant physiological systems.

Richardson explains that intelligence is based upon covariance:[6] "intelligence appears to be the ability to grasp that simple, superficial associations (between two variables) may themselves be conditioned by other variables, and that this conditioning may be conditioned by deeper variables, and so on." Predicting unpredictability allows us to understand why intelligence evolved.

Covariation and the developing organism

Covariant relations are present at the very moment of conception. As the cells multiply they do not do so in a random fashion but according to a 'geography' [7] that is consistent for all embryos. *Every* embryo has a north, south, east, and west pole. The head develops at the west pole and the tail at the east. The north pole is the top of the embryo and the south is the bottom. As every developing organism has this geography all organisms, whether a starfish or a human being, inherently know up, down, forward and back. As every organism has these orientations it indicates that genes that are responsible for the development of the organism have a rudimentary intelligence.

The evolution of perception and intelligence

Dawkins, in his book *The Blind Watchmaker*, shows how a bat's echolocation could have developed in an entirely mechanical way without recourse to any cause other than the interplay of physical forces. Echolocation is a kind of sonar that a bat uses instead of the organ of sight, and is a form of perception. Dawkins only describes half the echolocation system, the half that can be observed Objectively. He may have accurately described the evolution of the *executive structure*, or hardware of echolocation, the development of the ears of the bat, the way the bat emits sounds, and the circuitry of the bat's brain in processing the impulses that are sent and received — but he does not mention perception.

The acuity of the bat's perception must have progressed in tune with the evolution of the physical aspects of echolocation. The physical aspect of echolation and acuity of perception, that is the 'mental' aspects, are co-variants. Acuity of perception did not *cause* the evolution of the executive structure. Yet, without the evolution of acuity of perception, the evolution of the physical aspects would serve no purpose. Conversely, without the evolution of the brain, perception could not gain in acuity.

Let me use a very rough analogy of this co-relation of the 'mental' and the 'physical'. I go into a room in which the curtains are drawn and the room is quite dark. When I go into the same room later the curtains are still drawn but the room is not so dark. I look for the reason that the room is not so dark and find the curtains are different; the material of the second set of curtains is more translucent than the first set. The new curtains have not caused an increase in light. Indeed there has been no increase; the sun shines just as brightly. But the translucency of the curtains lets more light into the room. The curtains represent 'being': the neurological structure and perceptive organs of an animal. The light represents intention/knowing.

In a similar way, the development of the bat's ability to perceive increases, and this increase in ability is dependent in part on the development of the bat's nervous system and ears, but *intention and knowing do not necessarily increase*. Humans have more creativity than bats because our brains and nervous systems simply 'let through more light' of knowing and intention than the brains and nervous systems of bats. The more developed and the more integrated the brain and nervous systems become, the more easily does the light shine through. 'Integration' varies according to the degree of non-composed/non-complex simplicity that is allowed by the structure of the organism. To change the metaphor to one I have used already, knowing and being resonate more freely as the evolution of the nervous system evolves. Because of this, we can say that we humans are more creative than bats are.

On idea

Richardson used the word 'concept' to refer to "an internal representation of an object's deep covariant structure."[8] By internal representation Richardson is referring to what I have called *idea*. I have written extensively about the meaning of the word 'idea' in *Zen and Creative Management*[9] and in *Creating Consciousness*.[10] I use the word in the way that it was used before Descartes made it virtually synonymous with the term 'concept'. To show what I mean let me quote Jacques Maritain:

> "This determinative focus is what the Schoolmen [mediaeval philosophers] called the idea factiva, say the 'creative idea'. They took care, moreover, to warn us that the craftsman's creative idea is in no way a concept, for it is neither cognitive nor representative, it is only generative; it does not tend to make our mind conform to things, but to make a thing conform to our mind. They never even used the word 'idea' in the sense of 'concept' as we have done since the time of Descartes. And so, if we may continue to speak of the craftsman's creative idea, it is on the condition that we be aware of the fact that this word idea is merely analogous when applied to that creative idea and to what we usually call idea."[11]

In *Zen and Creative Management* I wrote that an *idea*[12] reveals relations between phenomena. I can now extend the definition to say *idea reveals covariance*. Ideas are never consciously known. In the definition of creativity that we are using the single idea within two contradictory frames of reference is what makes creativity possible. Concepts, thoughts and words are some of the ways by which the idea is expressed. Singing, dancing, and painting can also express ideas.

An example of the use of an idea is the following. My cat likes to jump up on to the TV cabinet and sit on the loudspeaker that is part of the TV surround sound. He cannot however jump up to the loudspeaker in one jump because it is too high. The contradictory frames of reference are 'I want to get up to the loudspeaker' and 'I cannot get up to the loudspeaker'. He solved the problem by simply jumping on another loud-speaker next to the cabinet and from there was able to make the leap without difficulty. No doubt he had met with other similar difficulties and simply used the idea that had been formed sometime before. But at some time the dilemma must have been a real one, even if only for a very short while. The dilemma was resolved by a creative idea, an insight, a coming together. All of this obviously would have been done without words and concepts.

It is well known that a magnifying glass can be used to focus the sun's rays to make some dried leaves or a piece of paper burst into flames from the concentrated light. In a similar way an idea focuses intention and makes activity possible. The focusing simplifies a field of phenomena by revealing patterns or covariant structures.

I said earlier that knowing makes simultaneity possible. I can now be more precise and say that knowing, through idea, makes the perception of covariance possible. Using this definition I would say that animals have ideas but not concepts. For example, the territory of an animal is a covariant structure of which the animal has an idea. All organisms that can perceive pattern will have ideas that will be expressed by intelligent behavior.

Normally, as Richardson points out,[13] this covariant structure, as well as its internal representation [idea], remains implicit, and we are 'unconscious' of them. For example, I recognize a friend in many different attitudes, postures, movements and distances. When she walks the movements of her arms and legs, head and shoulders covary. Richardson attached points of light to a person and took a sequence of photographs of these points of light in relation. He then showed these photographs to experimental subjects who readily identified the points of light as of a person walking. He says, "We showed that adults and children continue to recognize, quite quickly, an object's form from stimuli consisting of as few as four points, despite the fact that the stimuli contain no overt features".[14]

An example

To help in understanding what all this means, let me suppose that I am waiting for my son to come home. It is night and he is late. I hear a sound and wonder whether he has arrived. The simple auditory stimulus is a sound. A sound is not discrete, alone, isolated; a sound covaries with many different factors. The sound of a creaking stair and the sound of a footstep on concrete are different. The sound covaries also with its distance, the force with which it is made, the substance that makes the sound and so on. So I do not hear a sound. I hear a sound made by a foot, a hammer, or a pebble, and this within a covariant system. I hear a sound made by a small boy, a man, or an elephant. I also hear a sound made by someone creeping into the house, running into the house, striding into the house. I hear a sound followed by silence, a sound followed by a very similar sound, a sound followed by a dissimilar sound and so on. I also know the sound of my son's walk. I can distinguish the sound of his walking from others' walking. I also know that a person who is hurt walks differently from a person who is excited or afraid. All of these are elements within a covarying system, or covariations in a covariant system.

For the sake of brevity one could say that deciding by the sounds that I hear whether or not my son has come home depends on comparing a present set of covariances with a remembered set of covariances and inducing from that comparison whether they indicate my son. The remembered set of covariances is what I have called the 'idea' and what Richardson calls 'a representation' or a 'dynamic model'. In other words, an idea is not fixed and static but more like the theme in a symphony that, while constant, undergoes endless variations. Ideas are like whirlpools that drift along in the flow of awareness-as. Richardson says, "making sense of such a world depends on inducing a representation or dynamic model, of the covariant structure of objects and events experienced in ever-changeable forms, rather than fixed cues."[15]

A sound alone as a fixed cue tells me nothing. If someone were to make a recording of the sound and then ask me what makes the sound I would probably be unable to identify it. Identification requires the sound to be in a context and that context is a covariant system. Richardson goes on to say, "Animals living in complex environments need to be able to abstract and represent dynamic, ever changing, covariant structures because these are often the only consistent information available. These may be called hyperstructures."[16] One way of looking at a hyperstructure would be to see it as a hierarchy of nested ideas. Once abstracted, this hyperstructure is a kind of grammar from which all future images of objects and events can be created.

The hyperstructure of covariance

One mode of intelligence is the ability to use the environment to one's advantage. To accomplish this, not only perception but memory also is necessary. My memory retains the hyperstructure as idea and I use this idea to interpret my perception of the present covariance. All the ways that I have heard and interpreted sounds in the past are elements in the hyperstructure that I use when hearing the sound and wondering whether my son has come home. (Again let me say that I use the word 'I' simply for grammatical convenience. No self exists in me or in an animal that does these things.) Memory is not a static set of data waiting to be processed as in a computer memory. It is dynamic and we can only artificially separate memory from the dynamic process of perceiving. We do this when we *think* about 'memory' and 'perception' and reduce the living process to concepts. The hyperstructure, furthermore, gives what Richardson calls the *informational depth*, and this determines the level of intelligence necessary to make predictions. The greater the informational depth the more intelligence is necessary to make a decision.

The development of science arises from a steady progression in cultural perception and the possibility of communicating about deeper and deeper levels of covariance,[17] which is to say hyperstructures of increasing richness and depth. These deeper layers of covariant structures represent scientific knowledge. Geometry is a clear example of what is meant by covariance, and measurement is the means by which we standardize and conceptualize covariance. Mathematics could be called the *science of covariance:* it reveals relations between phenomena — covariances — that otherwise would not be obvious, which it then calls laws. Music and dance also explore covariance, the first in the tonal structure given by the natural harmonics, the second in the movement of the body. Richardson says, "there is abundant evidence . . . that what the most evolved cerebral or cognitive systems are most interested in are covariations, simple and complex."[18]

Physical structures as limits and resources

Creativity, and the exercise of intelligence that is dependent upon it, is not arbitrary and, to function as evolution, it has to wait until the right circumstances are present. These circumstances include among others: conflicts, random mutations, and physiological limits. Elliot Jaques developed a theory of company organization structure, which is now very well known among students of organization. One of his basic definitions was that *work is the exercise of discretion within limits in order to achieve a result.*[19] This definition is very similar to, but developed quite independently of, Arthur Koestler's definition of creativity: creativity arises when a single situation or idea is perceived in "two self-consistent but habitually incompatible frames of reference." As we have seen the definition of creativity is also very similar to Kenneth Boulding's definition of conflict:[20] "incompatibility of the position of two parties to a single position to which each is aspiring." When describing the creative process, Koestler uses words such as 'clash', 'explosion', 'collision', 'confrontation', words which can just as well, indeed often do, describe conflict.

Conflict, or what I have called dissonance, leading to what Darwin has called struggle to survive, is necessary for work, creativity and evolution. Conflict also creates the limits within which discretion is exercised, and discretion includes acuity of perception.[21] In the evolution of an organism, chance and mutation, the organism itself, as well as the environment, all provide the limits within which creativity can occur. As the limits become more refined, as the nervous system more evolved, and as covariance is perceived within the dissonance, so creativity becomes more precise; and. as the creativity becomes more precise, the limits will correspondingly be more refined.

The struggle to survive: is that all?

One of the basic dogmas of the neo-Darwinian theory of evolution says that all the traits and behaviors displayed by living things must be beneficial adaptations to some aspect of the natural environment, or they must optimize the chances of survival in the presence of competitors relying on the same resources. But can everything that an organism is or does be simply reduced to means in the struggle to survive? Are there not values other than utility in nature? If so how did they appear?

When I was an executive in a corporation in the 1960s and 70s the great question at the time was, "Why is a company in business?" It was the mantra of the day that a company was in business to make a profit.[22] The logic was clear-cut. If a company does not make a profit, it does not survive. It seemed indisputable. A similar mantra exists among the evolutionists. An organism must pass the test of the sieve; it must survive. The illogical conclusion is then drawn "All that it does must in some way be a survival strategy." We are survival machines, as someone said.

Peter Drucker, a management guru of the day, disagreed with the profit motive being the sole or even primary motive. He said, "Organizations do not exist for their own sake, they are a means; each is society's organ for the discharge of one social task. Survival is not an adequate goal for an organization as it is for a biological species."

According to the first point of view, profit is the cause; the social task is the consequence. According to Drucker, the social task is the cause; profit is the consequence. In other words the consumer market is as important as the money market.

To complete the picture, the economist Kenneth Galbraith disagreed with both views. In his opinion, the needs of the techno-structure were the cause. The techno-structure is made up of the management and professionals in the organization. The personnel of a company work there for a variety of reasons: money, challenge, the need to belong to a group, the need for structure in their lives and so on.

In the face of these three equally valid, but conflicting reasons, I suggested[23] that one viewed a company not as 'something', but as a dynamic, creative field, the outcome of the intentions and needs of stockholders, the market and the employees. Furthermore, this field was under tension induced by the conflicting needs of the three forces making up the field. This field of tension, or dissonance, was the field in which creativity within the company was released.

In a similar way, I question whether survival, and the strategies that come from the need to survive, are complete explanations for the evolution and behavior of organisms. I wonder whether a dynamic, creative and intentional field, similar to that of the field of a business, is not a better explanation of evolution and behavior of organisms.

Geoffrey Miller, who wrote the *Mating Mind*,[24] revives what Darwin put forward in his book *The Descent of Man*, and shows sexual selection to be of equal importance to natural selection. He states, "To date, it has proven very difficult to propose a biological function for creative human intelligence that fits scientific evidence."[25] Obviously, natural selection has been a factor in evolution, and Miller recognizes this. But, he also considers sexual selection another factor in evolution. Sexual selection would be a prime mover in the 'active struggle' to survive, and a prime mover in the active struggle becoming part of the evolutionary sieve.

Sexual selection, Miller says, arises through the competition for reproduction. He goes on to say, "the view of the mind as a pragmatic, problem solving survivalist has . . . inhibited research on the evolution of human creativity, morality and language."[26] He had said earlier, "Our minds evolved not just as survival machines, but as courtship machines."[27] Although the word 'our' suggests human minds, nevertheless the copious examples he gives from the animal world would suggest that it also includes other species. In other words, as a 'courtship machine' the organism has a social task. Reproduction could be to the theory of evolution what Drucker's social task was to the theory of management.

The third force in the field is simply the joy of creativity. Creative intelligence has not been brought into being by evolution, rather evolution is the unfolding of the creative and intelligent potential inherent in intention, knowing and being. Intention and knowing do not simply serve the function to survive, nor to compete sexually, although they play vital roles in both of these. Yet one could say equally well that the struggle to survive and the need to compete sexually serve creativity. Survival, sexual reproduction and creativity are, all three, both cause and consequence, just as satisfying the needs of the market, stockholders and employees are all cause and consequence.

If all this is so it will follow that at some stage in evolution creativity comes to be important for its own sake. For example, play is important among the young of many species, and this play often involves some kind of challenge and creativity. The traditional view of play is that the young are honing their skills for later in life. Yet as Darwin points out, "But nothing is more common than for animals to take pleasure in practicing whatever instinct they follow at other times for some real good. How often do we see birds which fly easily, gliding and sailing through the air obviously for pleasure? The cat plays with the captured mouse, and the cormorant with the captured fish. The weaver-bird (Ploceus), when confined in a cage, amuses itself by neatly weaving blades of grass between the wires of its cage. . . . Hence it is not at all surprising that male birds should continue singing for their own amusement after the season for courtship is over."[28] A cat plays with a mouse because the mouse is a challenge, a game; it only later kills and, sometimes but not always, eats the mouse. A bird wheels in the sky, perhaps looking for food, but, as Darwin suggests,[29] perhaps for the sheer joy of flying.

Even as I sit here typing I see that my cat is playing with a squirrel. The squirrel clings to a tree face down towards that cat, switching its tail back and forth, just out of reach. They stay looking each other in the eye. The squirrel suddenly takes off, descends the tree and scampers around in a figure of eight on the lawn with the cat hot on its heels. The squirrel dashes up the tree again and the ritual starts again. They have already done this three times.

This play may be the consequence of instinctive behavior, but is instinct the cause? To say so, one would have to say: the young do not play because they enjoy it, but because they have an instinct or the right genes that make them play. I have given reasons why teleonomy, and this includes instinct, is incomplete as a theory. Is it not simpler to say, as Darwin suggests, that the young play because they enjoy play, enjoy the creativity involved?

Curiosity also gives an opportunity to exercise creativity. Curiosity is searching out the novel, the unexpected, the challenging. While the same executive structure may be at work as when the animal seeks food, the fact of finding food may again be the consequence and not the cause of curiosity. Let Darwin instruct us again,[30] "When a pair of cockatoos made a nest in an acacia tree, it was ridiculous to see the extravagant interest taken in the matter by the others of the same species."[31] These parrots, also, evinced unbounded curiosity, and clearly had "*the idea of property and possession*"[32] (emphasis added).

One way we humans have claimed superiority is by claiming that we use tools and that animals do not. Generalizing, this could mean that humans use the environment to their advantage and animals do not. Ethologists, more recently, are finding that some animals do use tools, using rocks to break open nuts and sticks to extract ants from their nests and so eat them. Using tools is just one creative way to use the environment to one's advantage: seeking shade from the sun, using cover to hide from a predator, using the terrain as a way of trapping prey, these are all ways of using the environment to one's advantage. The environment itself becomes the tool. There is a difference in degree in the intelligence and creativity of human beings and the intelligence and creativity of other animals, but the difference is in degree, not in kind. Human creativity is not a quantum leap ahead of animal creativity, except in so far as we use language and animals do not.[33]

Miller said that twenty years ago his book that puts forward the theory of sexual selection could not have been written. This would have meant that twenty years ago Darwin's *Descent of Man* could not have been written either. Perhaps in twenty years' time intellectual fashions will change again, and maybe then people will accept that creativity is cause as well as consequence in all organisms and in evolution itself!

13 | On the Evolution of Consciousness

"The Self is a relation that relates itself to its own self."

SØREN KIERKEGAARD[1]

What is most typically human? What sets us apart from all other animals? Some say we differ because we use tools; others say that it is because we use language. Others again say it is because we are intelligent. But some people say that it is because we are conscious, and they feel and believe that in some way all the other attributes come out of consciousness. Descartes was the first to separate animals and humans in this way by saying that animals are machines.[2] He said that animals differ from humans because they lack language, and because they are not as flexible as humans in their response to situations.

One of the reasons that we are prone to believe that animals lack consciousness is because, generally speaking, we do not recognize that consciousness has evolved from the most primitive states. Of course, few people would doubt that the *content* of consciousness has evolved. But that consciousness itself has evolved is generally overlooked or ignored.[3] If we are to understand what makes the evolution of human nature possible we must at least understand the following points: the stages through which consciousness has passed in its evolution; how our sense of identity, 'I', has arisen; and why most of mankind has a profound need for other people. All of these are interrelated questions. In this chapter I will be responding to the first of these questions by showing the stages through which consciousness has evolved. I will show that *self-reflection*, symbolized by the ancients as the uroboros swallowing its own tail, must be used as an explanatory principle.

On awareness

Up until now I have said that intention, knowing, and being together constitute what we call life. In the interests of clarity, instead of using the word 'knowing' I will sometimes use another word that is more or less synonymous with it: *awareness*. You will understand shortly why I do this. Just as I distinguished between 'that I know' and 'what I know', so I need to distinguish between the *fact* of awareness and the *contents* of awareness. We will just be concerned with the evolution of the fact of awareness. As I have just said, that the contents of awareness — what we know — have evolved is common knowledge.

The analogy of a mirror will help explain the difference between the fact and the content of awareness. We can distinguish between the mirror and the reflections. They have different orders of reality because we are inclined to say that the mirror is real but the reflections are not. We are inclined in this way because the reflections depend for their existence upon the mirror; the mirror does not depend upon the reflections. The mirror is constant; the reflections are transient. The mirror is one; the reflections are multitudinous and varied. The mirror is analogous to the fact of awareness; the contents of awareness are the reflections. I made a similar distinction between 'that I know' and 'what I know'. If I say "I know it is raining," then *I know* it is raining is what I am calling the fact of awareness. I know *it is raining* is the content of awareness.[4]

The connection between awareness and consciousness

Those who have written about 'consciousness' and 'awareness' have used these words in many different ways. I am going to say that awareness is basic and that consciousness is derived from it. By using the words 'consciousness' and 'awareness' in this way, I am, to some degree, being arbitrary, but let me, as best I can, justify doing this. According to *Webster's Dictionary* the etymology of the word 'consciousness' is, on the one hand *con* that means 'with', 'together', 'jointly'; and on the other *scire*, meaning 'to know'. Furthermore, the word 'scire' is based upon another word *skei* meaning to 'split', 'to cut'. This means that consciousness has to do with putting together, through knowing, something that was split. The Sanskrit word for consciousness, *vijnana*, also implies a split.

It too is composed of two words, *vi* that means 'divided', and *jna* that means 'primordial knowing'. The 'something that was split' is awareness. The splitting, as we shall see, is the result of the advent of *reflexive awareness* or awareness of awareness.

The evolution of awareness

That consciousness evolves from awareness and not that awareness evolves from consciousness is given some support by the following. When we go to the cinema we *hear* the background music but rarely *listen* to it. We also say sometimes, "I was *looking* at it, but did not *see* it." So we can be *aware* of something and yet not be *conscious* of it. Furthermore we would not normally say, "I listened to the music but did not hear it," so we would not say, "I was conscious, but unaware." For all these reasons I prefer to say awareness is primary and evolves into consciousness. During this evolution awareness passes through several stages.

Knowing/being

One/(knowing/being) which Subjectively is *I-am*,[5] is the basic way of being aware. At this level being is awareness. This corresponds to a saying of Meister Eckhart[6] about God: "God's knowing is his being."[7] At this stage, knowing is awareness without reflection: it is pure knowing without content.[8] One could say that God does not know that he is God.[9] To know that He is God would require self-reflection, and this in turn would give content to awareness. Bohm was also at one time interested in knowing/being and its consequences. He preferred to use the expression *soma-significance* rather than knowing/being but the implication was the same. For example, he says,[10] "meaning and matter may not have the same sort of consciousness that we have but there is still a mental pole at every level of matter . . . and eventually if you go to the infinite depths of matter, we may reach something very close to what you reach in the depths of the mind."[11]

The hologram is the best metaphor for the pervasiveness of One/(knowing/being). In a hologram, each part is at the same time the whole. That all beings are Buddha is a basic understanding of Zen; these beings would include unicellular organisms as well as lions, tigers, and elephants. All beings are One/(knowing/being).

Awareness-as being

Consciousness evolves through an apparent separation of knowing from being and the first stage of evolution could be called 'awareness-as being'. This kind of awareness is often called automatic, preconscious or even 'unconscious'.

An example of awareness-as-being is the following. A woman wrote that she was standing at the edge of a low cliff overlooking the sea where birds were swooping in the sky when suddenly her mind switched gears. "I still saw the birds and everything around me but instead of standing looking at them, I was them and they were me. I was also the sea and the sound of the sea and the grass and the sky. Everything and I were the same, all one."[12] The expression, 'instead of standing looking at them, I was them' could be translated, using the terminology developed in this book, as 'instead of standing, aware *of* them, I was just *aware as* them'. This is an undifferentiated way of being aware, and the British philosopher F. H. Bradley spoke of it in the following way:

> "We in short have experience in which there is no distinction between my awareness and that of which it is aware. There is an immediate feeling, a *knowing and being in one* (my emphasis), with which knowledge begins; and though this in a manner is transcended, it nevertheless remains throughout as the present foundation of my known world. And if you remove this direct sense of my momentary contents and being, you bring down the whole of consciousness in one common wreck. For it is in the end ruin (as the history of philosophy has demonstrated) to divide experience into something on one side experienced as an object and on the other side something not experienced at all."[13]

At this stage awareness does not require a nervous system. It is a simple elaboration of the knowing inherent in the fundamental one/(knowing/being) of the universe. Quite likely elementary organisms are aware in this way: the oyster that evolutionary theorists use as an example of an organism with rudimentary vision would have rudimentary awareness to make perception possible.

We spend much of our day hovering close to this state and most spiritual traditions refer to it as 'being asleep'. As Bradley writes, "Although knowing and being in one (awareness-as) in a manner is transcended, it nevertheless remains throughout as the present foundation of my known world." You are presently *aware-as* the room you are sitting in, *as* the book that you are reading, *as* the sounds of the environment, *as* the pressure of the chair against your body. During any day you are aware *as* trees, houses, people, cars, the song of a bird, the rumble of traffic, the hum of a lawn mower, the smell of perfume and the taste of coffee; all this is known simultaneously and without the differentiation that is made possible by focusing attention.

Joggers sometimes enter a 'joggers' high' in which they are no longer aware *of* what is going on. They are not, however, simply unaware and certainly not unconscious; they are aware *as* all that is going on. When we see a movie we 'suspend disbelief'. Disbelief is a function of the discriminating mind, which basically is awareness-of. Seeing a movie is very much like dreaming which is the ultimate state of awareness-as.

Awareness-of

The next mode of awareness is 'awareness-of'. Awareness-of arises when intention directs awareness-as in a specific direction. Strictly speaking, if we want to develop a science of consciousness, we should be more precise and say this level is 'awareness-of-awareness-as being'. This may sound a little strange at first until we realize that neuro-scientists tell us that we do not see the world but we 'see' changes in neurological states. In other words they are saying the same as I am but from the perspective of being rather than that of knowing. Awareness-of is the first step into reflexive awareness: awareness is aware of itself.

Normally, when we are looking at birds, the sea, the waves, and so on, we say, "I am aware of them," although technically we are not aware *of* the world, but instead we are aware of awareness-as the world. The woman who was aware as the birds, the sea, the sound of the sea, the grass and the sky, let go of being aware-of, she reverted to a more primitive state of awareness.

Three paragraphs back I said, "You are presently aware-as the room you are sitting in, *as* the book that you are reading, *as* the sounds of the environment, *as* the pressure of the chair against your body." As I mentioned each of the different items you probably became aware of them and the simple awareness-as was lost. This is why talking about awareness-as is so difficult.

Michael Polanyi and Harry Prosch make a very similar distinction between two ways of being aware.[14] They call these two ways, 'from awareness' and 'focal awareness.' 'From awareness' corresponds to 'awareness-as' and 'focal awareness' to 'awareness-of'. They point out that knowing a skill involves these two different kinds of awareness. When I hammer a nail into a piece of wood I *watch* [am aware of] the effects of my hammering to ensure among other things that I hit the nail correctly, and to see how far it has gone into the wood. I am not aware of the handle of the hammer in my hand; I am aware of the head striking the nail. At another level though I am alert to the feelings in my palm and fingers holding the hammer [awareness-as]. These feelings ensure that I handle the hammer correctly. Moreover the awareness involved in the one is not more intense than the awareness involved in the other. But I am aware in a different way.

Polanyi and Prosch state, "The difference may be stated by saying that these feelings [in my hand] are not watched *in themselves*, but that I watch something else by being aware of them . . . I may say that I have a *subsidiary* awareness-of the feelings in my hand which is merged into my *focal awareness-of* my driving the nail."[15]

This distinction between 'awareness-as' and 'awareness-of' is crucial. When I spoke of knowing I pointed out that a difference exists between *knowing* it is raining and knowing *it is raining. Knowing* it is raining corresponds to awareness *as*; knowing *it is raining* corresponds to what I aware of; I am aware of the rain falling. Awareness-as is what I called Subjective; awareness-of gives rise to the Objective.

No sense of 'I' is involved at the level of awareness-as or awareness-of. Awareness-as is not subjective awareness where the word 'subjective' means colored by prejudices, emotions, and memories. It is Subjective awareness; indeed the word 'Subjective' is more or less synonymous with the word 'awareness'. Paradoxically, if one makes the distinction suggested earlier — that objectivity can mean knowing that is not clouded by subjectivity — then awareness-as is objective even though it is Subjective.

Because we are aware of awareness *as* the world, and not directly aware *of* the world, traditional teachings maintain that the world is a dream. We cannot be aware of 'being'; that is, we cannot be aware of the world, of the chair, of the book; we can only be aware-of-awareness-as-being; we are aware-of-awareness-as-the-world, as-the-chair, as-the-book. When I know it is raining I am aware-of-awareness-as-the-rain-falling. (I use the hyphens to emphasize the unitary nature of awareness as.) Invariably I ignore the knowing, the awareness, take it for granted, and ultimately forget it altogether, and just say, "It is raining." Because I, along with everyone else, ignore awareness in this way, only Objective knowledge remains, the Subjective is lost sight of and all talk of awareness-as may seem to us to be artificial, abstract even philosophical. But, awareness is the basis of our life and our experience and of all that happens to us.

Earlier I wrote that we 'hover' close to 'awareness-as' during much of the day. I used the expression 'hover' because awareness-of is most often present, even though frequently in a very rudimentary way. We say that we drive a car, or clean our teeth, 'unconsciously'. This means that awareness-of what we are doing is very rudimentary and we are mainly aware-as driving, as-cleaning-our-teeth.

Simultaneity and sequence

Awareness-as is space-like, and all that appears in awareness-as appears simultaneously, and all appears as present. Awareness-as is undiscriminating non-differentiating awareness and therefore simultaneous awareness; I am not now aware of this, now of that. Simultaneity is important because without it creativity is not possible. A creative situation arises within the presence of two or more incompatible frames of reference. If the two frames of reference do not arise simultaneously, then their incompatibility cannot be known; if their incompatibility is not known, the creative situation cannot arise.

Although all appears as present, because we cannot in fact separate knowing from dynamic unity, awareness-as is not a static awareness. Awareness-as is flowing; it is going towards, and this means that with awareness-as memory and perception are not differentiated. It is not going towards in time but as time. A metaphor for this is music. Music is going forward. If you saw the film *Death in Venice* you will no doubt remember the theme music, the Adagietto from Gustav Mahler's Fifth symphony. This music is full of yearning after, longing for, or going towards. Or if you have listened to the *Ride of the Valkyries* by Richard Wagner you will know that the music evokes feelings of galloping horses slowly unleashing momentum as they charge into battle. Life itself has the same underlying motion. We have the expression "I'm getting somewhere at last," and "my life isn't going anywhere." We get the feeling of being carried along on a stream. That life is a journey, that we are travelers, that life has a purpose, a goal which we are going towards, is part of our basic myth given form in the quest for the Holy Grail, Shangri la, or the crock of gold at the end of the rainbow. But in music time does not simply pass; it accumulates. This means that awareness-as and memory are not separate. This, no doubt, is what T. S. Eliot means when he said, "the difference between the present and the past is that the conscious present is an awareness of the past in a way and to an extent which the past's awareness of itself cannot show." He went on to say, "Someone said: 'the dead writers are remote from us because we know so much more than they did.' Precisely, and they are that which we know."[16]

In a similar way, the nine months of gestation time of an embryo do not simply pass; they are accumulated in the baby that is born. As Henri Bergson explained, "The more we study the nature of time, the more we shall comprehend that duration means invention, the creation of forms, the continual elaboration of the absolutely new."[17]

The arising of awareness-of

Three things occur with the arising of 'awareness-of': a point of view emerges; 'something' is selected from among the simultaneity of awareness-as; and present, past and future are projected. Differentiation comes with awareness-of. For example, with intention I focus my attention on the song of a bird. When I do this the birdsong stands out from the background, and I feel a sense of continuity in the song. One could say that the song 'exists'.[18] I could then shift my attention and focus on a flower in the hedgerow. The flower now exists, the birdsong sinks back into simultaneous, undifferentiated, awareness-as. In this way, by my action of focusing, 'objects' and 'things' exist in our environment. In this way also simultaneity gives way to 'paying attention to one thing at a time', and this, in turn, makes possible succession: past, present and future.

As Bradley pointed out, though knowing-being, that is awareness-as, is transcended by awareness-of, nevertheless awareness-as always remains present. Awareness-of — that is, seeing, listening, giving our attention to, concentrating, desiring — is like waves; the sea is what I am calling awareness-as. The waves cannot be separated from the sea because they arise out of it. The sea is there before the waves arise. And yet one can make a useful distinction between waves and sea. 'Awareness-of' cannot be separated from 'awareness-as-the-world' because awareness-of-things arises out of 'awareness-as-the-world'. In the same way 'awareness-as-the-world' cannot be separated from knowing/being as it arises out of One/(knowing/being).

Awareness-of and dualism

The arising of awareness-of is the first entrance into a perceived dualism or separation. This dualism is not the dualism 'me and the world', even though most of us, most of the time, are quite sure that it is. The dualism is not an extended substance and a thinking substance that Descartes believed in, a dualism that in various forms has been passed down to us ever since. The dualism comes from two different ways of being aware: awareness-of and awareness-as: it does not come from awareness-of on the one hand and the world on the other.

In the argument presented here I sometimes use words like 'discrimination', 'attention', 'concentration', 'interest in', and 'perception of' instead of awareness-of. Although all of these words have their own nuances, they are all variations of awareness-of and imply a direction and a focus. The word concentration, for example, means, 'with' [con] 'a center' [centration]. Most people can readily identify this focal center and move it at will although without knowing how this movement is made.[19] For example, you can put your attention on the tip of your right forefinger, then on your left elbow, then on the letter 'n' of the word 'on', then on a door knob, and so on. Intention is responsible for this center or focus.

A diagram will help sum up what I have said so far:

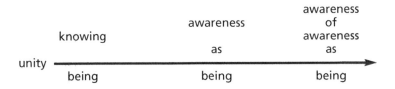

'Awareness-of' and me

After 'awareness-of' has appeared, a further evolution is possible. A point of view arises simultaneously with the arising of 'awareness-of'. By a point of view I do not mean an opinion. A point of view is just that: a point from which viewing, or 'awareness-of', originates. Because I will need to talk about it I must give it a name and I will refer to this point of view as 'me'.[20] I could also call it the 'self' but this seems to be a more abstract word than 'me', and I hope that the reader will pause a moment and savor the taste of 'me'. This point of view is not yet what we know as 'I'. 'I' is dependent upon language. 'I' is, so to say, 'out there'; 'me' is here, intimate. It is so intimate and immediate that we overlook its presence and fail to recognize its reality. Any organism that can be aware-of — that is to say, all organisms including fleas, flies, bees, and human beings that can perceive — 'have', or better still, 'are' this point of view. They all have, or are, 'me'. You can readily demonstrate this focal center or point of view simply by moving around the room. As you move the point of view moves as well because you are this point of view.

'Awareness-of' as a vicious circle: circular awareness[21]

Awareness-of is awareness-of awareness-as-the-world. Nevertheless, sometimes 'awareness-as' becomes less apparent, and then 'awareness-of' becomes 'awareness-of-awareness-of' itself. The focusing is also what is focused on. The focusing then becomes a *circular* 'awareness-of-awareness-of-awareness-of-awareness . . .'. Awareness-of feeds back into itself. Let us recall again Schopenhauer's *one being that perceives itself and is perceived by itself.* I will refer to this as *circular* awareness because it is awareness that can be focused on to itself in a vicious circle. It is a further evolution of reflexive awareness. Circular awareness is fraught with great danger. The ancients symbolized this state as the *uroboros* or snake swallowing its own tail. Jung quotes alchemical sources, "The substance (uroboros) devours itself and thus suffers no hunger; it does not die by the sword but slays itself with its own dart, like the scorpion, which is another synonym for the arcane substance."[22] Speaking clearly about circular awareness is difficult because it lies upstream of consciousness and language, both of which have evolved to protect us from the potential ravages of circular awareness. A metaphor for circular awareness would be given by holding a microphone up to a loudspeaker. Feedback occurs and the sound becomes unbearable. Another illustration would be if one were to look into one's own eyes in a mirror, and then lose track of who is the reflection and who is real. A circular momentum surges up. This circular momentum is the mechanism that underlies all our emotions, including anxiety, anger, depression, joy and romantic love. Extreme emotions, such as panic and rage, show this mechanism very clearly. 'I' am afraid, then afraid because 'I' am afraid, which circles until 'I' panic because 'I' am so afraid and then panic because 'I' am panicking, and a vortex erupts. Or, I am angry, then angry about being angry, then in a rage at being so angry, and so on until an eruption occurs.

A difficulty of the kind that I mentioned in the Preface, and which is created by the grammatical demands of language, arises as I write. I am writing of the ambiguity that arises within 'me'. However, our grammar as well as our logic, demands that I speak unambiguously. Failure to do so immediately brands one as a poor and shoddy thinker. Furthermore where I would like to use the word 'me' I am forced to use 'I'. Basic to what I am about to say is that I see myself. However, the difficulty that arises is two-fold. The first is the ambiguity because 'myself' that I see is the very same 'I' that sees. Moreover to speak correctly, as all this takes place within me, I should say, '*me*-that-sees/*me*-that-is-seen'; 'I' will not yet have appeared at the level of consciousness that we will be interested in throughout this chapter.

The connection between circular awareness and the logic of ambiguity is evident. The circularity is an attempt to resolve the ambiguity: I am the viewer and the viewed simultaneously, although I cannot be both at the same time yet each has equal claim and so I* try to destroy me.

* For grammatical reasons I have substituted 'I' for 'me'.

Awareness involved in *awareness*-of-*awareness*-of-awareness-of . . . is the same awareness, and yet it is awareness in two contradictory modes. Another analogy could be made: 'me' is simultaneously both actor on the stage and a member of the audience. These are contradictory modes of being: the actor is seen; the member of the audience sees. The first is a passive mode; the second is an active mode. Circular awareness is simultaneously actor and audience, seeing and being seen, simultaneously passive and active, noun and verb. An incipient civil war is ever present.[23]

Interaction between knowing and being

Let us now turn to a question that has recurred constantly throughout the history of the human race: what, if anything, is the connection between mind and matter (knowing and being)? More concretely, "How do mind and matter interact?" Let us take an ordinary, everyday situation and try to understand it, first by using common sense, and then by using the logic of ambiguity. For the sake of simplicity I will dispense with the complete formulation: awareness-of/awareness-as, and just use awareness-of. This will make what I mean clearer and easier to understand. Let us suppose that you are driving and come to some stoplights that are yellow, but about to turn red just as you come up to them. You check in your rear view mirror and see that another car is within a few feet of your trunk. You decide not to stop but instead go across the intersection just as the lights turn red.

A common sense, although admittedly very simplified way to interpret this is to say that the light waves from the stoplights enter the eye sending a stimulus to the brain and a red light is seen. (This could be understood as the activity of matter). You ask yourself, "Should I stop?" (This is the activity of mind). You look into the rear view mirror and see a car (activity of the brain). You think, "No he is too close. I dare not stop" (activity of mind). You then accelerate and go through the intersection. In this common sense way of looking at the situation, mind and matter, knowing and being, are intermixed at will.

The scientist who is a mechanist/materialist might well argue that as the world is simply a material world, no mind can be involved in the decisions. Thus a neuro-biologist, such as Crick, might well say that all that business about decisions and thoughts is unnecessary; all that occurs is the movement of molecules from beginning to end. He would see it all from the Objective point of view, the point of view of matter.

A psychotherapist would be more interested in what you felt, how you acted, what you decided, and so on. What you thought you saw would be as important as, perhaps even more important than, what you actually saw. As a psychotherapist he would not be interested in synapses, neural paths, brain chemistry or molecular movements; he would see it basically from the Subjective point of view of mind.

A parallelist would say that the neurologist and the psychologist are both right: each of the two worlds has its own laws and processes, but neither impinges upon the other as they run on parallel tracks.

Yet, we still have to face the fact that a mental decision did have a physical effect: the car went faster. On the other hand, the yellow light, the proximity of the other car, the intersection, the speed of the car, all that we call the physical, had an effect on the mind and brought about the mental question, 'should I stop?' At one moment equal pressure is on you to stop and to accelerate. The logjam is broken by a decision: the likes of neurologist Wilder Penfield or Karl Popper and Sir John Eccles[24] would say that the decision produced an interaction between the mind and matter.

Classical logic insists that only one of these points of view is valid. Yet, by using the logic of ambiguity a very simple resolution of the whole affair falls into place and we find that all four points of view are valid. In one way one must regret that it is so simple. One might well feel that a question that has racked the minds of so many should have a very complicated solution requiring very arcane mathematics for its resolution. Because the solution that I will offer is so simple, many will just want to reject it. In another way it is as well the resolution is simple because, as the question reaches down to the most fundamental ground of existence, the interaction between knowing and being at the unicellular level, its resolution cannot be complex. It must be a resolution that is valid at the simplest of levels. An amoeba perceives and reacts to its perception.

Resonance

We are interested in the interaction between body and mind, or, more generally, between being and knowing. This 'interaction' is a kind of resonance. Resonance arises out of the 'one is two: two are one' ambiguity with which we are now familiar. Strike the tone C_1 on a piano and the string of tone[25] C_2 an octave higher will resonate, although the strings on the piano adjacent to C_1 do not resonate. The strings of tone C_1 and C_2, an octave higher, vibrate in sympathy because they are One, they are both tone C. Yet the two vibrating strings are manifestly different and occupy quite different positions in the piano. To get from C_1 to C_2 one passes through six other notes. Let me use this as an analogy and see where it leads.

Tone C_1 and tone C_2 are One; both are C.
The tone C_1 is one tone, the tone C_2 is another; they are quite different.
However, because of the unity underlying C_1 and C_2, they resonate.

One/(Knowing /being) is a quantum.
Knowing and being are two and quite different.
However, because of the unity underlying knowing and being, they resonate.

Black and white shapes are one.
The young and the old woman are two.
However, because of the black and white shapes underlying them both, they 'resonate'.

As we have said, when we see the young woman she can have no interaction with the old woman simply because the old woman is nowhere to be found. To say the old woman is present in potential would be simply to start weaving a verbal web. Now, let us change something about the young woman, let us give her a necklace (on the following page).

We see that the mouth of the old woman is immediately changed. A change in the one has brought about a change in the other, although no interaction of any kind has occurred between the two. We now discover that all the different theories used to explain what happens when the light changes to red but I decide to pass through, are, in their own way, correct. The parallelist is right: the two — matter and mind — have no interaction. The materialist is right: one can investigate the Objective realm with the hypothesis that all is a modification of matter, because, from the Objective point of view, no Subject can be found. (If we see the old woman, where could we ever find the young woman?) From this point of view, all talk about decisions, values, judgments, and so on is just very sloppy thinking: we are machines, that is all. The psychotherapist is right in a similar way: one can look upon the mind as an autonomous field; what is at issue are what you thought, felt, imagined and feared. The interactionist is right; a change in the mind does make a change in the body and conversely, although no communication exists between the two. Furthermore, every change registered by knowing is reflected in being, and conversely. This means that the young and old woman, and by analogy, knowing and being, are perfectly correlated.

If I think, imagine, or even have a deep spiritual experience, a neuroscientist could detect modifications of my brain. This is not surprising because knowing and being are perfectly correlated: what happens to the young woman happens at the same time to the old. On the other hand, if I take LSD, which affects the functioning of the brain, I will have various experiences, some might even be what could be called spiritual. This is not surprising either, because knowing and being are correlated. The change in the brain does not *cause* the change in the mind, nor does a change in the mind *cause* a change in the brain. Each change is a *consequence* of the change in the other. A modification in thought may well occur every time and under all circumstances after a modification of the brain has occurred. Yet, to say that this means that the brain is the cause of thought is the logical fallacy *post hoc ergo propter hoc* (after this, therefore because of this).

We can now dispense with the resonance theory and by using the logic of ambiguity reconcile in a simpler way what otherwise is a set of contradictory theories: the theories of materialism, idealism, interactionism and parallelism. One/(knowing /being) is a gestalt, one field. The change in the young woman is a change of the one field; because the one field is changed, the old woman, as a manifestation of the one field, is also changed. Furthermore, the changes can occur via the young woman, via the old woman or via the one field, intention. Underlying the dilemma posed by the conflicting ways of explaining what happens when I passed through the traffic lights is the gestalt, intention/(knowing/being).

14 | The Ambiguity of 'I–You'

"Here we have the paradox, the potentially tragic paradox, that our relatedness to others is an essential aspect of our being, as is our separateness, but any particular person is not a necessary part of our being."[1]

R. D. LAING

Can animals feel love, empathy, altruism? Human beings can, so if we accept that evolution is a continuous process and no new elements may be introduced later into the evolutionary process to explain the appearance of new forms or qualities, it would seem that animals should be able to feel them too, even though perhaps in a different and more attenuated way. To justify my saying this I must elaborate on the assertion that humans can feel love. What is the 'structure' that underlies human love and which can also be found in other beings?

In order to answer this question I must refer the reader back to what I said in the previous chapter about the viewpoint and to chapter 3 in which I made the distinction between *what* I am and *that* I am. Each of us is a viewpoint. I called the viewpoint 'me'. All sights, sounds, smells, have 'me' as their destination. I furthermore distinguished 'me' from 'I'. All organisms that can perceive are 'me'. 'I' is dependent upon language. Most often the words 'I' and 'me' are looked upon as more or less synonymous, yet Subjectively we experience 'me' and 'I' quite differently. The viewpoint is ambiguous; it reflects on itself as awareness of awareness. Awareness of awareness is a common expression and most of us most of the time are unaware of the drama and tension that it contains. 'Me,' as I said in the previous chapter, is intimately present. It is so intimate and immediate that we invariably ignore it and fail to recognize it's reality. But me is also ambiguous: *me*-that-sees is *me*-that-is-seen and yet this same *me*-that-is-seen is *me*-that-sees. We become aware of the effects of this split in times of emotional upheaval, for example when we are anxious, and particularly when we panic. We get caught up in a spiraling vortex coming from the self reflecting the self. Except for psychotic states we are buffered from the most severe effects of the split viewpoint by consciousness, which is centered on a stable point. The next chapter will be devoted to enlarging upon this statement. In this chapter I want to concentrate on another effect of the split viewpoint, which is the emergence of 'me-you'. As we shall see this ambiguity *me*-that-sees/*me*-that-is-seen is the same ambiguity that underlies the relations that I have with others.

The drama of human relations — love and hate, altruism and violence — all arise from 'me/you'.

Ambiguity and life

Human relations are essentially ambiguous. This is not surprising as ambiguity is the basic theme in the symphony of life. The living ambiguity is One/(knowing/being). That such a simple formulation as this can integrate such a wide range of experience must in some way confirm its value. The test of a good theory is not simply whether it works or is heuristic, but also whether it is simple yet complete. We have seen that by using the logic of ambiguity we can understand more about evolution, creativity, conflict, intelligence, consciousness, the mind-matter problem, the antinomies of theoretical physics and even laughter. The same logic can help us to understand more about love, empathy, altruism, selfishness, and even mysticism and religion. These are of course very vast subjects, but I would like to show the direction in which to look and how, with the help of the logic of ambiguity, we can penetrate some of their mysteries. I have covered the ground much more extensively in my book *Creating Consciousness*, which is a study of consciousness, creativity, evolution and violence.

You as Object and as Subject

Before discussing love, empathy, and altruism among animals let us consider human love, as this will give us an entrance. In chapter 3 I explained that we can know ourselves Objectively as a body, or Subjectively as a self. Many authors have written about the ambiguity of our being both a body and a self, and about the torment that it can cause.[2] Another ambiguity, equally troubling, is the you/me ambiguity, which is an ambiguity within an ambiguity.

I can see you as a Subject, a self, or I can see you as an Object. When I see you as an Object I do not simply see you as the body; I see you as the 'role' in which you are operating. By this I mean that when I pass through the check-out counter in a supermarket, when I am stopped and given a speeding ticket, or when I go for a medical check-up, I rarely see another Subject or self: I see a check-out clerk, a policeman, or a doctor. I see the role and rarely do I see the self that is acting as the role.

I am even more likely to see you as an Object if I stereotype people — if I see wops, or yids, nips, or slopes. As we have seen, language distils 'things' — objects — out of the flow of life. Derogatory words like the above freeze the things ever more solidly. Stereotyping the enemy, turning them into objects, makes it easier for us to kill them, to 'waste' them.

I can, though, also know you as Subject. Now I am no longer concerned with *what* you are; *that* you are is enough. It is thus that love is blind. To see you as Subject is to be one with you, and to be one with you is to love you. Plato helps explain what 'to be one with you' means when he tells of the birth of romantic love: the earth was once populated by a race of hermaphroditic beings that possessed both male and female characteristics. They had both male and female sexual organs as well as two heads, four arms and four legs. They were so stable that the gods came to fear them, and decided to cut them in two. This gave rise to beings of one or the other sex, male or female. Each retained in his or her memory the earlier state of unity. Plato has Hephaestus ask the lovers, "Is it perhaps this for which you long, a perfect, mutual fusion so that you will never be sundered from each other by day or by night?"[3] Plato says that we long "to form one single nature from two distinct beings. . . . *It is really the burning longing for unity which bears the name of love*"[4] (emphasis added). The longing to be free from the underlying schism, the original sin of separation induced by ambiguity, is a longing for unity, and one of its most powerful expressions is the erotic encounter.

The philosopher, Martin Buber, in *I and Thou*,[5] wrote of the me/you ambiguity.* Buber says that you and me *arise simultaneously*, and so the word 'I' [me] should not be used on its own but always accompanied by 'you'. This is to see you Subjectively. When I see you Objectively, that is as simply the role that you are playing, Buber says that the basic word 'I–it' should be used. He said, "The world of experience belongs to the basic word I–it." That is to say, *what* you are belongs to the basic word 'I–it'. The basic word 'I–You', [me-you] on the other hand, "establishes the world of relation."[6] In chapter 3 I pointed out that '*that* I am' has no content; anything that I am, any content, is '*what* I am'. In the same way 'that you are' has no content. Buber says just this when he says that what I experience of you is "Nothing at all. For one does not experience you. What then does one know of you? Only everything. For one no longer knows particulars."[7]

This may sound strange: 'I experience nothing of you, and yet know everything of you'. When I encounter you, not as a thing in the world, the encounter is no longer in the world and I have no thing I can experience. I–you is transcendent, that is to say the relation I–you transcends experience. When Buber says that I can know everything of 'you', he obviously does not mean I know your complete history, because he says, "One no longer knows particulars." In other words *we have the same problem with 'that you are' as we had with 'that I am'*. I do not know everything about *what* you are; I know *that* you are. That you are and that I am are not different, and so I know everything of you in the same way that I know everything of me. I am is without content and yet is real. To know everything of I am is to dwell in the reality I am.

What you think you are, your body or your personality, belongs to the world of experience, that is to say to the world of particulars. The body can be found as an object among other objects; the personality is a collection of memories, thoughts, judgments, opinions, and ideas. They belong to the world of experience that Buber is calling I–it. Experience requires perceptions, images, ideas, and memories. I can only have ideas about the world of 'I–it', the world that has forms that can be perceived and remembered. If I should talk to an idea of you, then I do not talk to 'you'. 'You' are not an idea. 'You' cannot be found among objects but

---

* In what follows the same grammatical difficulty that I mentioned in the last chapter will also arise in this. Strictly speaking instead of writing I and Thou I should write me and Thou.

belong to the world of relations. This world, which is not a world of things or entities, cannot be experienced. That is why I cannot experience 'you', or anything about 'you', and also why I can know only *that* 'you' are, not *what* 'you' are. The encounter of Subject with Subject is love.

Love and unity

Love shows us that me–you cannot be found in the world of experience, but transcends it. Love has always been looked upon as something 'out of this world'. The love songs of the forties told us, "You came to me from out of nowhere." "Somewhere in heaven you were fashioned for me." "That old black magic." In Shakespeare's *Midsummer Night's Dream* the many and confused love affairs of the characters were all the result of a potion administered by Puck, a denizen of the world of fairies. Titania, one of the female characters in the play, even falls in love with an ass. We are not surprised to find that the whole drama is a Midsummer night's *dream*, nor that Cupid was the god of love, who with his arrows could drive a lover insane. Dreams, madness, fairies, and the Gods, all beyond the conscious reach of reason, have each in their time been invoked to explain the onset of love.

Love, in that its onset has always been seen to be sudden, shows its origins in unity. Love at first sight is a cliché in movies and novels, but is an explosive reality in life. Unity does not appear gradually, bit by bit. Another song in the forties summed it up, "All or nothing at all." The suddenness of love, its divine, transcendent quality, the feeling it gives of the complete absence of all conflict, can all be seen as the result of its origins in a transcendent unity expressed in the relation I–You.[8]

'That I am' needs no material support; it is not the result of any material cause. It does not need any verbal or conceptual support either. *This means that I–You relation is possible for animals, birds and even fish, as well as for human beings* Let me try to justify this stance.

The ambiguity of the look

The 'one' that is 'two', that is to say 'me' as both the actor and the audience at the same time, is most obviously encountered in the *look*. A cliché in movies and stories, and a constant theme in popular songs, is looking into the eyes of the beloved. In a film called *Damage*, in which a father falls in love with his son's girlfriend, the most dramatic moment of the film was when the father and the son's girlfriend first met and looked each other in the eyes. The look seemed to go on forever. To look with love and to be looked at in the same way can be enthralling. A circularity of affirmation affirming affirmation builds up in a mounting ecstasy.

In the previous chapter I spoke of the circularity of awareness that arose out of the wound in 'me'. I likened circular awareness to being simultaneously actor and audience, seeing and being seen, simultaneously passive and active, noun and verb, a one that is two. Schopenhauer also spoke of the "one being that perceives itself and is perceived by itself." The 'one being' of which he speaks is both you and me; me, perceiving you, and, simultaneously, being perceived by you; you simultaneously perceiving, and being perceived.[9] We are two, but one. I likened this also to holding a microphone up to a loudspeaker. When I look into the eyes of one whom I love, I am simultaneously audience and actor; she too, simultaneously, is both, and in this way we are one. You and me are not different, yet not the same: both are one and inseparable. Holy matrimony is making two into one. In the Christian marriage vows are the words, "Those whom God hath joined let no man break asunder." We cannot understand this using classical logic. Only by using the logic of ambiguity does it all make sense: the one that is two.

The look and babies

The power in the look is not something that is acquired or learned. Professor Richard Coss reports, "By the fourth week of age, many full-term infants will vigorously attempt to establish eye contact by visually searching for the eyes of another person. The duration of eye contact between mother and infant has been observed to last for several minutes if the mother deliberately sustains eye contact. Conversely, those same infants, when in a fussy mood prior to being changed or fed, may actively avoid eye contact by looking away or closing their eyes."[10]

One of the strangest of mother–child phenomena nowadays is the modern stroller in which the child, even the youngest, faces away from the mother when it is being pushed in the stroller. In earlier, and it would seem more enlightened times, the child in the stroller would face the mother who would engage the child in constant eye contact accompanied by smiles of reassurance as she pushed the stroller along.

Coss wonders "why the eyes alone are selected by the infant as 'high intensity stimuli' rather than other features of the body and face, such as the hands and mouth, which are equally conspicuous . . . Without the apparent effect of specialized reinforcement that could induce early learning of the eye schema, why do the eyes become a provocative source of stimulation so early in infancy?"[11] As we shall see in a moment, the same question could be asked about animals. Why is the look so important in their relations?

You are essential

I have been speaking of 'you' the beloved, but you are both very specific and not specific, that is to say that you are potentially anyone. As R. D. Laing states in the epigraph to this chapter, a potentially tragic ambiguity lies in the fact that our relatedness to others is an essential aspect of our being, as is our uniqueness; but any particular person is not necessarily part of our being. The feeling that we have that our love has in some way been predestined is founded in this truth that you are an essential aspect of my being, even though my meeting you the person may be quite fortuitous. Again a song from the forties tells us "Dearly Beloved how clearly I see/ Somewhere in heaven you were fashioned for me."

That you are an essential aspect of my being is confirmed by mystical experiences in which we seem to be in the presence of another without the other having any physical features. The following is an example of what I mean. "There was just the room with its shabby furniture and the fire burning in the grate and the red shaded lamp on the table. But, the room was filled by a Presence, which in a strange way *was both about me and within me*, like light or warmth. I was overwhelmingly *possessed by Someone who was not myself, and yet I felt I was more myself than I had ever been before*. I was filled with an intense happiness, and almost unbearable joy, such as I had never known before and have never known since."[12]

I have emphasized, 'was both about me and within me' and 'possessed by Someone who was not myself, and yet I felt I was more myself than

I had ever been before'. Both speak of the you/me ambiguity. A presence is simultaneously within me and around me. You possess me, but you who posses me are more myself than I have ever been before. Yet you are not a physical presence; the encounter is in the transcendent: in a time-less, spaceless moment the Subject is possessed by the Subject.

A Sufi poem relates:

"If then you perceive me, you perceive yourself.
But you cannot perceive me through yourself.
It is through my eyes that you see me and see your self,
Through your eyes you cannot see me."[13]

Biology and religion

A great deal of what can only be called nonsense has been written about the origin and meaning of religion. For example, in the book *Why God Won't Go Away,* the authors tell us, "All the world's great religions — and we believe all religious impulse — arise from the *brain's* ability to transcend the limited self and perceive a larger, more fundamental reality. Any attempt to create a biological theory of religion must address this point."[14] I have emphasized the word brain and can only ask what kind of brain can this be? The true religious impulse is found in a yearning for unity, for love, completeness.[15] The word 'religion' has its origins in *religio* which means 'to bind fast,' just as the word yoga has its origins in *yuj*, meaning 'to yoke, unite, or harness.' To be connected to unity, or to be 'one with', is the essence of all religious yearning for atonement. To yearn for unity is the Subjective experience of the cosmic imperative 'Let there be one!'

Not only is unity involved in the religious impulse, knowing also is involved and enhanced in the mystical experience. During a mystical experience one is intensely aware. In the above quotation the writer confirms this by saying, "I felt [I knew] I was more myself than I had ever been before. I was filled with an intense happiness, and almost unbearable joy, such as I had never known before and have never known since."

Research that has been conducted involving magnetic imaging people in spiritual states, by showing that neural activity occurs simul-taneously, confirms that the third aspect — being (the brain) — is likewise involved in the mystical. This is hardly surprising as most meditation traditions emphasize the importance of the physical, either in teaching the need for specific physical postures, or by teaching methods for regulating the breath. Many also use physical pain — going on long and painful pilgrimages for example — fasting, and other means to develop a concentrated mind. Unity, knowing and being are all involved. If we are to have a biological understanding of religion, then that biology must be a true study of life, as the name *bio*logy suggests, and not simply a study of the physical forms of life.

However, the authors do get one thing right. They say that mystical experiences are not simply isolated and unique events but appear at one end of a continuum. They rightly point out that at the other end of the continuum are feelings of love, compassion, and forgiveness, as well as community and family connections, ethics and morals. Underlying all of these is empathy. Empathy comes from the same one that is two; I empathize with you because I am one with you. But empathy is not an attribute of humans alone.

In his book *Lucy: Growing up*, an American psychotherapist, Maurice Temerlin, who with his wife conducted several years of research on a chimpanzee called Lucy, gives the following example of empathy. It appears in Frans de Waal's book *Good Natured: The origins of right and wrong in humans and other animals.*

Lucy was particularly tender with Temerlin's wife, Jane.

"If Jane is distressed, Lucy notices it immediately, and attempts to comfort her by putting her arm about her, grooming her, or kissing her. If I am the cause of the distress, for example, if we are arguing, Lucy will attempt to pull us apart or to distract me so that Jane's distress is alleviated. If Jane is sick, Lucy notices it immediately. For example, on every occasion when Jane was ill and vomited, Lucy became very disturbed, running into the bathroom, standing by Jane, comforting her by kissing her and putting her arm around her as she vomited. When Jane was sick in bed Lucy would exhibit tender protectiveness toward her, bringing her food, sharing her own food, or sitting on the edge of the bed attempting to comfort by stroking and grooming her."[16]

On violence

Looking into the eyes of another does not always explode into an ecstasy of love; on the contrary, it may provoke an explosion of rage. Throughout history the belief in the malevolent properties of the evil eye that expresses envy and hatred has been widespread throughout the world. The evil eye, the baleful, dead look of hatred, strikes terror in the one so looked at. The sudden appearance of staring eyes, of a cat, a doll, a blind man, or of Chucky, is a cliché in horror films. Even simple eye contact sometimes can be dangerous. This is why the biker or gangster may often sport dark glasses. Dark glasses prevent another seeing that the biker cannot hold the other's gaze. They protect him from showing his weakness, and also give him freedom to look without causing offence. Gaze aversion, used by animals and humans to avoid potential dangerous eye contact, is a term used by ethnologists to indicate the reflex of turning the eyes, head and sometimes the whole body away to avoid or break the contact. Dark glasses may sometimes be used as a form of gaze aversion.

Staring eyes are used as protection for sacred sites and vessels. Richard Coss in his article *Reflections on the Evil Eye* writes, "The Greek kylix drinking cup often depicts two painted staring eyes that may act as a protection device."[17] He tells us, "Facial paint enhancing the eye shape and masks with eyes portrayed by brightly painted concentric circles have been displayed by men in secret society rituals as protective devices to suppress the evil activity of suspected spirits and inhibit the intrusions of women and children."[18] A pair of staring eyes often protects the Buddhist stupas in South East Asia, which house the relics of the Buddha. Guardians, who also have staring eyes, protect temples of Japan.

The baleful consequences of the look are not only found among human beings. On the contrary they are found at all levels of life. Coss says, "The most primitive vertebrate animal examined, the African jewel fish, displays one large concentric eyelike spot on each gill cover that resembles the jewel fish eye. During territorial fights, jewel fish will rush a rival and suddenly flare open widely their gill covers, thus presenting the illusory image of two staring eyes from a larger, closer and more formidable opponent."[19]

He tells us moreover that English ethologist Robert Hinde has reported that an owl like model with eyes evoked a greater vocal disturbance in chaffinches than a similar model without eyes. More recent studies of predator recognition by German ethologist Eberhard Curio support these observations in other species of birds and suggest that recognition of eyelike shapes by some birds is a partially innate response.

My daughter experienced the aversion that her very young puppy also had for the staring eyes of an owl. She happened to put on the floor, near the puppy, a large wooden owl. As soon as he saw the owl he fled whimpering under the nearest shelter and stayed there. My daughter, remembering what I had told her about the power of eyes, covered up the owl's eyes but left it on the floor. The puppy emerged from his shelter and happily sniffed around the owl.

I had occasion, inadvertently, to verify for myself the truth of the aversion that birds have to eye shapes. I had some biscuits that had become stale and I decided to give them to the birds. I was in the habit of giving the birds food, and would always be rewarded by a great number swooping down to seize it. On the occasion of my throwing out the biscuits not a bird appeared. This mystified me until I remembered that the biscuits were round and had red circles of jam in the center. Suspecting that the birds were afraid that these were eyes, I broke up all the biscuits and was immediately rewarded by the birds flocking for their food.

Crowded barnyard chickens gaze avoid by turning their heads and bodies away from the nearest chickens. An ethologist, David Blest, found that hand-reared yellow bunting and great tit birds, isolated from frightening experiences with predators, avoided a butterfly with large eyespots conspicuously displayed on its hind wings. Different species of butterflies, caterpillars, insects, frogs and even fish have pseudo eyes as protective camouflage. That fish have this form of camouflage and the fact that the Jewelfish respond to pseudo eyes tells us that fish as well as birds and animals also have an aversion to the 'evil eye'.

Dominance and submission

The look can be used as a way to gain dominance and to force another into submission. Just before a boxing match begins the two adversaries will go to the center of the ring and touch gloves. At this moment they will most often look each other in the eye. If a boxer sees his opponent blink, unable to keep a steady gaze, he will know that he has the upper hand from the beginning. An ape too can be dominated by a look and, when confronted by a stare, blinks or turns his eyes away, normally by looking down. Gaze aversion is a very necessary survival mechanism and it is significant that it is one of our most rapid reflexes.[20]

Naval petty officers, concentration camp guards, kings, playground bullies all insist that the other lowers the eyes in their presence. This is why one should avoid eye contact in some environments, why bullies like to wear dark glasses, because eye contact is a potential threat, a potential challenge. Mammals, such as rats, confined in small cages where escape from close-range encounters with more dominant rats is limited, perform bouts of gaze aversion to avoid seeing the adversary's face and, at the same time, remove from view any threatening facial features of their own that could elicit an attack. Lemurs and lorises will gaze intently at a rival as a signal of threat intention. The closer proximity of a staring opponent can induce extreme gaze aversion in a submissive adversary, such as lowering the head and covering the eyes with the tail. Gaze aversion is especially apparent in zoo-kept ring-tailed lemurs.

The look as a trigger for love and aggression

In polite conversation we look at another in the eye but for a few seconds at the most and then turn away. As Coss says, "Among close friends or lovers, brief bouts of eye contact lasting a few seconds can be satisfying emotionally as long as the accompanying facial expressions are appropriate for generating pleasant moods. Conversely, prolonged eye-to-eye contact is invariably considered unpleasant, even among close associates. The unyielding stare of an approaching stranger is especially unnerving, but this also depends upon the social setting and the duration of the stare."[21] The same cause, in different contexts, gives contrasting effects.

Although eye contact is potentially dangerous, it is also the prerequisite among apes for reconciliation. "It is as if chimpanzees do not trust the other's intentions without a look into the eyes. In the same way, we do not consider a conflict settled with people who turn their eyes to the ceiling or floor each time we look in their direction."[22]

De Waal gives two examples of eye contact among primates that give two contradictory results. "A high ranking male may approach his opponent after a fight with all hair on end, locking eyes with him. If the other does not budge, another confrontation is inevitable."[23] In the second example he says, "First, the male and female looked at one another but avoided being caught looking. This phase was always accompanied by feigned indifference to the other, indicated by the concentrated interest in grooming one's own fur, or by staring intently at some imaginary object in the distance, (both ploys are commonly used by baboons in a wide variety of socially discomforting situations.) Eventually the coy glances were replaced by a more direct approach, usually initiated by the male."[24] These were two situations in which eyes locked, but they had two contradictory outcomes. The first resulted in a fight, the second in a romance.

How can the look be both loving and malevolent?

But how can the same action create two quite opposite reactions? Not only this, as we saw above, Coss wonders, "why do the eyes become a provocative source of stimulation so early in infancy?" Scientists have asked the same question about the gaze, about the evil eye, and about the use of eyes as a form of protection. Why does a butterfly have pseudo eyes on its wings? Why does specie of fish have pseudo eyes near its tail and its true eyes disguised by a black colored band that camouflages them? Why not pseudo teeth or a mouth? The answer of course lies in the ambiguity of the look.

In the look of love the lover wants to look and wants to be looked at and wants his lover to know he wants to look and be looked at. The beloved has the same desires. In this way the spiraling of the vortex builds up in a constant mutual reinforcement. In the look of hostility one wants to dominate the other by the look but does not want to be looked at. The other in turn resists the look and also wants to look but not be looked at. Each wants to be the one, the one who looks, the one of power. In the look of dominance one must not flinch or blink; this is critical. When one of the contestants begins to feel that his ability to hold the gaze is weakening he will then be most likely to resort to violence. Now the spiraling of the vortex leads to mutual destruction.

In love, compatibility and incompatibility are perfectly blended. I am I, but I am you; in being me, I am separate from you; in being one with you, the separation is transcended. With hostility I am I, not you. You in turn declare, " I am I, not you!" In declaring that I am I, I declare that I am the One; you do likewise. Whereas in love each yields to the other and yet is affirmed by the other, and so each affirms the other as

Unity, in hostility Unity is wounded and pain erupts. Violence is the endeavor to end the pain by vanquishing its source. Its source is the unbearable pain of divided unity.

When a gun is fired we could say that the cause was the finger pulling the trigger. Yet without the explosives in the bullet nothing would have happened. 'You' are the trigger, stimulus of my feelings of love, anger or pain, yet without the explosives within me there would have been no explosion. The explosion is caused by the internal wound inflicted by the impossible situation of being both the one and yet not one.

This wound in the heart is always present. We have seen in the previous chapter that it can give rise to anxiety, depression, anger and all the other negative emotions. The basis of Buddhism is that life is suffering, and the Sanskrit word for suffering is *duhkha*. Duhkha does not only mean suffering; it also means duality, division, and conflict.

What all of this shows is that reflexive awareness is not only present in human beings but is present *at all levels of life*. Species of fish, insects, frogs, and butterflies have false 'eyes' that protect them from predators. The predators are made afraid, not simply by the 'eyes', but more profoundly by the pain generated by the inherent reflexive or circular awareness. All of this might also answer the ongoing question of why the peacock has such an illustrious tail. The markings on the tail are in the shape of eyes. The peahen, looking at the peacock with his tail displayed, could well see a score of adoring eyes.

Summary

All organisms that can perceive have, or are, a 'viewpoint', a point from which viewing is possible. The viewpoint arises prior to the evolution of consciousness and language. I have called the viewpoint 'me'. In an introductory course that I conduct at the Montreal Zen Center I encourage participants to discern the difference between 'me' and 'I'. Most often the participants will announce that they feel 'me' to be warmer, more intimate, and more inclusive. They will feel that 'I' is objective, colder, and more divisive. Sometimes a person will reverse the order and give 'I' the attributes that others give to 'me'.

In this chapter I have written about 'me'. The main point that I have wanted to bring out is that me is ambiguous: *me*-that-sees/*me*-that-is-seen. I have hyphenated them to indicate that me is the seeing; an entity 'me' that sees does no exist. I have also italicized *me* to indicate that me *is the same me.* The [/] indicates ambiguity. Me which is the emissary of dynamic unity is therefore potentially torn, and this threat underlies our life giving us the incipient feeling of vulnerability and malaise. When the occasion occurs this malaise can erupt into anxiety, anger panic and rage.

We must now turn our attention to 'I' and this will be the subject of the chapter to follow.

15 | The Birth of Ego

"When we speak of a center we shall mean mostly the center of a field of forces, a focus from which forces issue and toward which forces converge."

ARNHEIM[1]

Reflexive consciousness and its more evolved version, self-consciousness, are both possible without 'I' necessarily being present. Human consciousness, nevertheless, is centered on 'I'. 'I', or better still, ' I–it' only comes into being with the emergence of language; this is why 'I–it' is only found in human beings. The function of 'I–it' in the ecology of mind is to fix a stable center,[2] which provides an escape from circular awareness and its ever-present threat. The importance of this dynamic center or stable point of reference becomes obvious in moments of extreme emotion, for example in moments of panic or profound anxiety. We often say, if these extreme emotions should arise, "I was beside myself with fear, or anger, or whatever". This suggests that the basic schism or wound is opened up.

With *me*-that-sees/*me*-that-is-seen — or to use the expression that I have used in other books me-as-center/me-as-periphery — the two aspects of me are incompatible and so set the stage for creativity. I–it is the single idea called for in Koestler's definition of creativity. But of course, at the same time the two aspects set the stage for conflict. Out of this arise the drama, the terror and joy of life.

Originally the dynamic center was a sacred tree, mountain, person, god or idol. The cosmic center, as idol or cosmic tree, protected the tribe from malignant forces that arose from the incipient circular build up of panic or violence within the members of the tribe, which could become

contagious and so threaten the whole tribe.[3] From this we can understand the immense importance of rituals and ceremony, which evolved
to preserve the dynamic center, and why so much time was taken up
among primitive people with these rituals. Indeed most religions even
today devote much of their time one way or another in the preservation
of the dynamic center. For example, the cross, an eternal symbol of the
dynamic center, is ever present in the Christian tradition.

Evolution of consciousness in the West has been accompanied by a
steady secularization and, at the same time, identification of the dynamic
center with 'me', first as the 'soul' then as the personality, and then
finally as 'ego'. We call this dynamic center, 'I'. 'I–it' and 'consciousness' are creations which, as the etymology of consciousness suggests,
have to do with putting together, through knowing, something that was
split. This 'something that was split,' as stated in chapter 13, is awareness. Language fixes the dynamic center and this allows a stable world
within consciousness to emerge. I have shown how language accom-
plishes this in several chapters of *Creating Consciousness* and will not
repeat the arguments here.

As an example of the value of the dynamic center as point of reference, and the panic that can arise if one should lose it, suppose you have
to make your way through a dense forest into which the sun's rays cannot
penetrate. You know that if you continue north you will be able to travel
through the forest in a few days. You have sufficient food supplies for
the journey and a compass. All that you need do is to follow the direction the compass is pointing.

Suppose that after a day's travel you lose confidence in the compass.
You wonder whether it is really pointing north. Every tree is similar to
every other tree and no central or stable point can be found. If one were
not an experienced woodsman this could well create panic. Indeed, not
a few people have died from panic because they were lost in this way.
Incidentally, in the book *Apollo 13*, which tells the story of that ill-fated
space capsule, the authors talk of the eight-ball, "a guidance system
containing a stationary component, which contained a stable element
that was inertially fixed in space relative to the stars."[4] A gimbal lock,
a loss of this stable element in a spacecraft, would be tantamount to
having no stable point in a forest of stars and galaxies, which would
result in a complete loss of orientation.

In a group the dynamic center is invested in the leader. For some animals the most central territory is the most valuable and the most powerful member of the group will take control of that territory.[5] Human beings know the importance of the center as the locus of power. The question of whose office is next to the CEO's, that is, who is closest to the center of power, can be of paramount importance in a company. When the peace talks between the USA and North Vietnam were getting underway, a great deal of time was spent on deciding the shape of table to be used. Eventually a round table was selected. Someone sitting at the head of an oblong table could have been seen as the dynamic center, the leader. King Arthur's roundtable was selected for the same reason. Even a flock of chickens has a strict hierarchy with the leader being the dynamic center of the flock, hence the expression 'the pecking order'.

The importance of the stable point, or 'I–it' can also be seen in that psychosis arises when a person loses the orientation that the stable point provides.[6] The importance and necessity of a stable point seems to have escaped the notice of modern-day psychology. The relation of psychosis with the absence of the center gives another means for testing the value of what I am saying. A study could be made of different kinds of people and their differing ways of investing the dynamic center thereby demonstrating whether I am right in my contention about psychosis, and providing clues as to how to deal with it.

Because we have a stable point, the encounter with the world of objects is, for most of us, an encounter without drama or tension. This is not so for everyone. In the book *An Autobiography of a Schizophrenic*, Renée, the author, says, "The stone jar, decorated with blue flowers, was there facing me, defying me with its presence, with its existence. To conquer my fear I looked away. My eyes met a chair, then a table; they were alive, too, asserting their presence. I attempted to escape their hold by calling out their names. I said, 'chair, jug, table, it is a chair'."[7] Renée was unable to maintain a stable point of reference and so saw things as alive, that is, as aware, because the basic schism, me-as-center/me-as-periphery, was unmediated by a stable point.

The dynamic center gives the feeling that I am something. But simply to be something is not enough. I must be something unique, a special something. Only one, unique, dynamic center is possible.[8] The dynamic center is the emissary of dynamic unity; it is a primordial creation arising through the incompatibility of being simultaneously actor and audience. The Subjective feeling of the dynamic center is the feeling of being unique.

On being unique

We have tended to look upon human beings as special, unique, something out of this world, created by God. We talk about Nature and the natural world as though we were something apart, outside so to speak. This sense of ourselves as being out of nature, observers, has been intensified with the growth of science and its insistence upon the Objective point of view, the view from outside.

The Christian religion has also intensified our sense of uniqueness and of being apart from nature with its insistence that each of us is a soul created by God and, we hope, looked after by him. On the other hand, since Descartes we have been assured that animals lack 'souls' and so are inferior to us, nothing more than complicated machines.

More recently things have changed and we too have been stripped of our souls and are now told that we are nothing more than complicated machines. This is the prevailing trend in evolutionary theory and neuroscience. Francis Crick said, "The main object of scientific research on the brain is not merely to understand and cure various medical conditions, important though this task may be, but to grasp the true nature of the human soul."[9] He had no doubt scientists will find this true nature in the movements of molecules.

The need to be unique

As human beings we would naturally say that we are unique.[10] Americans think that America is a unique nation. The English think England is unique. The Germans and Japanese also think their own country is unique. This is true of the members of all the different countries. If anyone is in any doubt about this they should tune into a TV broadcast of a world cup soccer game and observe the tribalism of the supporters. Members of most groups believe their group to be unique. A group's cohesive powers emerge out of this belief. When a sports team begins habitually to lose, supporters begin to fade. In his book *Closing of the American Mind*, the author, Harold Bloom, says, "[Non-Western cultures] think their way is the best way and all others are inferior . . . One should conclude from the study of non-Western cultures that not only to prefer one's own way but to believe it best, superior to others is primary and even natural."[11]

Yet, I am not unique because human beings are unique. On the contrary, human beings and Canadians are unique because I, a Canadian and a human being, am unique. You question my uniqueness if you question the uniqueness of humans. No wonder Darwinism has had such a tough time being accepted, and has aroused so much impassioned discussion. Similar difficulties were met with when people were asked to accept that the earth was just another planet having no special place in the universe. Not only was the earth dislodged, 'my' uniqueness as the dynamic center of the world also suffered.

From the need to be unique comes the notion of God having special care for me, as does the Calvinist notion of the elect, the claim of the Catholic Church to be the only true church, the Jews' claim to be the chosen people, and Allah's claim to be the true God. Adam Smith's economics, the basis of private enterprise, orders society so that, ideally, each person can find his own way to express uniqueness. Human beings love freedom because, as a free person, one can remain unique. The drive to remain unique, to be the only one, to be first, drives Olympic sportsmen and women to spend tortuous hours in training and drives others to sacrifice health, love and peace of mind in the rat race of earning money. Karen Horney, the neo-Freudian psychotherapist of the thirties and forties, said that we all have the need for power, prestige and possessions — the three principal ways of affirming uniqueness.

Uniqueness is absolute, it cannot be cannot be attained in bits and pieces. Each of us is dynamic unity/(knowing/being), each is the One manifest as the dynamic center. One cannot be more or less unique; uniqueness is an all or nothing deal. Because it is absolute, we do not like having to strive to attain uniqueness, but prefer to have it recognized without question. Striving is in part painful because, ideally, my uniqueness is me and must be taken for granted, or it is not uniqueness. This is why even a small slight from a perfect stranger can be extremely painful, and why we are rarely willing to expose our feeling of being unique to any kind of challenge. We hide this feeling, even from ourselves, behind diplomacy, good manners, being cultured and well bred, because even just to acknowledge it can be humiliating.

The need to be unique and the struggle to survive

Even the need to be unique is not special to humans. Harold Nicholson[12] realized that the greatest problems encountered by the primates do not come from physical challenges but from social ones. The primary challenge is how to remain unique in a tribe of others who seem to be identical to oneself, and who also believe in their own uniqueness. De Waal said that compromise and reconciliation among primates are as important as conquest.

An animal caught in a trap will gnaw its leg off to escape. What intention that indicates! The intention to be free is the intention to be autonomous, One. How many wars and revolutions have been fought in the name of freedom. The struggle to be autonomous can be seen as a more evolved expression of the struggle for survival. This is not a conscious struggle, but to see the need for autonomy as simply the result of a chain of cause and effect is to miss the drama. The struggle to survive is at first simply the intention to survive, to go on living, as an organism, as an integrated whole, that is as one. Then the struggle evolves into the struggle to survive as an autonomous unit; then, later still, to be unique, to be the only one. Eventually the struggle could become a striving for the transcendent: to be One with the origin and source that is itself One. In so far as intention is the drive to unity, that we have this drive to survive as an autonomous and unique individual is not surprising.

One might object to my saying that the struggle to survive, the desire for autonomy, the need to remain unique, and the striving for the transcendent, are evolving facets of the same dynamic impulse towards unity, and protest that the word 'struggle' is just a figure of speech. Dawkins sneers at Lamarck and says, "He spoke of animals striving as if they consciously in some sense wanted to evolve." Natural selection, these critics would say, simply wipes out the unfit. A new virus hits a population, or a severe drought occurs, and half of the population dies. Where is the striving? Yet animals, fish, birds, insects, all certainly strive to survive. As I pointed out at the beginning of this book the word 'struggle' is an ambiguous term. Sometimes to struggle means simply being winnowed; at other times it means actively fighting to survive. I called the first of these 'metaphorical' struggle, and the second 'active'. Writers on evolution sometimes seem not to be aware of this ambiguity and have a tendency to confuse the two.

I am not stretching language too far when I say that the active struggle to survive is the intention to survive. Certainly without the intention there would be no struggle or survival. I have also pointed out that cunning, deception, intelligent use of stratagems, are as important as sharp teeth and claws and that creativity and intelligence are not only necessary for survival, but they are also aspects of the evolutionary sieve and are ways by which the unfit are eliminated.

To be unique or to co-operate

With the struggle to be the one, to be unique, comes a further ambiguity with its ensuing dilemma. As Laing points out in the epigraph to this chapter, our relatedness to others is an essential aspect of our being, as is our separateness or, better still, our uniqueness. Karen Horney, the neo-Freudian of the thirties and forties, told us that the primary needs of a human being are the needs for power, prestige and possessions. These needs all come from our need for uniqueness. They are ways by which uniqueness is expressed.

But she also said that we had a need to belong. For too long has the drive to compete, to overcome, to triumph been extolled as *the* virtue. Survival of the fittest has become a credo in the West, drawing erroneously on Darwin's theory for support. Our commercial, industrial society, our nationalism, even much of our religion, favors above all else competition: we are better than you. Unfortunately the current theory of evolution, with its narrow understanding of the meaning of the struggle to survive, has been invoked as the natural support for this prejudice. Even our genes are said to be selfish. Yet, others are not simply our brothers or sisters, but are indeed much more intimate: they are the other halves of ourselves. Because we need to belong, but because we need to be unique, we live our lives in two incompatible contexts. We can see then that living among others is not simply a case of dog eat dog, but is the opportunity for living creatively.

16 | On Humans and Evolution

"The universal triumph of the secular state has thrown all religious organizations into such a definitely secondary, and finally ineffectual, position that religious pantomime is hardly more today than a sanctimonious exercise for Sunday morning, whereas business ethics and patriotism stand for the remainder of the week. Such a monkey-holiness is not what the functioning world requires; rather, a transmutation of the whole social order is necessary, so that through every detail and act of secular life the vitalizing image of the universal god-man who is actually immanent and effective in all of us may be somehow made known to consciousness."

JOSEPH CAMPBELL[1]

We have traveled far since I asked my opening question, "How has the evolution of human nature been possible?" According to the mechanistic/materialistic neo-Darwinian theory, it has not been possible: we are matter and only matter. As we saw when considering Mayr's teleonomy, only by making a caricature of human nature has this theory been able to approach the question of its evolution. In any case the theory of the evolution of human nature is not, nor ever can be, simply the province of scientists. It calls into question the meaning of who and what we are, and must account for the rise of religion as well as the development of the body. Religion, psychology and philosophy must make their contributions as participants in its creation.

Life, according to the neo-Darwinian, and as one of Shakespeare's characters assures us, is, "A tale told by an idiot. Full of sound and fury, signifying nothing." Or, as Dawkins would say, like a product of a monkey at a typewriter.[2] Kierkegaard laments, "If there were no eternal consciousness in a man, if at the foundation of all there lay only a wildly

seething power, which writhing with obscure passions produced everything that is great and everything that is insignificant, if a bottomless
void never satiated lay hidden beneath all — what then would life be
but despair."[3]

George Price knew well that the neo-Darwinian world could lead us
to this despair. Bertrand Russell knew it also. One is reminded of his
saying,[4] "Only on the firm habitation of unyielding despair, can the
soul's habitation henceforth be safely built."

Why do we despair in this way? Paradoxically, because we know deep
in our hearts that the materialist, mechanist dogma, is not complete. St.
Augustine said, "If you had not already found me you would not be
seeking me." We seek the truth because we know the truth. This is the
truth that, Jesus assures us, will set us free.

To understand this apparent paradox we must recall the definition
that I gave of faith. Faith means to *know* without recourse to understanding; faith is knowing that lies 'beyond' understanding. I contrasted
faith with belief, which is to *accept* without understanding. Faith is
constant, whereas beliefs may come and go. Faith underlies and upholds
all our knowledge and beliefs. It even underlies the mechanist/materi-
alist belief, which denies faith altogether. This, in someone sensitive to
ambiguity, can generate an irresolvable conflict that can lead to the kind
of despair about which Russell and Kierkegaard spoke.

Whether we are a mechanist, a neo-Darwinian, a creationist, a hierarchic creationist or a reductionist, beliefs pervade our knowledge and
they are intermingled with it. Often they go under the name of 'assumptions', 'presuppositions', 'premises' and 'axioms'. These are often
accepted without question. The difference between a belief and an
assumption is not hard and fast; an assumption may be subject to criticism, whereas a belief usually is not. Science, philosophy and theology
undertake a constant criticism of our assumptions, and sometimes find
them either unacceptable or else refine them into new theories.
Assumptions are held for their heuristic value; beliefs are held for their
subjective value. Beliefs support in some way or other the illusion of a
stable point of reference, or, in more common language, the ego.
Materialism may be an assumption or a belief. Neo-Darwinism has
become for some not simply a belief but a religion and, for these individuals, as Dawkins has shown us, the belief in materialism-mechanism
is held with passion.

Understanding can free us from beliefs, but at a price. One pays the price by surrendering pride. To attain humility we must often pass through the humiliation of finding that even our most cherished beliefs and assumptions may be wrong, and this is a price that for many people is too high. But we must also be freed from the tyranny of understanding itself, the tyranny that claims that the human intellect can grasp and solve the mystery of being. This claim serves what E. O. Wilson calls 'the Ionian enchantment' and which later he calls 'the dream of intellectual unity'.[5] The Ionian enchantment, as Wilson also recognizes, may be known as *hubris* and the difficulty with hubris is that it is pride in being proud, and so quite blind.

When I say we must free ourselves of the tyranny of understanding, I do not mean that we should turn our back upon it, but that we should see it against the background of the unknowable. The unknowable is the province of faith. But to surrender hubris we must surrender 'I'. This is only truly possible if we can make the leap from *what* I am to *that* I am.

How has the evolution of human nature been possible?

In asking, "How has the evolution of human nature been possible?" we have seen that animals share in almost all that in the past we thought was the province of human beings alone: reflexive awareness — and in some self awareness — awareness of the other, empathy, altruism, love, aesthetic feelings, intelligence, creativity. All of these naturally emerge as part of the evolutionary process and eventually, through the active struggle of life, become part of the evolutionary sieve. Evolution is not therefore mindless, uncaring and selfish as it appears when looked at through the 'glasses' of neo-Darwinism.

Evolution is normally looked upon as being 'anonymous'. By this I mean that in the metaphorical struggle to survive the individual does not matter. Chance alone determines whether one individual or another survives. The grim reaper scythes down whatever comes his way. This evolutionary sieve is blind to individual merit. But active struggle is concerned only with the individual. With active survival whether an individual survives or not depends upon the individual. The qualities of the individual that triumph become part of the evolutionary sieve. These qualities include the capacity to cooperate as well as to compete, the capacity to love as well as to strive, the capacity to be part of a group as well as to go it alone. Those qualities that we find in animals and human beings that triumph must also be part of the sieve. The evolutionary process, far from simply being all chance, just blind, unconscious and automatic, has the qualities of self-awareness, awareness of the other, empathy, altruism, love, aesthetic feelings, intelligence, and creativity, among others. This is the evolutionary process that has enabled human nature to evolve, not the neo-Darwinian evolutionary process that is dependent upon chance and metaphorical struggle, and that recognizes matter alone as fundamental.

What am I?

We saw that the need to be unique was a continuation of the active struggle to survive. 'I', or 'I–It' to use Buber's primary word, is a stable point of reference. 'I' is also a word; it is the *word* that gives 'I' its stability, and dynamic unity gives it the quality of being absolute. 'I,' as the dynamic center, orients us not only in the world of fact but also in the world of value. For most people 'I' is the supreme value and the measure of all values. That which approaches me [I] is important, that which is far is unimportant. Ten thousand people can die in China and I remain unmoved. A thousand in Europe and I am somewhat troubled. Several hundred in a nearby State and things begin to look serious; a hundred can be killed in my town and I am really worried. If ten are killed in my street, a catastrophe has struck; and if one is killed in my family then the bottom drops out of life. A reporter in the Montreal Gazette recently wrote, "When I heard of Cpl. . . . death, the war in Afghanistan became suddenly very close, very personal." Before the corporal had shipped out to Afghanistan, the reporter had been his supervisor in Montreal.

Proximity in time has the same effect. We do not give much attention to the dead of the American Civil War, and hardly remember those killed in the First World War, even the 60,000 that died or were wounded in one day on the Somme. We pay tribute to those who fell in the Second World War, but feel the deaths of the soldiers in Vietnam more acutely. (Of course that means American soldiers if we are

Americans.) But each soldier killed in Iraq (2007) is a renewed tragedy and we count the number with trepidation. 'I' can be invested, and whatever 'I' is invested in becomes 'mine' and acquires a new value: 'my' family, 'my' house, 'my' car, 'my' country acquires a value that 'the' family, 'the' car, 'the' country quite lacks.

The preservation of 'I' after death is ardently sought after, and solemnly assured by all the great religions. Some people will say, "I am not afraid of death, death means nothing to me!" That is until they get a call from the doctor's office in connection with the blood tests that were just done, and which unfortunately do not look too good. The loss of 'I' in death is dreaded even though we put 'I' aside each night, turn over and go to sleep. We can go to sleep in this way because 'I' is a creation. Eventually it too must pass, however much difficulty we have in accepting that truth, and however astonishing its passing appears to us while alive.

In answer to the question, "Where do I go after death?" the Christian is told, "To heaven!" 'I' is the name given to an amalgam of the need to be unique and the need for a dynamic center. The quality of being absolute, which is given by dynamic unity, and the impression that 'I' endures, turns it into an immortal soul. Ramana Maharshi, a Hindu saint who died in the 1950s, said on his deathbed, "I'm going nowhere, there's nowhere to go!" As long as we invest I, which endures and is absolute, in something, whether material, mental or spiritual which will inevitably perish, we must see death also as an absolute and live in terror of nowhere to go and so ward off truth by fairy tales. But we must persist in the bewilderment brought on by looking down the jaws of the basic ambiguity that yawn in the absence of 'I' and of all that I have invested it in, not in the hope of discovering some new understanding, but in the hope of awakening to the true meaning of the unknowable. When I can let go of all things, including bodies, minds and souls, and this after all was one of the basic teachings of Jesus,[6] then I can awaken to the truth *that* I am and that 'I' need go no-where.

Let us interpret religion then in the light of what we know, in the light of all that Darwin, Freud, Crick, Watson and Dawkins have shown us. Let us not be satisfied with "religious pantomime [that] is hardly more today than a sanctimonious exercise for Sunday morning", that is tolerated because people are superstitious, because they have a timorous nature that needs fairytales to comfort them in their distress. Let us not have a religion either that is the handmaiden of science, or stuck on to it like the flower is stuck on to a cactus. But, above all, let us not destroy the dignity and magnificence of what it means to be fully human, simply in the interests of some theory about what science is or is not.

Before we can creatively integrate our religion with what the sciences of biology, chemistry and physics have shown us, we must let go of our need to be unique, we must suspend disbelief and stray beyond the palisade of logic and wander in uncertainty. We must do this, not at a purely fanciful, intellectual level, as Crick, Dawkins, Gould and other evolutionists have sometimes done, but in the spirit of Christ, who said, "Unless a seed falls in the ground and dies it remains alone. If it dies, it brings forth much fruit." The seed, I–It, the dynamic center, must be relinquished. Christ is telling us that 'I' am not something: a body, personality, self, nor even a soul or spirit; my true home lies *beyond*.

Of humans and animals

Is this true also of the cockroach? Does the true home of the cockroach lie beyond? Or are humans special? Gould waxes indignant: "What beyond our dangerous and unjustified arrogance could even permit us to contemplate such a preferred status for one species among hundreds of millions that have graced the history of our planet? Therefore human existence must also be judged as a detail . . . left to chance."[7] Leaving the indignation aside, one has to agree with Gould that our arrogance, the certainty of our own uniqueness, has prompted us to take this stand. Just as, in the name of the certainty of our uniqueness, we pillage the rainforests, deplete the ocean of fish, pollute the atmosphere and destroy the ozone layer. But to exclaim, "therefore human existence must also be judged as a detail . . . left to chance," may be a statement as arrogant as the creationists' statement that humans are God's unique creation.

We humans are special because each is 'I'. All other qualities that we have reserved for human consumption alone turn out to be shared, although often in an attenuated form, by animals. 'I' alone is human. Because active survival is based upon the qualities of the individual, 'I' becomes a key element of the evolutionary sieve, but it might in time become the corrosive that destroys it. Most of the other qualities transcend the individual and so enhance not only the survival chances of the individual, but also of the group of which he or she forms a part. 'I' by definition is locked into an individual and so has the effect of setting the individual apart from the others in the group. This in turn weakens the bonds of the group, bonds that also are part of the evolutionary sieve. Animals that can cooperate and help each other are more likely to survive than individuals on their own. For evolution to continue — and with active struggle it can only continue through the struggle of the individual — 'I' must be transcended, a message that all the great mystics of the world have preached. But, alas the great religions of the world, the repository of their teachings, are in decline, and materialistic, mechanistic science has become their substitute.

Mysticism and science

Bertrand Russell said, "The greatest men who have been philosophers have felt the need both of science and of mysticism." Russell goes on to say, "The attempt to harmonize the two [science and mysticism] was what made their life, and what always must, for all its arduous uncertainty, make philosophy, to some minds, a greater thing than either science or religion."[8] And philosophy after all at its best is the love of wisdom. When speaking of Heraclitus, he said, "The facts of science, as they appeared to him, fed the flames in his soul, and in its light he saw into the depths of the world by the reflection of his own dancing swiftly penetrating fire. In such a nature we see the true union of the mystic and the man of science — the highest eminence, as I think, that it is possible to achieve in the world of thought."[9]

Perhaps now we can begin to answer this question, "Are human beings superior to animals?" Perhaps the superiority of the human being lies not in what he or she is, but in what he or she may become. It may be that each of us — man, woman, mouse, and wolf — carries within us the seed of our own immortality,[10] our own dancing swiftly penetrating fire, out of which the world and 'I' arise, and to which 'I' and the world return. As humans we can realize this, but such possibility is denied to the mouse and wolf, and thus what each of us as individuals may become, and not what we are, makes us superior. Our privilege, and our profound responsibility, is to cultivate this seed so that it does fall into the ground and die and so does bring forth much fruit.

And how do we begin? T. H. Huxley gives the simplest way to begin, a way that is in complete accord with the Zen Buddhist tradition: "Science seems to teach in the highest and strongest manner the great truth which is embodied in the Christian concept of entire surrender to the will of God. Sit down before every fact as a little child, be prepared to give up every preconceived notion, follow humbly wherever and to whatever abysses nature leads, or you will learn nothing. I have only begun to learn content and peace of mind since I have resolved at all risks to do this."[11]

Epilogue

Throughout the book I have avoided relying upon Zen teaching for support. My ideas are self-contained. I have wanted to tell how someone who has practiced Zen looks at the evolution of human nature, not how some abstraction called Zen would look at it. Nevertheless I think that to be fair I should let the reader know something about the Zen teaching that has led to these meditations. This would provide him or her with a context in which to place what I have to say.

The way of Zen Buddhism has its origins partly in the *Prajnaparamita school* of Mahayana Buddhism. This school first made its appearance at about the beginning of the Common Era. The etymology of the word *prajna* lies in two words: *pra* and *jna*. 'Pra' means 'aroused'; 'jna' means original mind, or knowing, and is closely related to the word 'gnosis'. I have referred to 'jna' throughout this book as *that* I know as opposed to *what* I know. *Paramita* means to cross to the other shore, or to go beyond experience. The 'other shore' refers to what I have called the transcendent. In the terms that I have been using, Prajnaparamita means: awakening from experience — from 'what I am' — to the transcendent, 'that I am'. Buddha summed up what this means in a phrase that is well known among followers of Zen: 'Throughout heaven and earth I alone am the honored One'.[1] Heaven corresponds to knowing; earth corresponds to being. 'Throughout heaven and earth I alone am the honored One', corresponds therefore to the Subjective declaration "I am." Thus the *Origin of Human Nature* is a twenty-first century meditation on the Prajnaparamita and Buddha's summation of it.

Central to the teaching of the Prajnaparamita school is the phrase that appears in the *Prajnaparamita Hridaya Sutra*: 'Form is emptiness: emptiness is form'.[2] That I am, that I know, and that it is, are without content; content belongs to the realm of what I am, what I know, what it is. To be without content is to be empty; it does not mean to be unreal.

Indeed, what I am depends on that I am; that I am comes first, not in time but in priority. We could use the mirror metaphor: the reflections depend upon the presence of the mirror: first the mirror, then the reflections. This would mean that the transcendent is real and the phenomenal, that which we experience, is an illusion or a dream.[3]

The question, "Who am I?" is a koan used by beginners. The Japanese way of posing this koan is, "What is my face before my parents are born?" Beyond the body, feelings, mind or consciousness: what am I? The question thrusts us into the very heart of the origin of human nature, but not in a conceptual or theoretical way. To ask the question is to live the question.

Insofar as the Prajnaparamita school teaches 'form is only emptiness' it teaches from the perspective of the Subjective. The sixth Zen Patriarch Hui Neng put it all in a nutshell when he said, "From the beginning not a thing is." Yet the Subjective perspective is not an Idealist perspective. Buddhism does not deny the Objective. The sutra also says, "Emptiness is form." A Zen Master, Bassui, tells us: "The universe and yourself are of the same root; you and every single thing are a unity. The gurgle of the stream, and the sigh of the wind are [your voice]. The green of the pine, the white of the snow, these are [your face].[4] Knowing and Being, though not the same, are one; the Subjective and Objective are ways of viewing this unity.

A recurrent theme in Buddhism is the theme of impermanence, and impermanence is a way of talking about change. In the West we have come to look upon permanence as the real. For us *things* are real; they pass away into nothing, the ultimate in the unreal. We therefore see a teaching that has the teaching of impermanence as one of its main tenets[5] as a negative, life denying, teaching, just as we see the Buddhist teaching of 'no-thing', or *anicca*, as nihilistic. The reputation that Buddhism has acquired of being a pessimistic teaching owes much to the teaching of impermanence. Yet the Western belief in things, in a mechanical universe put in motion by causes, its belief in a supreme being, an enduring Person that is somehow outside of the world He has created, is a pessimistic teaching: it is a teaching of a world going nowhere for no reason. This is the world that the neo-Darwinians would foist on us. By contrast the world that I am offering is creative, full of purpose and meaning.

Another word that could be used instead of impermanence is

'dynamic': Buddhism teaches us that the world is dynamic and living instead of static and dead. A dynamic world is one that is open to creative possibilities. Emptiness, instead of having nihilistic, nay saying overtones, now has vital, yea saying overtones. If all forms, that is all things — mountains and rivers, trees and animals, thoughts and theories — are empty, all are full of potential and possibility. This is the truth that erupts when one crosses over from *what* the world is to *that* it is, from *what* I am to *that* I am.

Seeing impermanence as the rule and the stable and static as temporary exceptions makes way for a new view of time. In the West we tend to see time as spacelike, as a fourth dimension. It is a void waiting to be filled, but which is forever passing away. As Rudyard Kipling said, it is like "an ever-rolling stream that bears all its sons away. They fly forgotten as a dream dies at the opening day." To see time as passing requires some Objectively fixed point of reference; to see impermanence as the rule is to no longer see time passing against an imagined background of eternity.

From the point of view of impermanence every thing is time; there is no background, no substratum. This is what Zen master Dogen calls *uji* or 'being-time'. Another contemporary Zen master, Shenryu Suzuki, explained the meaning of this by saying, "You do not have lunch at 1 o'clock; eating lunch is 1 o'clock." Bergson's notion of *durée* is very similar to uji. Because everything is time, everything, including the past and the future, is now. This is Subjective, 'organic' time, in place of an Objective, mechanical time. An organism does not grow in time but as time. A 9-month old embryo is not simply 9 months older than a recently fertilized ovum. Organic time makes evolution possible.

As long as we stay with the dogma that the world is a collection of absolute and unchanging abstractions that we call things — that is, as long as we insist that 'this is this and cannot be that', or, 'this is either this or that' — as long as we stay enchained in the prison, 'this is this and has to be this for ever and ever, amen', then all that I say, along with all the illustrious teachings of Buddha and the great Zen patriarchs, will remain foreign, alien and somewhat absurd. Yet, not everyone is willing, or even perhaps suited, to pull up the anchor of classical logic and venture into the uncharted waters of their own mind. Those who do, surrender the security and stability afforded by the dynamic center of ego, and flirt with chaos. Fear is a constant companion of the neophytes who feel the abyss of the primal schism opening behind them as the secure ground on which they have hitherto walked begins to crumble.

To help those for whom the risk is too great, or for whom the enterprise would be without value, I have offered another way to think, a way that I have called 'the logic of ambiguity'. With this logic the enigmatic quality of some of the koans will be less opaque, the paradoxes of the conversations between Zen masters and their disciples will seem less absurd, and the master who raised his hand and challenged his students, "If you call this a hand I will hit you thirty times with my stick; if you say it is not a hand I will hit you thirty times with my stick. Now what is it?" will not seem quite so mad. In the Diamond Sutra, another sutra celebrated by the followers of the Zen way, the Buddha tells us: "The world is not a world. That is why it is called a world." An apple is not an apple; that is why it is called an apple. With this new way of thinking we can broach some of the great mysteries of being with greater confidence.

Zen Buddhism has no doctrine of I–thou, and this is why I turned to the Jewish scholar and philosopher, Martin Buber, to help me explain the difficult truth that you and 'me'* are not separate, distinct beings, but arise simultaneously from a common living and creative source. *That* you are and *that* I am is indubitable; what you are and what I am can be questioned. Just as *that* I am has no content so the same can be said of *that* you are. I am not saying you and I are the same, quite the contrary. But we are not different.

Why then is Zen so silent on the great mystery of the 'Other'?

I once had the very good fortune to meet for a short while with a Tibetan Buddhist Lama, a very highly respected man and venerable teacher. I asked him, "What is Buddhism?" He replied, "It is the teaching of wisdom and compassion." I went on, "How does one acquire compassion?" "Through wisdom." I persisted, "What is wisdom?" His response, "Seeing all things are empty." I raised my hand and enquired, "Are you saying that this is empty?" He retorted, "If you know what you are talking about, it is; if you do not, then it is not."

Zen tradition tells us that Buddha went up the mountain for himself and came down the mountain for others. To go up the mountain is a Zen

---

*As you may remember our grammar is sometimes the enemy of truth. I should use me and not I as grammar demands, but I doubt whether my editor would let me get away with it. So I have done my best, sometimes using ' ' to help me out.

metaphor for awakening beyond experience; to come down the mountain is an expression of compassion. The exhortation of Christ, "Love God with all your heart and soul and love your neighbor as your self!" could be translated as, "Awaken to the truth *that* you are and to the further truth that you and your neighbor are One."

Zen Buddhism does not emphasize the importance of love and compassion as does the Christian tradition, but they are not less important to the one following the Zen way because of that. The *Prajnaparamita Hridaya* begins with, "The Bodhisattva of compassion from the depths of prajna saw the emptiness of all and broke the bonds of suffering." A bodhisattva is one who forgoes the bliss of eternal peace to help bear the sufferings of others. It is the bodhisattva of compassion who teaches wisdom, a subtlety that must not escape our notice.[6]

Why do I end on this note? Why did I subject the reader to the tortuous journey through the maze of I–thou in chapter 14? My feeling is that the great jewels in the crown of humanity have been our spiritual teachers. While their teachings have so often been distorted and forced into serving our debased and often cruel demands, this does not detract in any way from the loftiness and sublimity of their teachings. Christ, Buddha, the great Hindu teachers, Ramakrishna, Ramana Maharshi, Nisargadatta Maharaj, the wonderful teachers of Islam, Ibn 'Arabi, Jelludin rumi, Kabir, the great Jewish rabbis, Hillel and Shammai, all shone with love and compassion that was reflected in their teaching; the teaching of love is what they strove, and sometimes gave up their lives, to have us hear. In this way they radiated from the pinnacle of evolution what is potential in all life even in its lowest forms, and they exemplified the power that ultimately motivates the creativity that we call evolution: the power of compassion that is the highest expression of Unity itself. This truth — that wisdom and compassion sustain life and its processes — has led me and leads me still in my meditations on the origins of human nature.

Appendix I
Chance and Creativity in Evolution

On the notion of chance

About half of Americans are Creationists; only half accept that organisms have evolved. Even so the evidence in favor of evolution is so overwhelming that it cannot be denied. Nor can it be denied that some species are more adapted to their environment than others and that they are more likely to pass on their characteristics to their progeny. Most who are knowledgeable about the subject affirm that accident, chance or random processes must have played a part in bringing about changes leading to greater adaptation.

This affirmation is made in spite of the fact that 'chance' is a vague term. Richard Dawkins inadvertently illustrates the confusion surrounding it. He first says that one of his tasks, "Will be to destroy the eagerly believed myth that Darwinism is a theory of chance."[1] Yet later he tells us, "Cumulative selection is the key to all our modern explanations of life. We cannot escape the need to postulate a single step chance event in the origin of cumulative selection itself."[2]

Undoubtedly chance has played some part in evolution, but chance alone has not brought about all the changes; *creativity* too has played a part. This is cardinal. If chance alone accounts for the evolution of life, and that obviously would include the evolution of humans and all that we stand for, then E. O. Wilson is right: religion, ethics and philosophy must be subsumed under evolutionary biology. Not only this but art, that we consider to be essentially creative, must also be subsumed in the same way. If this were so the very idea of a way other than the Objective, physical way would be untenable.

It is on this question that the jury of public opinion is undecided: is accident the first cause uncaused or has intelligence and creativity too made a contribution?

Dawkins' five questions

Richard Dawkins, in *The Blind Watchmaker*, wants to eliminate any doubt about the role of chance in the evolutionary process. His book is a defense of mechanistic/materialistic biology and an attack on alternative theories. Dawkins is one of the leading exponents of the 'accidental' theory of evolution, and according to the accolades given by the text on the back cover of *The Blind Watchmaker*, it "is probably the most important book since Darwin." According to the *Times* review, "Dawkins in this book is tackling nothing less than the meaning of life and he attacks it with the evangelical fervor of a clergyman and the mind of a scientist."

Let us then take a look at his justification for the theory that chance is the sole motivator and means of evolution. He puts this justification at the beginning of his book and it is the basis of his theory and of the mechanistic materialistic theory generally. When reading the following one must not forget the importance that Dawkins has as apologist for neo-Darwinian theory: it is the very foundation of that theory.

Using the evolution of the marvelously complex human eye as a subject for discussion, he asks these five questions (the italics in what follows are mine):

The first question: *Could* the modern human eye have arisen directly from no eye at all, in a single step?

The second question: *Could* the human eye have arisen directly from something slightly different from itself, something that we may call X?

The third question: Is there a series of X's connecting the modern human eye to a state with no eye at all?

The fourth question: Is it *plausible* that every [X] was made available by random mutation of its predecessor?

The fifth question: Is it *plausible* that every [change] worked sufficiently well that it assisted the survival and reproduction of the animals concerned?[3]

Comments on the five questions

Only the most radical creationists would say yes to the first question —
could the modern human eye have arisen directly from no eye at all? —
but in doing so they would have to deny not only the discoveries of
science, but also the very value of human reason itself. This is too high
a price for us to pay. For any reasonable person the answer is unques-
tionably, "No, the modern human eye could not have arisen directly
from no eye at all."

One would have no trouble in saying yes in answer to the next two
questions. Most likely the eye did evolve through a succession of small
changes, and possibly a continuous series of small changes could account
for the development of the modern human eye from no eye at all.

So far the questions have been quite innocuous and we are almost
lulled to sleep by them. But the next two questions have a sting in the
tail. I have italicized the 'coulds' and the 'plausibles' in the questions to
draw your attention to them. I do this because we have come to the crux
of the argument. Why does Dawkins not just ask whether it is simply
possible that these changes are made by accident? Why does he insert
the phrase, "Is it plausible?"

Because he knows that if he just asks whether it is possible that these
changes are made by accident, his argument, for the following reasons,
evaporates. Dawkins asks, "Is it *plausible* that each of these changes was
made available by random mutation?" Let us change that to "Is it *possible*
that each of these changes was made available by random mutation?"
Anyone could agree that these changes *could* have been made available
by random mutation. Even a creationist could agree that it is *possible* that
this is so. But the creationist would likely to go on to say, "I am not
disputing that it is *possible* that accidents were the cause. I dispute that
they *were* the cause".

Plausible, according to the *Oxford English Reference Dictionary* means
both reasonable and *probable*. Using this definition of the word plausible,
I can agree that it is reasonable and *possible* that the changes were
wrought by accident or random mutation. I cannot agree that it was
probable. I could consider it plausible if I were to use the definition,
given by the *American Heritage Dictionary,* of the word plausible. "Giving
a deceptive impression of truth, acceptability, or reliability; specious:
the plausible talk of a crafty salesperson."

Dawkins in the first three questions asks about possibility; now with question number four he moves on to what is plausible: "Is it plausible that each of these changes was made available by random mutation?" After all, conceivably, that is possibly, the moon is made of green cheese, and many a debating society has shown that it is a reasonable proposition, but none has suggested that it is probably so. These debating societies are set up to test the debating skills of the participants, and the question about the moon being made of green cheese is chosen precisely because it is possible but not plausible. To move from what is possible to what is plausible requires a leap and that leap needs justification, a justification that Dawkins does not supply simply because he cannot supply it.

Dawkins gives some evidence in primitive organisms of crude eyes that nevertheless can perceive the world, even though the perception may be minimal. In this way he refutes the idea that half an eye is no use to an organism. He extrapolates from this rudimentary eye that the evolution of the human eye by small random changes is possible. One has to agree — it is *possible*. But that is all. But this gradual change through mutation brought about solely by chance is the lynch pin of the whole theory. Many scientific theories start with the feeling that something is possibly the case. One has a hunch. But the theory is only a theory after one has gone from the possible to probable. Dawkins, and the neo-Darwinians generally, start with the hunch and then turn it into a dogma.

The last question he asks is another wobbler. "Is it *plausible* that every change worked sufficiently well that it assisted the survival and reproduction of the animals concerned?" Again it may be possible that this is so, although, again, not plausible. The change must be great enough to make a difference, but small enough to be possible by random chance alone. How great a change that would be cannot be determined a priori. He should provide some evidence to support his contention.

The plausibility of these last two questions is precisely what concerns most serious critics of neo-Darwinians of Dawkins' persuasion. These concerns moreover are just what have led me to write this book.

The blurbs on the cover of the paperback version of *The Blind Watchmaker* tell us that Dawkins is an expert witness. But why does he use such a specious argument as these five questions as the foundation on which his whole theoretical edifice is built? With this elaborate shadow boxing, Dawkins has done nothing to show that chance or random mutation is the only way that species have evolved. He has simply shown that chance *may* have been responsible.

Professor Garret Hardin made an almost identical argument to the one presented by Dawkins as long ago as 1961. I quote from the book *Darwin Retried by* Norman Macbeth, who is quoting Hardin:

> "Were all other organisms blind, the animal which managed to evolve even a very poor eye would thereby have some advantage over the others. Oysters have such poor eyes — many tiny sensitive spots that can do no more than detect changes in the intensity of light. An oyster may not be able to enjoy television, but it can detect a passing shadow, react to it as if an approaching predator caused it, and — because it is sometimes right — live another day. By selecting examples from various places in the animal kingdom, we can assemble a nicely graded series of eyes, passing, by not too big steps, from the primitive eyes of oysters to the excellent (though not perfect) eyes of men and birds. Such a series, made up from contemporary species, is not supposed to be the actual historical series; but it shows us how evolution *could have occurred.*"[4] (italics added).

No progress has been made in 40 years to prove that chance is the only factor in change. Worse still, Hardin's and Dawkins' argument are both based upon Darwin's original attempt to show how eyes could have evolved, and he gave that argument 150 years ago.

Using Dawkins five questions to support creative evolution

Let me use the same questions that Dawkins has used, with one slight amendment to question four. By doing this I will show that one can use his very same argument to show that creativity is a factor in evolution.

The five questions

Question one: Using the human eye as a subject for discussion, could the modern human eye have arisen directly from no eye at all?

Question two: Could the human eye have arisen directly from something slightly different from itself, something that we may call X?

Question three: Could the eye have evolved through a succession of small changes?

Question four: Is it *possible* that each of these changes was made available by random mutation of its predecessor, *and by a creative resolu-*

tion of the dissonance that this randomness would have generated? (this is my addition). Please do not forget that, for the moment, like Dawkins, I am only asking whether it is possible. And in any case my argument for creative evolution is built upon a far wider foundation that just this.

Question five: Is it possible that some of these changes worked sufficiently well that they assisted the survival and reproduction of the animals concerned?

Dawkins uses the 'possible' and 'plausible' argument freely. 'It is possible and therefore it is so'. Professor Fischer, commenting on the 'fallacy of the possible proof' says, "The fallacy of the possible proof consists in an attempt to demonstrate that a factual statement is true or false by establishing the possibility of its truth or falsity. This tactic . . . never proves a point at issue. Valid empirical proof requires not merely the establishment of possibility, but an estimate of probability."[5]

Chance and creativity compared

Dawkins expects a 'yes' answer to each of his questions. I do as well. But this does not mean that we are necessarily in conflict. What does the word chance, or random, mean? A chance happening is unpredictable, and so is not the result of any plan, design or conscious intention. This means that it would be purposeless and quite fortuitous and the principle of cause and effect would not apply. Creativity too is unpredictable and, as I have shown, is not the result of *conscious* intention, plan, design or purpose. Cause and effect do not apply to creativity either. Moreover, as anyone who has created knows well, chance often plays a vital role in a creation. By advocating that creativity has played a part in evolution does not mean that we have to dismiss the contribution that chance has made. Adding creativity to what the neo-Darwinians have to offer, however, enhances our understanding.

Heuristic value

The theory of evolution based upon chance as the agent of change cannot be proven wrong. Falsification, according to Popper, is the test that a true scientific theory must pass. Darwin's theory of evolution is therefore not science in the way that physics, chemistry, and astronomy are sciences. The theory nevertheless has great heuristic value. It helps to bring together in a natural way many facts and observations, and is far more satisfactory than the Creationists' theory of the origin of the species, which, at the moment is the only alternative theory that is widely accepted.

Given that this is the case, given that Darwin's theory and the neo-Darwinian variations of it are judged to be acceptable theories because of their heuristic value, the test of the theory of evolution that I am offering must not then be based on whether it can be proven to be right, nor whether it is acceptable to the dogma of either the Creationists or the neo-Darwinians, but on its the heuristic merits. Which theory can account for the most data, including the prolific creativity of humanity, in the most complete and simple — not the most simplistic —way? This data must obviously also include our intelligence, creativity, ethical sense, our capacity for love and altruism, and our religious sensibility.

Appendix II
The Debate between Knowing and Being

The following is taken from Schopenhauer's *The World as Will and Idea*.[1]

> **Knowing:**
> I am, and besides me there is nothing. For the world is my idea.
>
> **Being:**
> What a crazy presumption! *I am,* and besides me there is nothing, for the world is my fleeting form. You are merely the sum of a part of this form, and entirely accidental.
>
> **Knowing:**
> What foolish arrogance! Neither you nor your form would be there without *me;* you are conditioned by me. Anyone who thinks me out of existence, and then believes he can still think you there, is in the grips of a gross delusion, for your existence apart from my idea is a direct contradiction, a nonsense. *You are* simply means that you are perceived by me. My idea is the place where you exist; hence I am the first condition of your existence.
>
> **Being:**
> Fortunately your impudent assertion will soon be refuted in a real way, and not by mere words. In a few more moments you will actually no longer be. With all your boasting, you will have lapsed into the void, will have drifted past like a ghost, and suffered the fate of all of my transient forms. But *I* will remain, unscathed and undiminished, from millennium to millennium, through infinite time, and without qualms I will observe the play of my changing forms.
>
> **Knowing:**
> This infinite time, through which you proudly claim to live, exists, like the infinite space you fill, only in my idea. Indeed, it is merely the form of my idea, the form I carry ready-made within me and in which

you show yourself, which receives you, and by means of which you exist in the first place. But the annihilation with which you threaten me does not affect me, for if it did, then you would be annihilated along with me. Rather, it merely affects the individual, which temporarily supports me and is, like everything else, my idea.

Being:

And if I concede this, and go so far as to regard existence (inseparably linked as it is, after all, to that of these fleeting individuals) as something which has an independent life, it will still remain dependent upon mine. For you are a subject only in so far as you have an object; and I am this object. I am its kernel and its content, the permanent part of it, the bonds that bind it together, and without which it would be as incoherent, tenuous and insubstantial as the dreams and fantasies of your individuals; and even their ostensible content they have borrowed, in the last analysis, from me.

Knowing:

You quite properly refrain *from* disputing my existence on the grounds that it is tied to individuals, for just as inseparably as I am linked to them you are linked to your sister, form, and have never appeared without her. No eye has yet seen either you or me naked and isolated; for we are both mere abstractions.

Appendix III
Should Clasical Logic be Superceded

I have argued that classical logic is inappropriate for the task of understanding evolution and other aspects of the life sciences, and that another, more inclusive, logic must be developed. As this is a considerable claim to make it will be as well for us to consider some of the objections to developing an alternative logic.

Michael Dummett, an influential analytical philosopher of our time, objects to introducing an alternative logic when he says, "It can scarcely advance our understanding of physics or anything else if the response to some perceived anomaly is to change the very ground rules that had hitherto defined what we should count as valid reasoning on the evidence and among whose more problematic entailments was precisely the anomaly in question. What this amounts to is merely a stipulative ruse for avoiding such problems by redefining the pertinence or scope of certain logical connectives and operators."[1]

As I have been at pains to point out, we are not responding to 'some perceived anomaly', some blip on the screen, but rather to many real and fundamental conflicts that I have listed in this book, including the conflict inherent in the two aspects, Subjective and Objective, of the statement, "I know it is raining." To brush off the question of changing the rules of thought, saying to do so is a 'stipulative ruse', or 'rhetorical device' is scarcely helpful in the discussion because it avoids the problem that is the core of the discussion.

Christopher Norris, a research professor in philosophy at Cardiff university, agreeing with Dummett declares, "If everything is called into question — from observational statements to logical 'laws of thought'– then nothing can any longer count as good reasons for rejecting this or that candidate hypothesis."[2]

Norris misses the point. Classical logic insists that one or other candidate hypothesis must be rejected. He is saying we must not change the rules that *demand* we reject one of two candidate hypotheses, because if we do we will not have grounds for rejecting one or other of them. The point that Norris is missing is that the evidence sometimes says that *neither of the two hypotheses may be rejected*, but only one may be accepted. In the knowing/being ambiguity, knowing has equal status to being. Or to make the point using more familiar words — mind is as important as matter and cannot be reduced to matter; or, to use Norris' words, mind cannot be rejected as a candidate hypothesis.

Quine, the recently deceased Harvard philosopher, mathematician and logician, seems to be in conflict with himself. On the one hand he agrees, "that certain developments in quantum physics may turn out to force revisions to the 'laws of thought' supposedly enshrined in classical logic."[3] On the other he denies, "We could ever, *in principle*, have rational grounds for preferring such a drastic response in the face of recalcitrant . . . evidence. Rather, we should suspect that there must be some problem with the evidence, some alternative (logic preserving) construal of it"[4] (my emphasis).

The laws of thought are not 'supposedly enshrined' in classical logic. Among philosophers and scientists they are tantamount to being sacred. They are firmly embedded, fixed, and taken for granted as being the only way to think. The complete reluctance that Quine has to changing the rules shows how deeply embedded they are. He denies *in principle* that we could *ever* have rational grounds for changing the rules of thought.

He says that we must suspect there is some problem with the evidence, or look for some alternative way of presenting it to overcome the problem. The problems of mind/body, of the priority of epistemology or ontology, idealism /realism, have been posed in many different ways for centuries and the problems just keep returning. The conflict between realism and anti-realism among quantum physicists has simply put the materialist/idealist problem in a new way; it is not a new problem. Quine's solution sounds like one of Dummett's ruses to get around the problem.

Leon Rosenfeld, in answer to questions posed by David Peat and Paul Buckley, said that Bohr was always very much against the idea that quantum mechanics called for a new logic. Rosenfeld goes on to say by way of explanation, "In order to understand [Bohr's] complementarity you must first put yourself at the starting point (which is pragmatism): otherwise you miss the point. If you are a strict logician, you will say: if it is mutually exclusive, then one of the two is false, one is right. That is obviously not the case."[5] In other words Bohr, according to what Rosenfeld said, is saying, let us use classical logic. But when, on pragmatic grounds, it is expedient, let us resort to complementarity. This, of course, is no foundation on which to build a secure science. Nadeau and Kafatos obviously agreed with this, hence the reason for their introducing their criteria for deciding when an alternative logic to classical logic is both necessary and appropriate.

Notes

Preface

1 R. C. Lewontin, *Biology as Ideology: the Doctrine of DNA* (Concord: House of Anansi Press, 1991), p. 41.
2 Gallup Poll (2004).
3 Please see my discussion on non-complex simplicity on pages 116 et seq.
4 Richard Dawkins, *The Blind Watchmaker* (Harmondsworth: Penguin, 1988), p. 3.
5 John Horgan, *The Undiscovered Mind* (New York: Touchstone, 1999).
6 Andrew Brown, *The Darwin Wars: The Scientific Battle for the Human Soul* (New York: Touchstone, 2000), p. 2.
7 While this is true of Zen Buddhism, Indian and Tibetan Buddhism collected a great number of outstanding philosophers. It worth noting moreover that as Florin Giripescu Sutton writes, "In this context of growing recognition of the originality and profundity of Buddhist insight into the nature of inner and outer realities, one is forced to consider the fact that Buddhism was the first religio-philosophical systems to assert and demonstrate, with great argumentative power, the ever-evolving nature of Reality, in both its subjective and objective aspects." Florin Giripescu Sutton, *Existence and Enlightenment in the Lankavatara-sutra: A Study in the Ontology and Epistemology of the Yogacara School of Mahayana Buddhism* (Albany: State University of New York Press, 1991), p. 39.
8 See justification for saying this in Albert Low, *Creating Consciousness* (Ashland: White Cloud Press, 2002), pp. 146–53.
9 Lucretius, *On the Nature of Things* <http://classics.mit.edu/Carus/nature_things.2.ii.html>.

Epigraph

1 Karl R. Popper, John C. Eccles, *The Self and its Brain: An Argument for Interactionism* (London: Routledge, 1998), p. 15.
2 Sean B. Carroll, *Endless Forms Most Beautiful: The New Science of Evo Devo* (New York: Norton, 2005), p. 286.
3 Michael Polanyi and Harry Prosch, *Meaning* (Chicago: University of Chicago Press, 1975), p. 29.

Introduction

1 Lucretius, *On the Nature of Things*, <http://classics.mit.edu/Carus/nature_things.2.ii.html>.

2 Karl Pearson, *The Grammar of Science* (London: J. M. Dent and Sons, 1937), p. 287.

3 See for example Marshall Berman, *All that is Solid Melts into Air* (Harmondsworth: Penguin Book, 1988).

4 Lewontin, *Biology as Ideology*, "Causes are usually seen to be at an individual level, the individual gene or the defective organ or an individual human being who is the focus of internal biological causes and external causes from an autonomous nature," p. 41.

5 Leda Cosmides and John Tooby, *Evolutionary Psychology: A Primer*, <http://www.psych.ucsb.edu/research/cep/primer.html>.

6 Bruce Chapman, former chief of the United States Census Bureau, and who serves as the president of the Discovery Institute says the following: "It can be argued that materialism is a major source of the demoralization of the twentieth century. Materialism's explicit denial not just of design, but of the possibility of scientific evidence for design has done untold damage to the normative legacy of Judeo-Christian ethics. A world without design is a world without inherent meaning." Quoted by Kenneth R. Miller in *Finding Darwin's God* (New York: Cliff Street Books, 1999), p. 188.

7 Richard Dawkins, *The Selfish Gene*, 2nd edn. (Oxford: Oxford University Press, 1989).

8 Francis Crick, *The Astonishing Hypothesis: The Scientific Search for the Soul* (New York: Touchstone, 1995), p. 3.

9 Stephen Pinker in an interview with the *Montreal Gazette* (Monday 21 October 2002), *Are we only such stuff as genes are made of?*

10 Jacques Monod quoted in Horace Freeland Judson, *The Eighth Day Of Creation* (New York: Simon and Schuster, 1979), p. 217.

11 Frank J. Tipler, *The Physics of Immortality: Modern Cosmology, God and The Resurrection of the Dead* (New York: Anchor Doubleday Books, 1994).

12 William Provine, quoted by Kenneth Miller, *Finding Darwin's God*, p. 171.

13 "The same [evidence given by biology and the brain sciences] favors a purely material origin of ethics." Edward O. Wilson, *Consilience: The Unity of Knowledge* (New York: Vintage, 1998), p. 263.

14 Brian Greene, *The Elegant Universe* (New York: Vintage, 1999), pp. 16–17.

15 Dawkins, *The Blind Watchmaker*, p. xiii.

16 Victor E. Frankl, *Man's Search for Meaning* (New York: Washington Square Press, 1969), p. 110.

17 See B. F. Skinner, *Beyond Freedom and Dignity* (New York: Bantam/Vintage, 1972).

18 Brown, *The Darwin Wars*, p. 2.

19 One only has to read some of the simplistic theories of what passes at the moment for Evolutionary Psychology to know what I mean. One good

place to start is the book Rose, Hilary and Rose Stephen, editors, *Alas, Poor Darwin* (London: Vintage, 2000), a collection of papers by respected scientists criticizing Evolutionary Psychology. In his introduction to the book, one of its editors, says on page 2, "To evolutionary psychologists, everything from children's alleged dislike of spinach to our supposed universal preferences for scenery featuring grassland and water derives from [a] mythic human origin in the African savannah."

20 See Euan Squires, *Conscious Mind in the Physical World* (London: Institute of Physics, 1990).

21 Howard Pattee is in the Department of Systems Science and Industrial Engineering, University of Binghamton. He is a theoretical biologist, specializing in evolutionary models of complex systems, and linguistic control of dynamic systems.

1 On Darwin's Theory

1 Stuart Kaufmann, *The Origins of Order* (Oxford: Oxford University Press, 1993), p. xiii.

2 Darwin, *The Origin of Species*, Last sentence of the Introduction, <http://www.talkorigins.org/faqs/origin.html>.

3 Charles Darwin, *The Origin of Species* (London: The Collector's Library, 2004), p. 74.

4 *Ibid.*, p. 75.

5 Lewontin, *Biology as Ideology*, p. 83.

6 Gabriel Dover, *Dear Mr. Darwin* (London: Phoenix, 2001), p. 9.

7 Darwin, *The Origin of Species*, p. 75.

8 A gestalt, according to *Webster's New Collegiate Dictionary* (1976) is a "configuration of physical, biological, or psychological phenomena so integrated as to constitute a functional unit with properties not derivable from its parts in summation."

9 Erich Jantsch, *The Self-Organizing Universe: Scientific and Human Implications of the Emerging Paradigm of Evolution* (Oxford: Pergamon Press, 1980), p. 8.

10 See note 6.

11 Dawkins, *The Blind Watchmaker*, p. xv.

2 On Subjectivity and Objectivity

1 Howard Pattee, *The Physics of Symbols: Bridging the Epistemic Cut*. Special issue of BioSystems, Vol. 60, No 1–3. pp. 5–21. <http://informatics. indiana.edu/rocha/pattee/pattee.html>.

2 *Ibid.*, p. 3.

3 Lee Nichol (ed.), *The Essential David Bohm* (New York: Routledge, 2003), p. 16.

4 James D. Watson, *The Double Helix* (New York: Signet, 1968).

5 Heisenberg, Werner, *Physics and Philosophy: The Revolution in Modern Science* (New York: Harper Torchbooks, 1962), p. 52.

6 Max Born, "Symbol and Reality," in *Physics in My Generation* (New York: Springer-Verlag, 1969), pp. 132–46. I have substituted the capital 'S' for the small 's' to tie the quote into what I am saying about Subjectivity.

7 Euan Squires, *The Mystery of Quantum Reality* (Bristol: The Institute of Physics Publishing, 1996), p. 123.

8 *Ibid.*, p. 16.

9 Nick Herbert, *Quantum Reality* (New York: Doubleday Anchor, 1987), pp. 15–29.

10 Karl R. Popper, *The Logic of Scientific Discovery* (New York: Harper Torchbooks, 1965), p. 38.

11 Dawkins, *The Blind Watchmaker*, p. ivx.

12 Robert Pollack, *The Faith of Biology, the Biology of Faith* (New York: Columbia University Press, 2000), p. 12.

3 'Knowing', the Basis of Experience

1 Arthur Schopenhauer, *The World as Will and Idea*, abridged in one volume by David Berman, translated by Jill Berman (New York: Everyman, 1997), p. 5.

2 "It may turn out that certain features of the living cell, including perhaps replication, stand in a mutually exclusive relationship to the strict application of quantum mechanics, and that a new conceptual language has to be developed to embrace this situation." Quoted by Howard Pattee, *The Physics of Symbols: Bridging the Epistemic Cut.*

3 A more precise word would be *gnosis*, which according to the Wikipedia means "the unconditioned ground (and source) of phenomenal reality." The Sanskrit equivalent is *jna* 'primordial knowing'. *Jna* is the basis of *prajna*, a word which signifies awakened or aroused knowing. *Prajna* is a basic term in Zen Buddhism. Unfortunately the word *gnosis* has all kinds of dubious mystical connotations and so it would not be appropriate to use it here.

4 The goal of Zen is to awaken to the transcendent. The enigmatic quality of the koans derives from their speaking about the unspeakable transcendent level. The first koans that one works with are called 'breakthrough koans'. *"The Sound of One Hand Clapping"*, *"What is your face before your parents were born?"* and *Joshu's "Mu!"* are all designed to help the one practicing to breakthrough the conceptual barrier. See Albert Low, *Hakuin on Kensho: The Four Ways of Knowing* (Boston: Shambhala, 2006) and Albert Low, *The World a Gateway: Commentaries on the Mumonkan* (Boston: Charles E. Tuttle, 1995).

The subsequent koans that one works with are used to refine the original awakening and to see that the transcendent and our ordinary mind, while not being the same, cannot be separated.

5 The distinction between 'that I know' and 'what I know' is made in the *Surangama Sutra*. In this sutra a dialogue occurs between Buddha and his chief disciple, Ananda, in which Buddha seeks to show Ananda the differ-

ence between *that* one hears and *what* one hears. During this dialogue Buddha tells Ananda, "Sound and no sound come and go, while hearing and no hearing are permanent. Sound and no sound are imaginary; hearing belongs to the pure Essence of Mind. Ananda you are mistaken when you say that you no longer hear simply because there is no longer a sound. You heard the sound again when the gong was struck again, so it means that hearing was there all along." See Albert Low, *Zen and the Sutras* (Boston: Charles E. Tuttle, 2000), pp. 145–7. This same distinction has some similarity with the distinction made in the study of consciousness between the 'hard' question and the 'easy' question.

6 Although I have italicized the 'that,' the emphasis must still be put on the knowing. The emphasis is made to distinguish 'that I know' from 'what I know'. I do not mean I know 'that' over there.

7 A beautiful poem by Basho, the Japanese haiku poet put all of this thus:

> "No-one
> Walks along this path
> This autumn evening".

8 *Qualia*, or qualities perceived directly by the Subject — such as red, the feeling of pain, or a sweet taste — and which correlate with neural activity, are included in 'what I know'.

9 In certain transcendental states, the distinction can drop away. This is why it is said that an awakened person does not know that he is awakened.

10 While some materialists may acknowledge that one can meaningfully use the expression, "I know that something or other is the case," nevertheless knowing is still considered by them to be a function of the brain and, presumably, in strict scientific terms, by using Occam's razor, can be dispensed with altogether.

11 This is explored more completely in Chapter 13.

12 This awakening is known in Zen as the 'awakening before the awakening,' *bodhicitta*, the awakening of the Mind that seeks the Way.

13 Martin Heidegger, translated by John Macquarrie and Edward Robinson, *Being and Time* (New York: Harper and Bros., 1962), p. 1.

14 Heidegger was profoundly influenced by Zen Buddhism. See Graham Parkes, editor, *Heidegger and Asian Thought* (Honolulu: University of Hawaii Press, 1990), and Reinhard May, translated with a complementary essay by Graham Parkes, *Heidegger's Hidden Sources* (London: Routledge 1996).

15 It is for this very reason that Zen has such a profound distrust of words and conceptual thought. It warns us not to confuse the finger with the moon towards which it points.

16 René Descartes, *A Discourse on Method and Other Works*. Abridged and edited and with an introduction by Joseph Epstein (New York: Washington Square Press, 1965), p. 20.

17 *Ibid.*, p. 24.

18 Karl Popper, *The Logic of Scientific Discovery*, p. 39.
19 Consciousness, as I shall explain shortly (chapter 13) has evolved from 'pure knowing'.
20 The discipline of 'waking up', 'being present', or 'recollected' during the day, is an important discipline in most spiritual ways. One may use a rosary and/or an accompanying mantra to help combat the tendency to 'sleep'. Only after one has truly struggled to remain 'awake' can one realize how much of our lives are passed in 'sleep'. When we are told we are asleep, for the few seconds that it take so to register what that means, we are awake, which makes it difficult for many to accept that we are, most of the time, asleep.
21 For more on the meaning of *samadhi*, please see Albert Low, *The Butterfly's Dream* (Vermont: Charles E. Tuttle, 1993), chapter 8.

4   Knowing and Evolution

1 Charles Darwin, The *Origin of Species*, 1859, <http://www.talkorigins.org/faqs/origin/chapter14.html>, last paragraph.
2 J. D. Bernal, *The Origin of Life* (London: Weidenfeld, 1969).
3 See Pattee, *The Physics of Symbols: Bridging the Epistemic Cut*, "It has turned out that for even the simplest known case, the gene, an adequate description requires the two irreducibly complementary concepts of dynamical laws and non-integrable constraints that are not derivable from the laws." I am suggesting that "non-integrable constraints that are not derivable from the laws," are related to knowing.
4 David Deutsch, *The Fabric of Reality* (Harmondsworth: Penguin Books, 1998), p. 189.
5 *Ibid.*, p. 190.
6 Carroll, *Endless Forms Most Beautiful: The New Science of Evo Devo*, p. 89.
7 Nichol, *The Essential David Bohm*, p. 171.
8 See Albert Low, *Hakuin on Kensho: the Four Ways of Knowing*.

5   On a New Way of Thinking

1 Herbert, *Quantum Reality*, p. 21.
2 R. C. Lewontin, Quoted in Miller *Finding Darwin's God*, p. 186.
3 Amit Goswami, *The Self-Aware Universe: How Consciousness Creates the Material World* (New York: Jeremy P. Tarcher), pp. 10–11.
4 Arthur Schopenhauer, *The World as Will and Idea*.
5 *Ibid.*, p. 24.
6 *Ibid.*, p. 216.
7 *Ibid.*
8 Heisenberg, *Physics and Philosophy: The Revolution in Modern Science*, p. 49.
9 Christopher Norris, *Quantum Theory and the flight from Realism: Philosophical Responses to Quantum Mechanics* (London: Routledge, 2000), p. 8.
10 *Ibid.*, p. 87.

11 Amit Goswami, *The Self-Aware Universe: How Consciousness Creates the Material World* (New York: Jeremy P. Tarcher, 1995), p. 116.

12 Nick Herbert, *Quantum Reality*, p. 21.

13 Robert Nadeau, and Menas Kafatos, *The Non-Local Domain* (Oxford: Oxford University Press, 1990), p. 101.

14 Nichol, *The Essential David Bohm*, p. 29.

15 Alfred Korzybski, *Science and Sanity* (Lancaster: The International Non-Aristotelian Library Publishing Co., 1941). In the 1950s *Science and Sanity* was listed as one of the most influential books of the twentieth century by a survey of most of the prominent scientists of the day.

16 Martin Heidegger, *Identity and Difference* (New York: Harper Torchbooks, 1969).

17 Lamouche, André (1955) *Le Principe de Simplicité Dans les Mathématiques et les Sciences* (Paris: Gautier Villiers).

18 Stéphane Lupasco, *L'Energie et la matière psychique* (Paris: Editions du Rocher, 1974).

19 Nadeau and Kafatos, *The Non-Local Domain*, p. 94.

20 I have slightly modified the third criterion.

21 *Ibid.*, p. 95.

22 Nadeau and Kafatos, *The Non-Local Domain*, p. 88.

23 *Ibid.*, p. 89.

24 Renée Weber, *Dialogues with Scientists and Sages* (London: Arkana, 1986), p. 41.

25 Martin Heidegger, *Discourse on Thinking* (New York: Harper Torchbooks, 1966), p. 56.

26 For a full discussion of the meaning of complementary relation see Archie J. Bahm, *Polarity, Dialectic and Organicity* (Albuquerque New Mexico: World Books, 1988), pp. 5 –11.

27 Heisenberg, *Physics and Philosophy: The Revolution in Modern Science*, p. 41.

28 *Ibid.*, p. 52.

29 Schopenhauer, *The World as Will and Idea*, p. 24.

30 C. G Jung, *Mysterium Coniunctionis* (The collected works of C. G. Jung, Vol. 14, Bollingen series XX; New York: Pantheon Books, 1963) pp. 536–7.

31 The word 'atom' is derived from the Greek *atomos:* that which cannot be divided.

32 The Sufis refer to it as the *unoambus.*

33 Simone Weil, *An Anthology* (London: Virago, 1986), p. 260.

34 I have given a full justification for saying this in *Low, Creating Consciousness.*

6 On Intention

1 Schopenhauer, *The World as Will and Idea*, p. 24.

2 I use the word 'directional' in the same way that one uses the term when speaking of the direction of a piece of music. Music is the perfect medium for the expression of human intention. See Low, *Creating Consciousness*, chapter 23, pp. 272–300.

3   Norris, *Quantum Theory and the flight from Realism: Philosophical Responses to Quantum Mechanics*, p. 6.
4   Quoted by Antonio T. de Nicolás, *Meditations through the Rg Veda: Four Dimensional Man* (New York: Nicolas Hay,1976) pp. 240–1.
5   <http://www.google.com/search?hl=en&lr=lang_en|lang_fr|lang_de&client=safari&rls=en&defl=en&q=define:Noumenal&sa=X&oi=glossary_definition&ct=title>.
6   William K. Mahony, *The Artful Universe* (New York: State University of New York Press, 1998), p. 1.
7   *Ibid.*, p. 3.
8   *Ibid.*
9   Herbert V. Guenther, *Wholeness Lost, Wholeness Regained* (New York: State University of New York Press, 1994), p. 2.
10 Herbert V. Guenther, *Matrix of Mystery* (Boulder and London: Shambhala, 1984), p. 5.
11 Philip Kapleau, *The Three Pillars of Zen* (New York: Harper and Row, 1966), p. 74.
12 No doubt this "true substance of things" is what Zen master Rinzai referred to when he tells us,

> "In the eye it is called seeing,
> In the ear it is called hearing.
> In the nose it smells odors,
> In the mouth it holds converse.
> In the hands it grasps and seizes,
> In the feet it runs and carries.

Fundamentally it is one pure radiance; divided it becomes the six harmoniously united spheres of sense." Ruth F. Sasaki, *The Record of Lin Chi* (Kyoto: The Istitute for Zen Studies 1975), p. 9
13 Henry Corbin, *Creative Imagination in the Sufism of Ibn 'Arabi* (Princeton: Bollingen Series XCI Princeton University Press, 1979), p. 47.
14 *Ibid.*, p. 220.
15 *Ibid.*, p. 228.
16 Heisenberg, *Physics and Philosophy: The Revolution in Modern Science*, pp. 78–9.
17 Goswami, *The Self-Aware Universe*, p. 116.
18 Herbert, *Quantum Reality*, p. 21.
19 David Bohm, *Wholeness and the Implicate Order* (London: Routledge and Kegan Paul, 1980), p. 11.
20 *Ibid.*, p. 11.
21 *Ibid.*, p. 11.
22 Roger Penrose, *The Large, the Small and the Human Mind* (Cambridge: Cambridge University Press: 1999), p. 93.
23 *Ibid.*, p. 94.
24 Schopenhauer, *The World as Will and Idea*, p. 32.

7 Intention as Dynamic Process

1 Ernst Mayr, *Towards a New Philosophy of Biology: Observations of an Evolutionist* (Cambridge, MA: Harvard University Press,1988), p. 64.

2 J. L. Mehta, "Heidegger and Vedanta: Reflections on a Questionable Theme," in *Heidegger and Asian Thought*, edited by Graham Parkes (Hawaii: University of Hawaii Press, 1990), p. 39.

3 Schopenhauer, *The World as Will and Idea*, p. 32.

4 Frans De Waal, *The Ape and the Sushi Master: cultural reflections of a primatologist* (New York: Basic Books, 2001), p. 65.

5 Howard Pattee, "Causation, Control and the Evolution of Complexity." in Peter Bøgh Anderson et al. (eds), *Downward Causation: Mind, Bodies and Matter* (Langelandsgade: Aarhus University Press), p. 63.

6 *Ibid.*

7 Lewontion, *Biology as Ideology: the Doctrine of DNA*, p. 51.

8 *Ibid.*, p. 51.

9 Bertrand Russell, *Mysticism and Logic* (Harmondsworth: Pelican Books, 1954), p. 190.

10 See the entry in *Cambridge Dictionary of Philosophy* general editor Robert Audi, under 'causal law'.

11 Dawkins took this expression from Julian Huxley's criticism of Henri Bergson.

12 David Bodanis, $E=MC_2$ (New York: Anchor Books, 2000), p. 11.

13 Dogobert Runes and 72, Authorities, *The Dictionary of Philosophy* (Littlefields, Adams and Co.: Totowa, 1997).

14 *Webster's New Collegiate Dictionary*, 1976.

15 Bohm, *Wholeness and the Implicate Order*, p. 11.

16 Popper, *The Logic of Scientific Discovery*, p. 10.

8 The 'Blind, Unconscious, Automatic' Process of Intention

1 Schopenhauer, *The World as Will and Idea*, p. 30.

2 If the reader feels that this is too naïve an experiment he or she should consult Lynn McTaggart's book *The Intention Experiment* (New York: Harper Perennial, 2007). This contains a series of experiments, many conducted by physicists, which show that intention can have an effect on the material world.

3 This has been proven by scientific experiment in which it has been shown that a time lapse of about a second occurs between the time that an intention is made and is registered by brain activity, and the conscious recognition of its having been made. Roger Penrose refers to this experiment in his book *The Large, the Small and the Human Mind*, p. 136. See also Daniel M. Wegner, *The Illusion of Conscious Will* (Cambridge, MA: MIT Press, 2002).

4 Dawkins, *The Blind Watchmaker*, p. 5.

5 The point has been made that perhaps God is not a creator, but creativity.

This would be close to my own understanding, although I feel that the word 'God' in this instance is superfluous.

6 The word 'automatic,' according to *Webster's Heritage Dictionary*, goes back to the Greek word *automatos*, 'acting of one's own will, self-acting, of itself.' The word 'automatic' is made up of two parts: *auto* 'self,' and *matos*, 'willing,' or, in the words that I am using 'intention'.

7 Lamouche, *Le Principe de Simplicité Dans les Mathématiques et les Sciences.*

8 Superstring theory promises to provide the complete unification of physics, the *Theory of Everything*. It would enable the fundamental building blocks of matter to be identified. The theory is based upon the assumption that the universe is made of small vibrating strings.

9 The term *therblig* was coined by Lilian and Frank Gilbreth, pioneers of modern management techniques, who developed a method for this kind of analysis. Therblig is Gilbreth spelt backwards.

10 Henri Bergson, *Creative Evolution* (New York: Modern Library, 1944), p. 14. "It is true that in the universe itself two opposite movements are to be distinguished . . . 'decent' and 'ascent'. The first only unwinds a roll ready prepared. In principle, it might be accomplished almost instantaneously, like releasing a spring. But the ascending movement, which corresponds to an inner work of ripening or creating, *endures* essentially, and imposes its rhythm on the first, which is inseparable from it."

9 On Causation and Programming

1 Frans De Waal, *Our Inner Ape: A leading primatologist explains why we are who we are* (New York: Riverhead Books, 2005).

2 *Ibid.*, p. 41.

3 *Ibid.*, p.170.

4 *Ibid.*, p.170.

5 *Ibid.*, p. 40.

6 Mayr, *Towards a New Philosophy of Biology: Observations of an Evolutionist*, p. 60.

7 *Ibid.*, p. 41.

8 *Ibid.*, p. 45.

9 *Ibid.*, p. 45 my emphasis.

10 *Ibid.*, p. 45.

11 *Ibid.*

12 *Ibid.*, p. 49.

13 *Ibid.* p. 52.

14 *Ibid.*, p. 46.

15 For more on metaphor see Low, *Creating Consciousness*, chapter 19, pp. 193–208, The Word as Metaphor.

16 Please see Low, *Creating Consciousness*, p. 198, for my reasons for saying this.

17 Alfred North Whitehead, *The Function of Reason* (Princeton: Princeton University Press, 1929).

18 I have said that the origin of an organism is One/(knowing/being).

19 Mayr, *Towards a New Philosophy of Biology: Observations of an Evolutionist*, p. 50.
20 *Ibid.*, p. 49.

10 What is Creativity?

1 T. S. Eliot, *On Poetry and Poets* (Faber and Faber: London, 1957), p. 112.
2 In *Low, Creating Consciousness*, I have given a great number of ways in which the value of this definition can be seen, and the reader who wishes to have some indication of these ways is referred to that book. See in particular Chapter 14, pp. 146–53.
3 Arthur Koestler, *The Act of Creation* (London: Pan Books, 1964), p. 35.
4 Barry Sanders, *A is for Ox* (New York: Vintage Books, 1994), p. 89.
5 Brian P. Copenhaver, *Hermetica* (Cambridge: Cambridge University Press, 1992).
6 Kenneth E. Boulding, *Conflict and Defense* ((New York: Harper and Row, 1962), p. 5.
7 For a much more sophisticated critique of the gradualists' theory of evolution see Henri Bergson, *Creative Evolution*, chapter 1.
8 Marie Louise von Franz, Tr. Andrea Dykes, *Number And Time: Reflections Leading Toward A Unification Of Depth Psychology And Physics* (Evanston: Northwestern University Press, 1974), p. 60.
9 J. G. Bennett writes of evolving systems in chapter 37 of the third volume of his four-volume work *The Dramatic Universe*. He points out that the systemic attribute, or quality, of a system changes as elements are added. Thus a system with three elements will be qualitatively different from a system with four. J. G. Bennett, *The Dramatic Universe*, Vol. III (London: Hodder and Stoughton, 1967).
10 Geoffrey Miller, *The Mating Mind* (New York: Anchor Books, (2001), p. 398.
11 *Ibid.*, p. 405.
12 *Ibid.*
13 Brewster Ghiselin, *The Creative Process* (Berkeley: Mentor Books 1952), p. 36.
14 *Ibid.*
15 Von Franz, *Number And Time: Reflections Leading Toward A Unification Of Depth Psychology And Physics*, p. 22.
16 T. S. Eliot, *On Poetry and the Poets* (London: Faber and Faber, 1957), p. 98.

11 Creative or Mechanical Evolution?

1 A. Zee *Fearful Symmetry, The Search for Beauty in Modern Physics* (Princeton: Princeton University Press, 1999, p. 3.
2 Dawkins, *The Blind Watchmaker*, p. 60.
3 The opening chords of Rickard Strauss' 'Thus Spake Zarathustra' were used to herald the dawn of creation in the film 2001.

4 Dawkins, *The Blind Watchmaker*, p. 66.

5 Eliot, *On Poetry and the Poets*, p. 98.

6 *Ibid.*, p. 98.

7 Dawkins, *The Blind Watchmaker*, p. 4.

8 *Ibid.*

9 *Ibid.*, p. 5.

10 *Ibid.*

11 Nichol, *The Essential David Bohm*, p. 166.

12 Eliot, *On Poetry and the Poets*, p. 98.

13 John Briggs, *Fire In The Crucible* (Los Angeles: Jeremy Tarcher, 1990), p. 299–300.

14 Gregory Bateson, *Ecology Of Mind* (New York: Ballantyne Books, 1972), p. 14.

15 Ghiselin, Brewster, *The Creative Process*, p. 29.

16 Jacques Maritain, *Creative Intuition in Art and Poetry* (New York: Meridian Books, 1955), p. 69.

17 *Ibid.*, p. 58.

18 Brewster Ghiselin, *The Creative Process*, p. 14.

19 D. T.Suzuki, *Zen and Japanese Culture* (London: Routledge and Kegan Paul, 1959), p. 159.

20 *Ibid.*, p. 153.

21 *Ibid.*

22 Erich Jantsch, *The Self Organizing Universe*, p. 6.

23 *Ibid.*, p. 10.

24 Dawkins, *The Blind Watchmaker*, p. 139.

25 Francis Crick, *Life Itself: Its Origin and Nature* (New York: Touchstone, 1981).

26 *A question of Physics: Conversations in Physics and Biology*, conducted by Paul Buckley and F. David Peat (Toronto: University of Toronto Press, 1979), p. 92.

27 Howard Pattee, *Evolving Self-Reference: Matter Symbols and Semantic Closure*, <http://citeseer.ist.psu.edu/cachedpage/518567/2>.

28 "Only by virtue of the freely selected symbolic aspects of matter do the law-determined physical aspects of matter become functional (i.e., have survival value, goals, significance, meaning, self-awareness , etc). It is well known that replication and evolution depend crucially on how the material behavior of the organism is influenced by symbolic memory. Biologists call this matter-symbol distinction the phenotype and genotype. Computationalists call this the hardware-software distinction. Philosophers elevate this distinction to the brain-mind problem". Pattee, *ibid.*

29 Pattee, *Evolving Self Reference*, <http://citeseer.ist.psu.edu/cachedpage/518567/2>.

30 *Ibid.*

31 The following gives an example of the extraordinary lengths to which

scientists go in order to avoid using the word consciousness. In a symposium on theoretical biology Pattee said that measurement, "includes the purpose of the observer in order to say whether or not measurement has occurred. It cannot be stated objectively that it has or has not occurred without introducing the *meaning* of the interaction." He was asked whether this means that consciousness is necessary for measurement to take place. He replied, "Well, I just say 'life' instead of consciousness." Another scientist, Robert Rosen, interjected, "I would say 'subjectivity'." In spite of Pattee's reticence, it is difficult to see how one can have a symbolic organization without an intelligence capable of interpreting those symbols. It is because of this difficulty that I relate his symbolic structure to knowing. Buckley and Peat, *A question of Physics: Conversations in Physics and Biology*, pp. 104–5.

32 Every system contains the seed of it own destruction.

33 Chang, Garma C, *The Buddhist Teaching of Totality* (University Park: Pennsylvania University Press, 1977).

34 *Ibid.*, p. 165.

35 Michael J. Behe, *Darwin's Black Box: The Bio-Chemical Challenge to Evolution* (New York: Touchstone, 1996), pp. 232–53.

36 *Ibid.*, p. 252.

37 *Ibid.*, p. 250.

38 *Ibid.*, p. 251.

39 Lewontin, Quoted in Miller *Finding Darwin's God*, p. 186.

12 The Evolution of Intelligence

1 Charles Darwin, *Descent of Man* (Harmondsworth: Penguin Books, 2004), p. 86.

2 Darwin, *The Origin of Species*, p. 230.

3 The French use the word hearing *entendre* in a similar manner.

4 Ken Richardson, *The Making of Intelligence* (London: Phoenix. 1999), p. 157.

5 *Ibid.*, p. 152.

6 *Ibid.*, p. 155.

7 Carroll, *Endless Forms Most Beautiful: The New Science of Evo Devo*, p. 92 et seq.

8 *Ibid.*, p. 183.

9 Albert Low, *Zen and Creative Management* (New York: Anchor Books, 1976).

10 Low, *Creating Consciousness.*

11 Maritain, Jacques, *Creative Intuition in Art and Poetry* (New York: Meridian Books, 1955), p. 100.

12 See Low, *Zen and Creative Management*, Chapter 16, pp. 156 et seq., and Low, *Creating Consciousness*, Chapter 15, pp. 154 et seq. for more on the 'idea'.

13 Richardson, *The Making of Intelligence*, p. 184.

14 *Ibid.*, p. 153.
15 *Ibid.*, p. 152.
16 *Ibid.*
17 *Ibid.*, p. 185.
18 *Ibid.*, p. 219.
19 In *Zen and Creative Management* I explore fully the implications of this very simple definition. It has great heuristic value.
20 Kenneth E. Boulding, *Conflict and Defense* (New York: Harper and Row 1962), p. 5.
21 See Low, *Zen and Creative Management*.
22 For more on this see Low, *Zen and Creative Management*, pp. 16–21.
23 *Ibid.*
24 Miller, *The Mating Mind*.
25 *Ibid.*, p. 7.
26 *Ibid.*, p. 6.
27 *Ibid.*, p. 3.
28 Darwin, *The Descent of Man*, p. 419.
29 *Ibid.*, p. 419.
30 *Ibid.*, p. 463.
31 *Ibid.*
32 *Ibid.*
33 We must make a clear distinction between a language and communication. See Low, *Creating Consciousness*, pp. 186–8.

13 On the Evolution of Consciousness

1 Søren Kierkegaard, *Fear and Trembling: The Sickness unto Death* (New York: A Doubleday Anchor Book, 1954), p. 146.
2 Descartes René, *A Discourse on Method and Other Works*. Abridged, edited and with an introduction by Joseph Epstein (New York: Washington Square Press, 1963), p. 115.
3 A notable exception is Jean Gebser. See Jean Gebser *The Ever-present Origin* (trans. Noel Barstad with Algis Mikunas (Athens, OH: Ohio University Press, 1986).
4 In the Buddhist *Lankavatara* sutra a similar distinction is made between "the Alaya (supreme awareness) as it is in itself, and the Alaya as a mental representation." The Alaya itself is pure awareness; the Alaya as mental representation is a stage between pure awareness and consciousness. See Albert Low, *Zen and the Sutras*, pp. 116–25.
5 Nisargadatta Maharaj makes a thorough investigation of the role of I-am in the ecology of human beingness in his book *I Am That* (Durham: Acorn Press, 1973). This is a compilation of conversations conducted by Nisargadatta, a Hindu sage, who died quite recently.
6 Franz Pfeiffer, *Meister Eckhart Vol. 1* (London: John M. Watkins 1956), p. 33.
7 Earlier I gave a number of sources that have referred to what I am calling

One/(knowing/being). Among these was the Tibetan *rDzogs-chen* Buddhist tradition, "That fundamental pervasive, unified, holistical process [that is One] whose highly energized dynamics set up the variety of sub-processes and their associated structures." This indicates both the dynamic nature of unity as well as its all pervasiveness. The Tibetans call this dynamism the Ground (*gzhi*), and it is "the ground and reason for everything . . . [it is] thoroughly dynamic . . . [and] responsible for the variety of structures, things, and experiences that are said to make up Reality." This is to say that *gzhi* is the ground of all experience and of all existence.

In chapter six also I said that in Zen One/(knowing/being) is *ku*, which, although unknowable, "is not mere emptiness. It is that which is living, dynamic, devoid of mass, unfixed beyond individuality or personality — the matrix of all phenomena." It is "unfixed, devoid of mass, beyond individuality or personality — is outside the realm of imagination. Accordingly, the true substance of things that is their Buddha or Dharma-nature, is *inconceivable and inscrutable*" (emphasis added).

8 Alaya, knowing, is without support and is its own being, See Low, *Zen and the Sutras*, pp. 116–25.

9 This is similar to Zen Master Dogen saying that an awakened person does not know that he or she is awakened.

10 Zen master Bassui put it this way, "The universe and yourself are of the same root; you and every single thing are a unity. The gurgle of the stream, and the sigh of the wind are [your voice]. The green of the pine, the white of the snow, these are [your color]." Kapleau, *The Three Pillars of Zen*, p. 183.

11 Nichol, *The Essential David Bohm*, p. 174.

12 Meg Maxwell and Verena Tschudin, *Seeing the Invisible* (London: Arkana, 1990), p. 47.

13 F. H. Bradley, *Essays on Truth and Reality* (Oxford: Clarendon Press, 1914), p. 159–60.

14 Michael Polanyi and Harry Prosch, *Meaning* (Chicago: University of Chicago Press, 1975), p. 33.

15 *Ibid.*, p. 33

16 T. S. Eliot, *The Sacred Wood* (London: Methuen and Co., 1969), p. 52.

17 T. S. Eliot, *The Four Quartets* (London: Faber and Faber, 1952).

18 Henri Bergson, *Creative Evolution*, p. 14.

19 The etymology of the word 'exists' is *ex*, meaning 'outside', and *sistere* meaning 'to stand'. To exist is therefore is to stand out, or to stand outside of.

20 We know that it occurs and so we often assume that we also know how it occurs.

21 In religious and spiritual literature this is often referred to as the 'heart'.

22 In *Creating Consciousness* I referred to circular awareness as *iterative awareness*. However, this seemed to make it into an exotic, rather than a normal every day, occurrence. Hence the change of name.

23 Jung, *Mysterium Coniunctionis*, p. 60.

24 This could well be the foundation for the First Noble Truth of Buddhism: Life is suffering.

25 Popper and Eccles, *The Self and its Brain: An Argument for Interactionism*.

26 Tones are not simply physical sounds; they are sounds with meaning. The meaning is paramount and this fact enabled Beethoven to compose music in spite of being deaf. See Victor Zuckerkandl, *Man the Musician* (Princeton: Bollingen series, Princeton University Press, 1976). In *Creating Consciousness* I said that music is the voice of Dynamic Unity, see Low, *Creating Consciousness*, chapter 24.

14 The Ambiguity of 'I–you'

1 R. D. Laing, *The Divided Self* (Harmondsworth: Pelican Books, 1965), p. 26.

2 Jean Paul Sartre also wrote about the significance of the 'look' in *Being and Nothingness: An Essay on Phenomenological Ontology* (Methuen: London 1957), pp. 252–64.

3 See for example Ernest Becker, *The Denial of Death* (New York: The Free Press, 1973) and Sheila MacLeod, *The Art of Starvation* (London: Virago Books, 1981).

4 Julius Evola, *The Metaphysics of Sex* (London: East West Publications, 1983), p. 43.

5 "Suppose Hephaestus, with his instruments, to come to the pair who are lying side by side and to say to them, 'What do you people want of one another?' they would be unable to explain. And suppose further, that when he saw their perplexity he said: 'Do you desire to be wholly one; always day and night to be in one another's company? for if this is what you desire, I am ready to melt you into one and let you grow together, so that being two you shall become one, and while you live a common life as if you were a single man, and after your death in the world below still be one departed soul instead of two — I ask whether this is what you lovingly desire, and whether you are satisfied to attain this?' there is not a man of them who when he heard the proposal would deny or would not acknowledge that this meeting and melting into one another, this becoming one instead of two, was the very expression of his ancient need. And the reason is that human nature was originally one and we were a whole, and the desire and pursuit of the whole is called love."

Plato, *The Symposium*, translated with an introduction by Benjamin Jowett, <http://classics.mit.edu/Plato/symposium.html>.

6 Martin Buber, *I and Thou*, trans. Walter Kaufmann (New York: Touchstone, 1996).

7 *Ibid.*, p. 56.

8 *Ibid.*, p. 61.

9 Richard Coss, "Reflections on the Evil Eye" in *The Evil Eye* Alan Dundes, editor (Wisconsin: University of Wisconsin Press, 1992), p. 184.

10 *Ibid.*, p. 185.

11 F. C. Happold, *Mysticism, A Study and an Anthology* (Harmondsworth: Penguin Books, 1970), pp. 133–4.

12 Corbin, Henry, *Creative Imagination in the Sufism of Ibn 'Arabi*, p. 174.

13 Andrew Newberg, Eugene D'Aquili, and Vince Rause, *Why God Won't Go Away* (New York: Ballantine Books, 202), p. 174.

14 A sample of what religions have said about unity is the following:

Hear, O Israel, the Lord our God, the Lord is One! (Hebrews)
No divinity if not One divinity. (Mohammed)
The entire universe is one bright pearl. (Gensha)
One fist is the entire universe. (Dogen)
There exists just the One Mind. (Huang-po)
I and the Father are One. (Christ)
Above the heavens, below the heavens, I alone am the Honored One. (Buddha)
The way is one and only One. (Mencius)

15 Frans de Waal, *Good Natured: The Origins of Right and Wrong in Humans and Other Animals* (Cambridge, MA: Harvard University Press, 1996), p. 57.

16 Coss, *Reflections on the Evil Eye*, p. 182.

17 *Ibid.*, p. 182.

18 *Ibid.*, p. 186.

19 *Ibid.*, "If eye contact occurs inadvertently, gaze aversion can occur in less than one-fifth of a second, making it one of the faster body reflexes," p. 183.

20 Coss, *Reflections on the Evil Eye*, p. 183.

21 Frans de Waal, *Peacemaking Among Primates* (Cambridge, MA: Harvard University Press, 1989), p. 43.

22 de Waal, *Good Natured: The Origins of Right and Wrong in Humans and Other Animals*, p. 103.

23 B. B. Smuts, *Sex and Friendship Among Baboons* (New York: Aldine, 1985), p. 223. Quoted by de Waal, *Peacemaking Among Primates*, p. 156.

15 The Birth of Ego

1 Arnheim, *The Power of the Center*, p. 2.

2 For more on the dynamic center please see Low, *Creating Consciousness*, pp. 167–82. Mircea Eliade, the mythologist, also refers to the importance of the dynamic center in many of his books. See for example, Chapter One, "The Symbolism of the Centre" in *Images and Symbols* (London: Harvill Press, 1961), pp. 27–51.

See also the T. S. Eliot, *The Four Quartets* (London: Faber and Faber, 1952).

At the still point of the turning world.
Neither flesh nor fleshless;
Neither from nor towards;

at the still point , there the dance is,
But neither arrest nor movement.
And do not call it fixity,

3   For more on this please see René Girard, *Violence And The Sacred*, (Baltimore: Johns Hopkins University Press, 1977). Also see *Creating Consciousness*, p. 214.

4   Jim Lovell, and Jeffrey Kluger, *Apollo 13* (New York: Pocket Books, 1995), p. 127.

5   See Robert Ardrey, *The Territorial Imperative* (New York: Dell, 1969).

6   A man who had bouts of mania gives some inkling of this world without a center in the following account:
"Psychosis leaves you with fear; you lose all sense of yourself as a person among other persons. You feel yourself dissipating; your distinctiveness vanishes. No voice in the universe sounds like your voice; yet all voices sound like yours. You see yourself as a vast multitude; and these millions in the multitude become you. This voice, this multitude that is me, has a detached quality to it without substance or body. *This multitude drowns me; it swallows me up.* With its persistent hollowness, *the voice blots out any sense of an I* and this hollow sound, like drums beating in a huge cavern, encircles me and paralyzes my thoughts" (emphasis added), James M. Glass, *Private Terror/Public Life: Psychosis and the Politics of Community* (Ithaca: Cornell University, 1989), p. 36.

7   Anon, *An Autobiography of a Schizophrenic Girl: With analytic interpretation by Marguerite Sechehaye* (New York: New American Library, 1951), p. 40.

8   Rudolph Arnheim wrote of the importance of the unique dynamic centre in art in *The Power of the Center* (California: University of California Press, 1982). Much of what he says in that book about the center could be used to help explain the point that I am now making.

9   Crick, *The Astonishing Hypothesis*, p. 7.

10 What is surprising is that even Gould and Mayr claim uniqueness for human beings. In Gould *More things in Heaven and Earth*, p. 103, he said, "Human cultural change operates fundamentally in the Lamarckian mode, while genetic evolution remains firmly Darwinian. Lamarckian processes are so labile, so directional and so rapid that they overwhelm Darwinian rate of change. Since Lamarckian and Darwinian systems work so differently, cultural change will receive only limited and metaphorical illumination from Darwinism."

As I quoted above, Mayr made a similar statement when he excluded human behavior from his teleonomic explanation. "Intentional, purposeful human behavior is, almost by definition, teleological." In this way, in spite of the protests that both have made earlier, both recognize that humans are in some way special and so they claim a hiatus exists in the evolutionary flow.

11 Allan Bloom, *Closing of the American Mind* (New York: Simon and Schuster, 1987), p. 36.

12 Humphrey Nicholson, *The Inner Eye: Social Intelligence in Evolution* (Oxford: Oxford University Press 2002).

16 On Humans and Evolution

1 Joseph Campbell, *The Hero with a Thousand Faces* (Princeton: Bollingen Series XVII, 1973), p. 389.
2 Dawkins, *The Blind Watchmaker*, p. 46.
3 Kierkegaard, *Fear and Trembling: The Sickness unto Death*, p. 30.
4 Russell, *Mysticism and Logic*, p. 51.
5 Wilson, *Consilience* the *Unity of Knowledge*, p. 4.
6 He said, "Be ye perfect as your Father in heaven is perfect."
7 Gould, *Rocks of Ages: Science and Religion in the Fullness of Life*, p. 202.
8 Russell, *Mysticism and Logic*, p. 9.
9 *Ibid.*, p. 11.
10 A basic axiom of Zen Buddhism is that all beings are Buddha.
11 Quoted by Gould, *Rocks of Ages: Science and Religion in the Fullness of Life*, p. 40.

Epilogue

1 A number of koans are devoted to this phrase for example Koan Number 57 of *The Blue Cliff Record*. See *The Blue Cliff Record* translated by Thomas and J. C. Cleary (Boulder: Prajna Press, 1978), p. 378.
2 For a further explanation of this sutra please see Low (2000), pp. XXX.
3 See Diamond Sutra (Low, *Zen and the Sutras*, p. 82):

> *Thus shall you think of all this fleeting world*
> *star at dawn, a bubble in a stream;*
> *flash of lightning in a summer cloud,*
> *flickering lamp, a phantom and a dream.*

4 Kapleau, *The Three Pillars of Zen*, p. 183. Zen has three principal bodhisattvas: the Bodhisattva of Compassion, who, in Sanskrit, is called Avalokita and in Chinese, Kwan Yin. For many Buddhists, this bodhisattva plays the same role as the Virgin Mary plays for Christians. Avalokita is said to have a thousand eyes and a thousand arms. The thousand eyes are to see the suffering of the world; the thousand arms arm to offer succor to those who suffer. She is often depicted in icons as having multiple heads and many arms. Then there is the Bodhisattva of Commitment, or the Bodhisattva of Vows, called Samanthabhadra. He is depicted in icons as seated on an elephant. Finally there is the Bodhisattva of Wisdom, Manjusri. Manjusri is depicted wielding a sword and seated on a lion. The sword is said to cut in One, not two. In other words, it is a sword that cuts through the delusion of duality. What is surprising and so very instructive is that the *Prajnaparamita sutra*, a sutra about wisdom or *prajna*, is not presided over by Manjusri, the Bodhisattva of Wisdom, but by Avalokita the Bodhisattva of Compassion.

5   The three basic tenets of Buddhims are *anatman* (no-self), *anicca* (no-thing) and *duhkha* (suffering).

Appendices

Appendix I

1   Dawkins, *The Blind Watchmaker*, p. 9.
2   *Ibid.*, p. 140.
3   *Ibid.*, pp. 77–9.
4   Norman Macbeth, *Darwin Retried* (New York: Dell Publishing, 1973), p. 100.
5   David H. Fischer, *Historical fallacies* (San Francisco: Harper and Row, 1970), p. 53.

Appendix II

1   Schopenhauer, *The World as Will and Idea*, pp. 22–4.

Appendix II

1   Norris *Quantum Theory and the Flight from Realism: Philosophical Responses to Quantum Mechanics*, p. 216.
2   *Ibid.*, p. 216.
3   *Ibid.*, p. 216.
4   *Ibid.*, p. 216.
5   Buckley and Peat, *A question of Physics: Conversations in Physics and Biology*, pp. 215–16.

Bibliography

Anon, (1951). *An Autobiography of a Schizophrenic Girl* with analytic interpretation by Marguerite Sechehaye (New York: New American Library).

Ardrey, Robert (1969). *The Territorial Imperative* (New York: Dell).

Arnheim, Rudolph (1982). *The Power of the Center* (Berkeley: University of California Press).

Audi, Robert, general editor (1995). *Cambridge Dictionary of Philosophy* (Cambridge: Cambridge University Press).

Bahm, Archie J. (1988). *Polarity, Dialectic and Organicity* (Albuquerque New Mexico: World Books).

Bateson, Gregory (1972). *Ecology of Mind* (New York: Ballantyne Books).

Behe, Michael (1996). *Darwin's Black Box* (Touchstone Books: New York).

Bennett J. G. (1967). *The Dramatic Universe, Vol. III* (London: Hodder and Stoughton).

Bergson, Henri (1944). *Creative Evolution* (New York: The Modern Library).

Bernal, J. D. (1969). *The Origin of Life* (London: Weidenfeld).

Bernstein, Richard J. (2005). *The Abuse of Evil: the Corruption of Politics and Religion since 9/11* (Malden: Polity Press).

Bloom, Allan (1987). *The Closing of the American Mind* (New York: Simon and Schuster).

Bodanis, David (2000). $E = MC_2$ (New York: Anchor Books).

Bohm, David (1980). *Wholeness and the Implicate Order* (London: Routledge and Kegan Paul).

Born, Max (1969). "Symbol and Reality" in *Physics in My Generation* (New York: Springer-Verlag).

Boulding, Kenneth E. (1962). *Conflict and Defense* (New York: Harper and Row).

Bradley, F. H. (1914). *Essays on Truth and Reality* (Oxford: Clarendon Press).

Briggs, John (1990). *Fire in the Crucible* (Los Angeles: Jeremy Tarcher).

Brown, Andrew (2000). *The Darwin Wars: The Scientific Battle for the Human Soul* (New York: Touchstone).

Buber, Martin (1996). *I and Thou* trans. by Walter Kaufmann (New York: Touchstone).

Campbell, Joseph (1973). *The Hero with a Thousand Faces* (Princeton: Bollingen Series XVII).

Carroll, Sean B. (2005). *Endless Forms Most Beautiful: The New Science of Evo Devo* (New York: Norton).

Chang, Garma C. (1977). *The Buddhist Teaching of Totality* (University Park: Pennsylvania University Press).

Copenhaver, Brian P. (1992). *Hermetica* (Cambridge: Cambridge University).

Corbin, Henri (1979). *Creative Imagination in the Sufism of Ibn 'Arabi* (Princeton: Bollingen Series XCI).

Cosmides, Leda and Tooby, John *Evolutionary Psychology: A Primer* <http://www.psych.ucsb.edu/research/cep/primer.html>.

Coss, Richard "Reflections on the Evil Eye," in Dundes, Alan, editor (1992). *The Evil Eye* (Wisconsin: University of Wisconsin Press).

Crick, Francis (1995). *The Astonishing Hypothesis: the Scientific Search for the Soul* (New York: Touchstone Books).

Crick, Francis (1981). *Life Itself: Its Origin and Nature* (New York: Touchstone).

Darwin, Charles (2004). *The Origin of Species* (London: The Collector's Library).

Darwin, Charles (2004). *The Descent of Man* (Harmondsworth: Penguin Classics).

Dawkins, Richard (1988). *The Blind Watchmaker* (Harmondsworth: Penguin).

Dawkins, Richard (1989). *The Selfish Gene*, 2nd edn. (Oxford: Oxford University Press).

de Nicolás, Antonio T. (1976). *Meditations through the Rg Veda: Four Dimensional Man* (New York: Nicolas Hay).

Dennett, D. (1995). *Darwin's Dangerous Idea* (NewYork: Simon and Schuster).

De Waal, Frans (1989). *Peacemaking Among Primates* (Cambridge, MA: Harvard University Press).

De Waal, Frans (1996). *Good Natured: The Origins of Right and Wrong in Humans and other Animals* (Cambridge, MA: Harvard University Press).

De Waal, Frans (2001). *The Ape and the Sushi Master: Cultural Reflections of a Primatologist* (New York: Basic Books).

De Waal, Frans (2005). *Our Inner Ape: A Leading Primatologist Explains Why We Are Who We Are* (New York: Riverhead Books).

Descartes, René (1963). *A Discourse on Method and Other Works*. Abridged, edited and with an introduction by Joseph Epstein (New York: Washington Square Press).

Deutsch, David (1998). *The Fabric of Reality* (Harmondsworth: Penguin Books).

Dover, Gabriel (2001). *Dear Mr. Darwin* (London: Phoenix).

Eliade, Mircea (1961). *Images and Symbols* (London: Harvill Press).

Eliot, T. S. (1952). *The Four Quartet* (London: Faber and Faber).

Eliot, T. S. (1957). *On Poetry and the Poets* (London: Faber and Faber).

Eliot, T. S. (1969). *The Sacred Wood* (London: Methuen and Co.).

Evola, Julius (1983). *The Metaphysics of Sex* (London: East West Publications).

Frankl, Victor E. (1969). *Man's Search for Meaning* (New York: Washington Square Press).

Gebser, Jean (1986). *The Ever-present Origin*, trans. Noel Barstad with Algis Mikunas (Athens, OH: Ohio University Press).

Ghiselin, Brewster (1952). *The Creative Process* (Berkeley: Mentor Books).

Girard, René (1977). *Violence and the Sacred* (Baltimore: Johns Hopkins University Press).

Goswami, Amit (1995). *The Self-Aware Universe* (New York: Jeremy P. Tarcher).

Gould, Stephen Jay (1999). *Rocks of Ages: Science and Religion in the Fullness of Life* (New York: Ballantyne Books).

Gould, Stephen Jay "More things in Heaven and Earth" In Rose, Hilary and Rose, Stephen, editors (2000). *Alas, Poor Darwin* (London: Vintage).

Greene, Brian (1999). *The Elegant Universe* (New York: Vintage).

Guenther, Herbert V. (1984). *Matrix of Mystery* (Boulder and London: Shambhala).

Guenther, Herbert V. (1994). *Wholeness Lost, Wholeness Regained* (New York: State University of New York).

Happold, F. C. (1970). *Mysticism: A Study and an Anthology* (Harmondsworth: Penguin Books).

Heidegger, Martin (1962). trans. by John Macquarrie and Edward Robinson, *Being and Time* (New York: Harper and Bros).

Heidegger, Martin (1966). *Discourse on Thinking* (New York: Harper Torchbooks).

Heidegger, Martin (1969). *Identity and Difference* (New York: Harper Torchbooks).

Heisenberg, Werner (1962). *Physics and Philosophy: The Revolution in Modern Science* (New York: Harper Torchbooks).

Herbert, Nick (1987). *Quantum Reality* (New York: Doubleday Anchor).

Horgan, John, (1999). *The Undiscovered Mind* (New York: Touchstone).

Jantsch, Erich (1980). *The Self-Organizing Universe: Scientific and Human Implications of the Emerging Paradigm of Evolution* (Oxford: Pergamon Press).

Judson, Horace Freeland (1979). *The Eighth Day of Creation* (New York: Simon and Schuster).

Jung, C. G. (1963). *Mysterium Coniunctionis* (New York: Collected Works of C. G. Jung, Vol. 14, Bollingen Series XX; Pantheon Books).

Kapleau, Philip (1966). *The Three Pillars of Zen.* (New York: Harper and Row).

Kaufmann, Stuart (1993). *The Origins of Order* (Oxford: Oxford University Press).

Kierkegaard, Søren (1954). *Fear and Trembling: The Sickness unto Death* (New York: A Doubleday Anchor Book).

Koestler, Arthur (1967). *The Ghost in the Machine* (London: Pan Books).

Korzybski, Alfred (1941). *Science and Sanity* (Lancaster: The International Non-Aristotelian Library Publishing Co.).

Laing, R. D. (1965). *The Divided Self* (Harmondsworth: Pelican Books).

Lamouche, André (1955). *Le Principe de Simplicité Dans les Mathématiques et les Sciences* (Paris: Gautier Villiers).

Lewontin R. C. (1991). *Biology as Ideology: the Doctrine of DNA* (Concord: House of Anansi Press).

Lovell, Jim and Kluger, Jeffrey (1995). *Apollo 13* (New York: Pocket Books).

Low, Albert (1976). *Zen and Creative Management* (New York: Anchor Books).

Low, Albert (1993). *The Butterfly's Dream* (Boston: Charles E.Tuttle).

Low, Albert (1995). *The World a Gateway: Commentaries on the Mumonkan* (Boston: Charles E. Tuttle).

Low, Albert (2000). *Zen and the Sutras* (Boston: Charles E. Tuttle).

Low, Albert (2002). *Creating Consciousness* (Ashland: White Cloud Press).

Low, Albert (2006). *Hakuin on Kensho: The Four Ways of Knowing* (Boston: Shambhala).

Lupasco, Stéphane (1974). *L'Energie et la matiére psychique* (Paris: Editions du Rocher).

McTaggart, Lynn (2007). *The Intention Experiment* (New York: Free Press).

Mahony, William K. (1998). *The Artful Universe* (New York: State University of New York Press).

Press).

Maritain, Jacques (1955). *Creative Intuition in Art and Poetry* (New York: Meridian Books).

Maxwell, Meg and Tschudin, Verena (1990). *Seeing the Invisible* (London: Arkana).

May, Reinhard (1996). trans. with a commentary essay by Graham Parkes, *Heidegger's Hidden Sources* (London: Routledge).

Mayr, Ernst (1988). *Towards a New Philosophy of Biology: Observations of an Evolutionist* (Cambridge, MA: Harvard University Press).

Miller, Geoffrey (2001). *The Mating Mind* (New York: Anchor Books).

Miller, Kenneth (1999). *Finding Darwin's God* (New York: Cliff Street Books).

Nadeau, Robert and Kafatos, Menas (1990). *The Non-Local Domain* (Oxford: Oxford University Press).

Newberg, Andrew, D'Aquili, Eugene and Rause, Vince (2002). *Why God Won't Go Away* (New York: Ballantine Books).

Nichol, Lee (editor) (2003). *The Essential David Bohm* (New York: Routledge).

Nicholson, Humphrey (1992). *The Inner Eye* (Oxford: Oxford University Press).

Nisargadatta Maharaj (1973). *I Am That* (Durham: Acorn Press).

Norris, Christopher (2000). *Quantum Theory and the Flight from Realism: Philosophical Responses to Quantum Mechanics* (London: Routledge).

Parkes, Graham (editor) (1990). *Heidegger and Asian Thought* (Honolulu: University of Hawaii Press).

Pattee, Howard *Evolving Self-Reference: Matter Symbols and Semantic Closure* <http://citeseer.ist.psu.edu/cachedpage/518567/2>.

Pattee, Howard *The Physics of Symbols: Bridging the Epistemic Cut*. Special issue of BioSystems, Vol. 60, No 1–3.

Pearson, K. (1937). *The Grammar of Science* (London: J. M. Dent and Sons).

Penrose, Roger (1999). *The Large, the Small and the Human Mind* (Cambridge: Cambridge University Press).

Pfeiffer, Franz (1956). *Meister Eckhart, Vol. I* (London: John M. Watkins).

Plato, trans with an introduction by Benjamin Jowett, *The Symposium* <http://etext.library.adelaide.edu.au/p/plato/p71sy/symposium.html>.

Polanyi, Michael, and Prosch, Harry (1975). *Meaning* (Chicago: University of Chicago Press).

Pollack, Robert (2000). *The Faith of Biology, the Biology of Faith* (New York: Columbia University Press).

Popper, Karl (1965). *The Logic of Scientific Discovery* (New York: Harper Torchbooks).

Popper, Karl R. and Eccles, John C. (1998). *The Self and its Brain: An Argument for Interactionism* (London: Routledge).

Richardson, Ken (1999). *The Making of Intelligence* (London: Phoenix).

Russel, Bertrand (1954). *Mysticism and Logic* (Harmondsworth: Pelican Books).

Sanders, Barry (1994). *A is for Ox* (New York: Vintage Books).

Sartre, Jean-Paul (1957). *Being and Nothingness: An Essay on Phenomenological Ontology* (London: Methuen).

Schopenhauer, Arthur (1997). *The World as Will and Idea* (abridged in one volume by David Berman, trans. by Jill Berman) (New York: Everyman).

Skinner, B. F. (1972). *Beyond Freedom and Dignity* (New York: Bantam/Vintage).

Squires, Euan (1990). *Conscious Mind in the Physical World* (London: Institute of Physics).

Squires, Euan (1996). *The Mystery of Quantum Reality* (Bristol and Philadelphia: The Institute of Physics Publishing).

Sutton, Florin Giripescu (1991). *Existence and Enlightenment in the Lankavatarasutra: a Study in the Ontology and Epistemology of the Yogacara School of Mahayana Buddhism* (Albany: State University of New York Press).

Suzuki, D. T. (1959). *Zen and Japanese Culture* (London: Routledge and Kegan Paul).

Tipler Frank J. (1994). *The Physics of Immortality: Modern Cosmology, God and The Resurrection of the Dead* (New York: Anchor Doubleday Books).

Von Franz, Marie-Louise, tr. Dykes, Andrea (1974). *Number And Time: Reflections Leading Toward a Unification of Depth Psychology and Physics* (Evanston: Northwestern University Press).

Watson, James D. (1968). *The Double Helix* (New York: Signet).

Weber, Renée (1986). *Dialogues with Scientists and Sages* (London: Arkana).

Wegner, Daniel M. (2002). *The Illusion of Conscious Will* (Cambridge, MA: MIT Press).

Weil, Simone (1986). *An Anthology* (London: Virago).

Whitehead, Alfred North (1929). *The Function of Reason* (Princeton: Princeton University Press).

Wilson, Edward O. (1999). *Consilience: the Unity of Knowledge* (New York: Vintage).

Zee, A. (1999). *Fearful Symmetry, The Search for Beauty in Modern Physics* (Princeton: Princeton University Press).

Zuckerkandl, Victor (1976). *Man the Musician* (Princeton: Bollingen Series, Princeton University Press).

Index

Printed and bound by CPI Group (UK) Ltd, Croydon, CR0 4YY

13/04/2025

14656582-0008